STAR WARS AND PHILOSOPHY STRIKES BACK: THIS IS THE WAY

The Blackwell Philosophy and Pop Culture Series
Series editor: William Irwin

A spoonful of sugar helps the medicine go down, and a healthy helping of popular culture clears the cobwebs from Kant. Philosophy has had a public relations problem for a few centuries now. This series aims to change that, showing that philosophy is relevant to your life – and not just for answering the big questions like "To be or not to be?" but for answering the little questions: "To watch or not to watch *South Park*?" Thinking deeply about TV, movies, and music doesn't make you a "complete idiot." In fact it might make you a philosopher, someone who believes the unexamined life is not worth living and the unexamined cartoon is not worth watching.

Already published in the series:

Alien and Philosophy: I Infest, Therefore I Am
Edited by Jeffery A. Ewing and Kevin S. Decker

Avatar and Philosophy: Learning to See
Edited by George A. Dunn

The Avengers and Philosophy: Earth's Mightiest Thinkers
Edited by Mark D. White

Batman and Philosophy: The Dark Knight of the Soul
Edited by Mark D. White and Robert Arp

Battlestar Galactica and Philosophy: Knowledge Here Begins Out There
Edited by Jason T. Eberl

The Big Bang Theory and Philosophy: Rock, Paper, Scissors, Aristotle, Locke
Edited by Dean Kowalski

BioShock and Philosophy: Irrational Game, Rational Book
Edited by Luke Cuddy

Black Panther and Philosophy: What Can Wakanda Offer the World?
Edited by Edwardo Pérez and Timothy Brown

Doctor Strange and Philosophy: The Other Book of Forbidden Knowledge
Edited by Mark D. White

Dune and Philosophy: Minds, Monads, and Muad-Dib
Edited by Kevin S. Decker

Dungeons and Dragons and Philosophy: Read and Gain Advantage on All Wisdom Checks
Edited by Christopher Robichaud

Ender's Game and Philosophy: The Logic Gate is Down
Edited by Kevin S. Decker

The Expanse and Philosophy: So Far Out Into the Darkness
Edited by Jeffery L. Nicholas

Game of Thrones and Philosophy: Logic Cuts Deeper Than Swords
Edited by Henry Jacoby

The Good Place and Philosophy: Everything is Fine!
Edited by Kimberly S. Engels

The Ultimate Harry Potter and Philosophy: Hogwarts for Muggles
Edited by Gregory Bassham

The Hobbit and Philosophy: For When You've Lost Your Dwarves, Your Wizard, and Your Way
Edited by Gregory Bassham and Eric Bronson

LEGO and Philosophy: Constructing Reality Brick By Brick
Edited by Roy T. Cook and Sondra Bacharach

Metallica and Philosophy: A Crash Course in Brain Surgery
Edited by William Irwin

The Ultimate South Park and Philosophy: Respect My Philosophah!
Edited by Robert Arp and Kevin S. Decker

The Ultimate Star Trek and Philosophy: The Search for Socrates
Edited by Jason T. Eberl and Kevin S. Decker

The Ultimate Star Wars and Philosophy: You Must Unlearn What You Have Learned
Edited by Jason T. Eberl and Kevin S. Decker

Terminator and Philosophy: I'll Be Back, Therefore I Am
Edited by Richard Brown and Kevin S. Decker

Wonder Woman and Philosophy: The Amazonian Mystique
Edited by Jacob M. Held

Forthcoming

Mad Max and Philosophy
Edited by David Koepsell

Ted Lasso and Philosophy
Edited by David Baggett and Mary Baggett

Wheel of Time and Philosophy
Edited by Jacob M. Held

For the full list of titles in the series see www.andphilosophy.com

STAR WARS AND PHILOSOPHY STRIKES BACK: THIS IS THE WAY

Edited by

Jason T. Eberl and Kevin S. Decker

WILEY Blackwell

Published by John Wiley & Sons, Inc., Hoboken, New Jersey.
Published simultaneously in Canada.

For general information on our other products and services or for technical support, please contact our Customer Care Department within the United States at (800) 762-2974, outside the United States at (317) 572-3993 or fax (317) 572-4002.

Wiley also publishes its books in a variety of electronic formats. Some content that appears in print may not be available in electronic formats. For more information about Wiley products, visit our website at www.wiley.com.

Library of Congress Cataloging-in-Publication Data

Names: Eberl, Jason T., editor. | Decker, Kevin S., editor.
Title: Star Wars and philosophy strikes back : this is the way / edited by Jason T. Eberl, Kevin S. Decker.
Other titles: Star Wars and philosophy
Description: Hoboken, NJ : Wiley-Blackwell, 2023. | Series: Blackwell philosophy and pop culture series | Includes bibliographical references and index.
Identifiers: LCCN 2022041342 (print) | LCCN 2022041343 (ebook) | ISBN 9781119841432 (paperback) | ISBN 9781119841449 (adobe pdf) | ISBN 9781119841456 (epub)
Subjects: LCSH: Star Wars films. | Philosophy in motion pictures. | Philosophy in literature.
Classification: LCC PN1995.9.S695 S76 2023 (print) | LCC PN1995.9.S695 (ebook) | DDC 791.43/75–dc23/eng/20221108
LC record available at https://lccn.loc.gov/2022041342
LC ebook record available at https://lccn.loc.gov/2022041343

Cover Design: Wiley
Cover Image: © MEHAU KULYK/Getty Images

Set in 10.5/13pt Sabon by Straive, Pondicherry, India

SKY10077052_060724

Contents

The Bad Batch

Joel Archer holds a PhD in philosophy from Saint Louis University and is pursuing a PhD in religion at Duke University. His research has appeared in journals such as *Philosophical Studies*, *Religious Studies*, *Journal for the Study of the New Testament*, and *New Testament Studies*. Why two PhDs? Some think he draws inspiration from Ahsoka Tano, who fights evil with two lightsabers instead of one.

Daniel Banning is a Field Service Engineer with Marel. He received a BA in history from Franciscan University of Steubenville. He underwent years of informal training in philosophy as a result of having professional philosophers as best friends and roommates, and he has engaged in many deep discussions of both philosophy and *Star Wars*. He has a special interest in the history of the *Star Wars* universe, particularly the Old Republic era. This book marks his first step into the larger world of academic publishing.

Michael Baur teaches in both the Philosophy Department and the Law School at Fordham University. He holds a PhD from the University of Toronto, and a JD from Harvard Law School. He has served as general editor of the "Cambridge Hegel Translations" series for Cambridge University Press, and is President of the Metaphysical Society of America for 2023/24. He has published on a variety of thinkers (including Aristotle, Aquinas, Kant, Fichte, Hegel, Heidegger, and C.S. Peirce) and on a variety of topics (including metaphysics, ethics, jurisprudence, German Idealism, pragmatism, existentialism, and hermeneutics). They say he has never heard the tragedy of Darth Plagueis the Wise – but perhaps the archives are incomplete.

Steve Bein is wondering, why is he here? Associate Professor of Philosophy he is, at the University of Dayton. Deep is his nerdery in science fiction, and often does he contribute to volumes on pop culture and philosophy. Many chapters has he written, on subjects ranging from Wonder Woman to Mr. Rogers. A novelist is he as well, and several black belts has he earned, but he is not a Jedi yet.

Philipp Berghofer is a postdoc researcher and lecturer at the University of Graz, Austria. His research focus centers around epistemology, phenomenology, and philosophy of physics, aiming at establishing a phenomenological experience-first epistemology. He is the author of *The Justificatory Force of Experiences*, co-editor of *Phenomenological Approaches to Physics*, and president of the Austrian Society for Phenomenology. Ultimately, he is just a simple man trying to make his way in the universe, one pursuing a complicated profession.

Lance Belluomini did his graduate work in philosophy at the University of California, Berkeley; San Francisco State University; and the University of Nebraska–Lincoln. He's recently published essays on *Tenet* and *The Mandalorian* in *The Palgrave Handbook of Popular Culture as Philosophy* (2021). He's also contributed chapters to *The Philosophy of Christopher Nolan* (2017) and the Wiley-Blackwell volumes on *Inception*, *The Walking Dead*, *Ender's Game*, *The Ultimate Star Wars*, and *Indiana Jones* (forthcoming). Still swept away by *The Mandalorian*, he currently loves to end his sentences with the inscrutable catchphrase "I have spoken."

Isabel Bishop is a freelance writer living in St. Louis, Missouri. She has a BA in English from the University of Dallas with an interest in film, art history, and culture. She writes for *The Take* and for *Think Christian*, as well as her own pop culture blog on Medium. Her work explores feminist, political, and Christian thought in relation to film and television. She is a fervent defender of *The Last Jedi*, her favorite of the sequel series, and much of her work explores the Jedi mind-trick of the patriarchy.

Jeffrey P. Bishop is Professor of Philosophy and Professor of Theological Studies at Saint Louis University, where he holds the Tenet Endowed Chair in Bioethics. Bishop is also the founding Director of the Center for Culture, Religion, Ethics, Science, and Technology (CREST) at SLU, which conducts interdisciplinary research on topics at the intersection of science, technology, and culture. His own scholarship explores the historical, political, and philosophical foundations of medicine, science, and technology. His books include, *The Anticipatory Corpse: Medicine, Power, and the Care of the Dying* (2011) and *Biopolitics After Neuroscience: Morality and the Economy of Virtue* (2022), co-authored with M. Therese Lysaught and Andrew A. Michel. Bishop is currently working on a three-volume series at the intersection of philosophical anthropology and philosophy of technology. He can often be found ruminating over a fire, smoking Bantha brisket in his native Texan "low and slow" BBQ style, pondering the technological enframing of humanity represented in the trash compactor scene in *A New Hope*, which he considers the most philosophically rich and important scene in the *Star Wars* canon.

Dear *Star Wars* Powers That Be: My Experimental Clone Force 99 Lego set came without an Omega figure. In addition, the Wrecker figure is the same size as the rest of the other clones. As you know, part of Wrecker's mutation was greater height than the Fett clone standard 1.83 meters. The Omega figure, as a young girl, "little sister" should be smaller than the rest of the figures at one meter. This is obviously a *Clone Wars* animated series era set, not a *Bad Batch* animated series era set, which should have the appropriately sized Wrecker and the *Bad Batch* series new figure Omega, including her laser crossbow. Please rectify this by issuing a new Bad Batch set with the correct characters with appropriate dimensions and weaponry.

The Force be With You,

Dr. Patricia L. Brace, Professor of Art and Humanities, Southwest Minnesota State University; co-editor with Robert Arp of *The Philosophy of J.J. Abrams*.

Timothy Challans identifies with the clone troopers in many ways, not the least of which is his white beard and bald head, which helped him pull off his older (*Rebels*) Captain Rex costume last Halloween. Tim retired from the Army as an infantry lieutenant colonel and has spent over a dozen years as a professor teaching over a thousand military students a range of subjects at a number of military colleges, starting with the teaching of philosophy and military ethics at West Point. He has an award-winning (Choice Award Bronze Medal) academic book, *Awakening Warrior: Revolution in the Ethics of Warfare*

(2007). His fascination with clone troopers comes from his empathy for the people transformed into soldiers of an imperial army who could so easily and unwittingly be manipulated by their masters – through discipline, pressure, and propaganda – to cross a "thin red line" into an abyss of immorality, following orders to commit heinous acts of torture, murder, and treason. Given the requisite conditions, any army is capable, unfortunately, of following Order 66.

Roy T. Cook is CLA Scholar of the College, Setterberg Fellow of Philosophy, and Professor at the University of Minnesota. He works on the philosophy of mathematics, logic, and the philosophy of art. He has two R2-D2 tattoos, because he realizes that R2-D2 is actually the main character of the Star Wars fictional universe, and the only character who consistently understands what is really going on.

Kevin S. Decker is Professor of Philosophy at Eastern Washington University. He has edited or co-edited more than a dozen anthology books in philosophy and popular culture, including *Dune and Philosophy*, and is the author of *Who is Who? The Philosophy of Doctor Who*. If you look closely in the scenes from *The Force Awakens* when Maz Kanata's castle on Takodana is under assault, you can see him cowering under the second table to the left.

Jason T. Eberl is Professor of Health Care Ethics and Philosophy and Director of the Albert Gnaegi Center for Health Care Ethics at Saint Louis University. He teaches and publishes on bioethics, medieval philosophy, and metaphysics. He's the editor of *Battlestar Galactica and Philosophy* (Wiley-Blackwell, 2008), co-editor (w/ Kevin S. Decker) of *The Ultimate Star Trek and Philosophy* (Wiley-Blackwell, 2016) and *The Ultimate Star Wars and Philosophy* (Wiley-Blackwell, 2015), as well as the original *Star Trek and Philosophy* (2008) and *Star Wars and Philosophy* (2005), and co-editor (w/ George A. Dunn) of *Sons of Anarchy and Philosophy* (Wiley-Blackwell, 2013) and *The Philosophy of Christopher Nolan* (2017). He's also contributed to similar books on Stanley Kubrick, J.J. Abrams, Metallica, the Marvel Cinematic Universe, *Harry Potter*, *Terminator*, *The Hunger Games*, *The Big Lebowski*, *Hamilton*, *Westworld*, and *Avatar*. As a bibliophile, the most disturbing moment for him in the entire *Star Wars* saga isn't when Luke gets his hand cut off or makes out with his sister, but when he nearly destroyed the sacred Jedi texts on Ahch-To.

Noam Ebner was in the wrong place at the wrong time. Naturally, he became a lawyer. Reprogrammed as successfully as IG-11, he's now a professor of negotiation and conflict resolution at Creighton University, teaching that wars not make one great. Noam lives in a swamp with his wife and four younglings. He is co-editor of *Star Wars and Conflict Resolution* (forthcoming), and swears by the Maker that everything in this bio is literally true.

Umut Eldem is an assistant professor at Doğuş University Sociology Department. He teaches history of philosophy, ethics, philosophy of science, and occasionally the ways of the Force. He has published articles on Kant, Heidegger, Rick & Morty, and now, Yoda. In his spare time he likes to visit swamps to look for buried X-wings.

Thomas D. Harter is the director of the Department of Bioethics with Gundersen Health System. After his Jedi-esque training in philosophy at the University of Tennessee he was seduced to the "dark side" of clinical ethics, realizing the great power that comes with helping ill patients and their families overcome challenging ethics questions at the bedside. However, Harter has attempted to remain in balance with the Force, continuing with academic pursuits while battling forces of evil as a knight of the Order of Clinical Ethics. When not in frontline clinical battles, Harter writes about issues at the intersection of medical ethics, business ethics, medical professionalism, and philosophy, and teaches bioethics courses and lectures on bioethics topics with other health professions rebels and teachers of the Jedi-esque health professions.

A.G. Holdier is a scruffy-looking nerf-herder doing graduate work in philosophy and public policy at the University of Arkansas (which is probably why he has a bad feeling about this). When he's not researching social and political epistemology or philosophy of language in his local Dex's Diner, you can find him still trying to "do the magic hand thing."

David Kyle Johnson is a professor of philosophy at King's College, in Wilkes-Barre, Pennsylvania, who also produces lecture series for The Teaching Company's *The Great Courses*. His specializations include metaphysics, logic, and philosophy of religion and his "Great Courses" include *Sci-Phi: Science Fiction as Philosophy*, *The Big Questions of Philosophy*, and *Exploring Metaphysics*. Kyle is Executive Officer of

GCRR (The Global Center for Religion Research), the editor-in-chief of *The Palgrave Handbook of Popular Culture as Philosophy* (forthcoming), and has also edited other volumes for Blackwell-Wiley, including *Black Mirror and Philosophy: Dark Reflections* and *Inception and Philosophy: Because It's Never Just a Dream*. Kyle generally likes his *Star Wars* like the Sheev likes his Empire: Jedi free.

Russell P. Johnson is a professor in the Religious Studies program at the University of Chicago, where he teaches "Villains: Evil in Philosophy, Religion, and Film" and "*Star Wars* and Religion." If you haven't visited it, the University of Chicago combines the pleasant weather of Hoth with the wild nightlife of the Jedi Archives. Dr. Johnson's research focuses on the philosophy of communication and nonviolent conflict resolution, so naturally he writes about movies where people solve their problems with laser swords. In addition to his monthly columns for *Sightings*, he wrote a chapter titled "Lifting Rocks: Camus, Sainthood, and the Anti-heroic in *The Last Jedi*" for the upcoming book *Theology and the Star Wars Universe*.

Joshua Jowitt is from a small coal-mining town in the North of England and holds undergraduate and graduate degrees in law and the philosophy of law from the Universities of Cambridge, Warwick, and Durham in the United Kingdom. He is currently a lecturer at Newcastle Law School, where he works mainly in legal theory, but has recently gotten obsessed with the idea of what it means to be a "person" in both philosophy and law. His strong accent means that, when he was younger and had more hair, he was frequently mistaken for Chewbacca. The illusion was quickly shattered, since whenever he was asked to make practical repairs to literally anything, he was about as dexterous as a Bantha.

Nathan Kellen is Instructor of Philosophy at Owensboro Community & Technical College. In the time since the publication of the previous *Star Wars and Philosophy* volume, he has passed his trials to become a Jedi Knight, started training his own Padawans, and for some unknown reason finally gotten around to watching the *Star Wars Holiday Special*.

Aikaterini-Maria Lakka is currently finishing her PhD in comparative literature at the Sorbonne. Her interest in all kinds of stories began from an early age, so she studied classics in Greece (DUTH) and France (Bordeaux Montaigne), and did graduate studies in French literature at the Sorbonne. One of her main research interests revolves around Foucauldian heterotopias, spaces caught up in between reality and imagination, hence her love for the Star Wars universe. She is also a novelist herself; her debut novel, *Someone Named Galatea*, was published in Modern Greek in 2021. When she was young, she decided to become fluent in over 6 million forms of communication to rival C-3PO, but only managed to become fluent in French, and is currently struggling to speak better Spanish, German, Russian, and Italian. Watching Princess Leia being a badass turned her into a feminist. She dreamed of showing up at the *Star Wars* auditions for Episode VII in London, but ended up losing track of time inside an antique bookshop.

Sheepishly confessing that, unlike Socrates, he has never heard from the Oracle of Delphi, **James Lawler** recently revealed, nevertheless, that his roommate in college used to call him "Soc." Perhaps the roommate was an oracle in disguise? Possibly. The reader who wishes to climb the ladder of the love of philosophy can do no better than to begin with Jim's book, *The God Tube: Uncovering the Hidden Spiritual Message in Pop Culture* (2010). For advanced lovers adapted to more rarified levels, there is *Matter and Spirit: The Battle of Metaphysics in Modern Western Philosophy before Kant* (2006). The next rung is, of course, *The Intelligible World: Metaphysical Revolution in the Genesis of Kant's Theory of Morality* (2013).

Terrance MacMullan is an award-winning educator and author who has loved teaching at Eastern Washington University since 2002. He is the author of *Habits of Whiteness: A Pragmatist Reconstruction* as well as numerous publications on American philosophy and pop culture and philosophy. He has served as the EWU Faculty President, earned the President's Award for Academic Excellence, and was voted the Faculty of the Year by the Associated Students of EWU. Most importantly, he came in second place at the 2014 Lilac City Comicon Costume Contest as Qui-Gon Jinn, though every day he looks more and more like Episode IV Obi Wan!

Daniel P. Malloy teaches philosophy at Aims Community College in Greeley, Colorado. He has published numerous chapters on the intersections of philosophy and popular culture, including chapters on *Terminator*, *Inception*, *The Walking Dead*, *Orphan Black*, and *The*

X-Files. He was fired by Figrin D'an and the Modal Nodes for being a bit too scummy and villainous.

Nick Munn did his PhD in philosophy at the Centre for Applied Philosophy and Public Ethics at the University of Melbourne, and currently works as a Bounty Hunter Senior Lecturer in Philosophy at Waikato University in New Zealand. His philosophical interests are many and varied: democracy, enfranchisement, emerging technologies, virtual worlds, moral evaluation, friendship ... Sometimes he thinks it would be a lot easier to pursue them all if, like the IG-88 series of assassin droids, his consciousness was distributed over multiple bodies.

James M. Okapal is Professor of Philosophy at Missouri Western State University, Area Chair for Philosophy and Culture at the Pop Culture Association/American Culture Association National Conference, and the Ethics and Culture Series Editor for McFarland. His research focuses on issues of friendship and moral status in literature and philosophy and he hopes that someday he will be able to count a Wookiee as a close friend. Well, a Wookie not named Krrsantan.

Edwardo Pérez was one of a handful of Padawans who managed to escape the Jedi Temple and survive Order 66. Giving up his Jedi ways (but not his green lightsaber) and settling down with a purple Twi'lek, Edwardo eventually began instructing English students in the ways of the rhetorical force, raising two broom-wielding, force-sensitive children in the Outer Rim, and practicing the Chindinkalu flute in case Max Rebo decides to get the band back together.

James Rocha, unable to locate a kyber crystal, gave up his dream of becoming a Sith Lord and instead turned to philosophy, which he teaches at Fresno State. For the past few years, he has practiced being a Mandalorian by never letting anyone see him without a mask, and he has also published three books: *The Ethics of Hooking Up* (2019), *Joss Whedon, Anarchist?* (co-written with Mona Rocha; 2019), and *Philosophical Reflections on Black Mirror* (co-edited with Dan Shaw and Kingsley Marshall; 2022).

Mona Rocha, unable to locate a kyber crystal, gave up her dream of becoming a Jedi, and instead turned to history and classics, which she teaches at Fresno State. In between putting together a protocol droid from scrap parts, Mona spends her time writing on history, classics, and popular culture. Her latest books are *The Weatherwomen* (2020) and *Joss Whedon, Anarchist?* (co-written with James Rocha; 2019). She has also written book chapters and articles on TV shows, such as *Psych*, *Veronica Mars*, *Buffy*, *Angel*, *Grimm*, and *Supernatural*.

Mohammed Shakibnia is currently a graduate student in public policy at Oregon State University. He studied philosophy and political science in his undergraduate studies, growing to be an admirer of philosophical work aimed at creating a more socially just world. His interests include political and social philosophy, contemporary politics, and popular culture. When he isn't rewatching his favorite *Clone Wars* episodes in Jedi robes and with a purple lightsaber in hand, he's probably reading, playing soccer on the streets of Coruscant, or rearranging his *Star Wars* action figure collection.

Matthew Shea is an assistant professor of philosophy at Franciscan University of Steubenville. His research focuses on human flourishing, natural law and virtue ethics, and biomedical ethics. When teaching philosophy to young padawans, he uses as many Star Wars references as possible. One of the highlights of his life is meeting John Williams and being conducted by him while singing in the University Chorale at Boston College.

Corry Shores teaches philosophy at the Middle East Technical University in Ankara, Turkey. He works primarily on Gilles Deleuze and phenomenology, at times in relation to film and painting. He recently authored the book *The Logic of Gilles Deleuze: Basic Principles*. Though he claims to be completely insensitive to the Force, his college poker buddies often accused him of winning by using Jedi mind tricks.

Patrick Tiernan is a doctoral candidate in education at Gwynedd Mercy University. While Bounty Hunter is not listed on his resume, he has been known to act like an outlaw while serving as Principal of St. Mary Magdalen School in Wilmington, Delaware. His two boys often require more supervision than watching Grogu scarf down rare frog eggs, and his wife is always there to remind him about "the Way" to do things around the house.

Dan Weijers researches well-being and the ethics of new technologies in his role as a senior lecturer in the Philosophy Programme at the University of Waikato in New Zealand. The Philosophy Programme at Waikato is a tight-knit team, an alliance if you will. Dan's role in the team is mainly comic relief, but unfortunately for Dan, and much like the infamous Jar Jar Binks, most of the comedy is about him rather than by him. Despite much bumbling, and again like Jar Jar, Dan has managed to achieve some successes as a philosopher, including authoring chapters in this volume and *Inception and Philosophy* from the same series (he argued that reality didn't matter!). The best example of his fortuitous bumbling must be accidentally putting "International" in the name of the journal he co-created, the *International Journal of Wellbeing*, which has attracted over one million article reads.

Eric Yang trains Padawans for a living, trying to remember that "we are what they grow beyond." Since the probability of getting something published is low, his approach to writing is the same as Han Solo's piloting: "Never tell me the odds!"

Introduction

"Boba Fett Riding a Rancor"

In 2005, when we published *Star Wars and Philosophy: More Powerful Than You Can Possibly Imagine*, the release of the *Star Wars* prequel trilogy was about to be concluded with *Episode III: Revenge of the Sith*. Fan response as well as critics' reviews were generally tepid. The best we could've hoped for was that George Lucas might redeem himself by completing the last three films in a planned nine-film arc that would come to be known as the "Skywalker Saga."

At that time, we couldn't have predicted that Disney would purchase the franchise from Lucasfilm in 2012 for $4.05 billion in cash and stock. The next year, Disney announced an ambitious slate of stand-alone *Star Wars* films as well as hinting at a sequel trilogy. It also announced that the *Star Wars* Expanded Universe would be rebranded "Legends" and no longer be canon; only Lucas's episodic films and television series *The Clone Wars* would be considered canon in addition to new works. For fans of Mara Jade, the Yuuzhan Vong, and Borsk Fey'lya, it was tantamount to literary genocide. Would Disney/Lucasfilm recreate the post-*Return of the Jedi* galaxy in an equally entertaining and philosophically interesting way?

Although *Star Wars* had become an integral part of American culture, we also couldn't have predicted the extent to which it would become a touchpoint for controversy in the American culture wars of the early twenty-first century. Plenty of fans didn't care for *The Force Awakens*, *The Last Jedi*, or *The Rise of Skywalker* for aesthetic, canonical, or personal reasons. Yet, sequel trilogy directors Rian Johnson and J. J. Abrams made precisely the right move in writing characters and casting actors and so declaring that women and people who hail from marginalized groups are part of grand narratives too. Using codes such as "keep politics out of entertainment" and projecting their own toxicity onto Lucasfilm and Disney, the reprehensibly anti-feminist, anti-diversity-casting "Fandom Menace" movement politicized the films in a way surprising and distressing to OG fans like ourselves. Yet, the very fact that such a distasteful response occurred shows that, like other great sci-fi/fantasy narratives, *Star Wars* can hold a mirror up to our current culture and offer a poignant critique.

Finally, we wouldn't have guessed in 2005 that *Star Wars* could have been revivified through its television presence. After all, prior to Gennady Tartakovsky's 2003 *Clone Wars* miniseries, *Star Wars* on TV existed as little more than formulaic children's programming, from the "intentionally lost canon" of *The Star Wars Holiday Special* in 1978 to the 1980s *Droids* and *Ewoks* animated series and live-action Ewok specials. The seven seasons of *The Clone Wars* that premiered on Cartoon Network in 2008, however, offered a serious and multi-layered set of story arcs for Obi-Wan Kenobi, Anakin Skywalker, Padmé Amidala, and their opponents. Further miniseries airing on the Disney+ streaming network, created and guided by Dave Filoni and Jon Favreau, have shown that it's still possible to "get *Star Wars* right" – that magical mix of humor, action, empathy, characterization, exciting quests, and fan service. On the premiere of *The Mandalorian*, one of us told his classes that it was the best *Star Wars* film to be released since *Return of the Jedi*. And yes, we finally got to see what must be the fantasy of so many franchise enthusiasts: Boba Fett riding a rancor!

This volume is a little different from our previous ones. We want to thank Marisa Koors, formerly an editor at Wiley-Blackwell, for her insistence that this book follow a chronological structure, beginning with topics from *Episode I* like "what does the ethics of the Force share with natural law theories of morality?" and moving forward in time through the original trilogy to a critical assessment of the value of friendship between Rey, Finn, and Poe in the sequel films. Because of this chronological structure, we've been able to include chapters that focus on philosophical topics in the animated series *Rebels* and *The Bad Batch*, stand-alone films *Rogue One* and *Solo*, and *The Mandalorian*. We've also been able to encourage our authors to reflect on how their topic fits into the history of the greater *Star Wars* universe. Sometimes, they delve into Legends material to make their claims, a move licensed by the argument of Roy T. Cook and Nathan Kellen in *The Ultimate Star Wars and Philosophy: You Must Unlearn What You Have Learned*:

> The conventions and practices that were shaped and encouraged by Lucasfilm themselves with regard to the canon/non-canon divide – in particular, the dynamic, negotiable, and participatory nature of this

> distinction – throw some doubt onto whether or not Lucasfilm truly has the authority to unilaterally dictate which *Star Wars* stories, or versions of stories, fans should take to be "genuine" parts of the central story.

"*Star Wars* is, after all, about rebellion," they add.[1]

If you're interested in the ways in which newer *Star Wars* narratives demonstrate the importance of ethnicity on alien worlds or how love and sex with a droid like L3-37 would work ("It works"), you'll find answers within. If you've ever wondered if Count Dooku's Separatist Freedom Movement has anything to say about the struggle for social justice in the USA in the twenty-first century, we've got you covered. The metaphysics of time and why we ought to maintain hope in dark times are both addressed in the coming pages. Our contributors even explore defenses of director Rian Johnson's take on a defeatist Luke Skywalker and pose the question, "Should you eat Baby Yoda?"

As *Star Wars*' "galaxy far, far away" continues to expand, so do the philosophical questions that inspired some of the brightest minds in our own galaxy. We invite you to join our Clan of Thirty-Seven. Sometimes the dark side makes it hard to see what other philosophical lessons *Star Wars* has yet to teach us, and yet here we are: This is the Way.

Note

1 Roy T. Cook and Nathan Kellen, "Gospel, Gossip, and Ghent: How Should We Understand the New *Star Wars*?" in Jason T. Eberl and Kevin S. Decker, eds., *The Ultimate Star Wars and Philosophy: You Must Unlearn What You Have Learned*, (Malden, MA: Wiley-Blackwell, 2015), 305–306.

Part I

EPISODES I–III

1

"Another Solution Will Present Itself": *The Phantom Menace*, Daoism, and Doing without Trying

Russell P. Johnson

The Phantom Menace (*TPM*) is one of the most polarizing films in the *Star Wars* franchise. When it was first released in 1999, some fans claimed that it ruined their childhood. But for many fans since then, it's *been* their childhood. Ironically, Daoism – the philosophical religion that rejects controversy and division – has a lot to do with this controversial and divisive movie. If we watch this film with some classical Chinese philosophy in mind, the different narratives, themes, and characters start to make more sense. In short, the philosophy in *TPM* is to Daoism what Taco Bell is to Mexican food: *TPM* may not be most authentic example of Daoist philosophy, but it's got some of the same flavors.[1]

"This Is the Way"

Classical Daoist thinking, found in texts like the *Daodejing* and the *Zhuangzi*, says that everything we experience is always changing, often into its apparent opposite.[2] Day is always turning into night, and night is always turning into day. Cold weather becomes warm in the springtime, and warm weather turns cold in the fall (at least, this is how it works in China. On Hoth, the weather just tends to stay cold). There's a rhythm in the natural world – the sky produces water, which nourishes trees, which are then burned in fires, which send

Star Wars and Philosophy Strikes Back: This is the Way, First Edition.
Edited by Jason T. Eberl and Kevin S. Decker.

smoke back into the sky, and so on forever. When living things die, they become food for other living things, and so on forever. This constant flow from one state of being to another is the nature of all things. Nothing is permanent ... except for change.

This is true not just of the natural world, but also of the political one. Totalitarian, rigid empires tend to become overbearing, which causes rebellions and anarchy. Anarchy creates a power vacuum, which leads to new rulers (like the First Order) who become increasingly rigid in their use of power, and so on forever. In our own lives, too, we see this fluid, changing process. If you are calm and permissive, you let things happen that'll ultimately make you angry, yet expressing your anger ultimately calms you down. Everything flows into its apparent opposite; nothing is static and fixed for all time.

Apparent opposites also *depend* on one another. "Warm" means nothing without "cold." There's no such thing as being cold unless warmth also exists. If it were not for darkness, there could be no light. We would not be able to label anyone "tall" unless we are comparing them with other people who are "short." We could not recognize Chewbacca as "strong" unless we contrast him with someone who's "weak," like C-3PO. The distinctions we use to separate things into "good" and "bad," "hard" and "soft," "calm" and "angry," can make us forget that these apparent opposites depend on one another and are always turning into one another.

According to Daoism, there's a fundamental unity to all of reality that we forget when we try to separate what's valuable from what's worthless. We have the tendency to make sense of the world by privileging one side of a dichotomy over the other. Happy is better than sad, young is better than old, moral is better than immoral, smart is better than dumb, sharp is better than dull, fast is better than slow. After making these distinctions, we tend to find value only in one side and not the other: "I'm wealthy and not poor. I worked very hard to be wealthy and not poor. I'm proud of myself for being wealthy and not poor." By doing so, we forget that any one side in a dichotomy depends upon its apparent opposite, flows into its apparent opposite, and is part of a more fundamental unity. Wealth depends upon poverty and is always coming from and returning to poverty. To think otherwise is to be deluded.

A classic example is dirt and flowers. Flowers grow out of the dirt, and then they die and decompose and become dirt. In *The Last Jedi*, Rey gets a glimpse of this when she's meditating on Ahch-To: "Life. Death and decay, that feeds new life." For Daoists, the human problem is basically that we want there to be flowers without dirt. We want to hold on to one thing at the expense of its apparent opposite, but that's impossible. Symbols like the well-known Taiji diagram (the "Yin/Yang" symbol that's emulated in the Jedi temple on Ahch-To) can help us remember the fundamental unity of all things and free us from our tendency to think in terms of stark opposites. Everything contains within itself the seed of its opposite, so apparent opposition is always misleading. In addition to those symbols, Daoist writings also feature many stories where someone who may seem useless ("another pathetic life-form") turns out to be successful, or something that seems to be worthless turns out to be invaluable. One classic example is a tree so gnarly and curved that it cannot be turned into planks for building. The tree grows to a great height and provides shade for the emperor, and it's able to do that precisely because of its worthlessness. As the *Daodejing* says, "The soft, the weak, prevail over the hard, the strong"[3] – just as we see the tiny, primitive Ewoks help topple the technologically sophisticated and powerful Empire.

"A Symbiont Circle"

In *TPM*, there's similar emphasis on the inevitability of change and the tendency for opposites to depend on each other. In one scene, young Anakin Skywalker has just been freed and is saying goodbye to his mother, Shmi. He complains, "I don't want things to change," and Shmi responds, "But you cannot stop the change any more than you can stop the suns from setting." This sounds a lot like the *Zhuangzi*. Just as we cannot keep the sun (or suns) from setting, so all of our efforts to hold on to happiness, wealth, or reputation are ultimately going to fail. But since the sun has to set in order for there to be a new morning the next day, we too can let ourselves change without really suffering any loss.

TPM also features many examples of those who are apparently useless and worthless triumphing over those who have better training, technology, or skills. The "local boy" Anakin implausibly defeats Sebulba, who "always wins." The "young and naive" queen of Naboo drives out the powerful Trade Federation. The "little droid" R2-D2 restores power to the shield generator. The "primitive" Gungan militia holds their own against the vastly superior droid army. *TPM* emphasizes that we should not rely too much on our judgments of who is capable and who is not. The seemingly insignificant slave boy is in the process of becoming a Jedi Knight, and the seemingly indestructible Droid Control Ship is in the process of becoming space dust.

Symbiosis is also a theme that runs through *TPM*. Two civilizations on the same planet – the Naboo and the Gungans – depend upon one another. As Obi-Wan Kenobi explains to Boss Nass, "You and the Naboo form a symbiont circle. What happens to one of you will affect the other." Flowers depend on dirt which depends on flowers, light depends on dark which depends on light, cold depends on warm which depends on cold. The opposition between the Naboo and the Gungans only conceals their fundamental unity. Qui-Gon Jinn echoes this idea when teaching Anakin about midi-chlorians. He says that living beings and midi-chlorians are "symbionts ... life-forms living together for mutual advantage." Mutual dependence, not opposition, is the natural order of the world.

Doing without Trying

If we agree with the Daoist picture of the natural order, what should we do about it? Do we just do nothing? Well, yes and no. Instead of striving to be rich, virtuous, or famous, the better way to live is to recognize the fluid nature of reality and act accordingly. This is the idea of "non-action," or *wu wei* in Chinese.

If, when we act, we are striving to grasp one side of a dichotomy but not the other – to have flowers without dirt – we'll constantly fail and be frustrated. The more we try to make things turn out the way we want them to, the more we'll mess them up – just as Anakin's turn to the dark side in order to save Padmé tragically results in her death. Striving to achieve one side of a dichotomy ironically drives one further into its opposite. The more a nation clings to security and pursues it at all costs, the more insecure and ultimately susceptible to fear and war it becomes. The more a parent tries to control a child, the more rebellious the child will become. The harder you concentrate and try to accomplish something, the more you'll psych yourself out and become unable to do it. Daoists read history this way, too: one dynasty overreaches and tries to control too much or govern too strictly, and then that dynasty collapses, making room for the next dynasty – the Old Republic, out of fear and war, becomes the Empire, which later collapses and the New Republic is born, which then falls to the First Order until the last is defeated, not by a navy, but "just people."[4]

If our actions align with the natural flow of reality, however, we'll be able to succeed without really having to do anything: the person who moves fastest down the river is not who swims the hardest but who positions themselves so they are carried along by the current. Daoist sages (*zhenren*) give up anxiously trying to make things turn out how they want them to be; instead they let their actions be governed by the same fundamental unity that governs the constant flow of change in the natural world, the social world, and the emotional world.

The *Daodejing* says, "Act on things, and you will ruin them. Grasp for things, and you'll lose them. Therefore the sage acts with non-action and has no ruin. Lets go of grasping and has no loss."[5] The way to gain power and long life and peace is paradoxically by *not* trying to achieve them. Acting organically instead of intentionally, you can live in the moment rather than using all of your energy to try fruitlessly to bring about a specific future. So, if you had to give a one-sentence summary of Daoism, you could do a lot worse than, "Do or do not. There is no try."

"Concentrate on the Moment"

TPM is filled with characters who are not living in the moment but are focused on the future. More specifically, it's filled with people making predictions that turn out to be wrong.

The Jedi assume the trade negotiations will go smoothly. They are right, but not in the way they expect. The Trade Federation leaders assume the Jedi will be no match for their destroyer droids. They are wrong. Jar Jar predicts that the bosses will do terrible things to him. That does not happen. Amidala thinks the Senate will side with her. They will not. Nute Gunray thinks Amidala will be easy to control. Wrong. Palpatine says that the Jedi will be no match for Darth Maul. Half-true. Watto says he knows Sebulba's going to win. He does not. Captain Panaka thinks this is a battle they cannot win. They do. I could go on, but you get the idea. Every story involves characters not knowing what's going to happen – this creates dramatic tension and is art being true to life. But more than most movies, *TPM*'s characters keep thinking they know what's going to happen, keep trying to make things happen, and keep misjudging the future. One theme in *TPM* is that predictions and assumptions are, in general, best avoided, which connects with the

Daoist emphasis on existing in the moment rather than trying to discern the future and make it turn out the way you want it to. To be empty and open to what happens is wiser than being fixated on your expectations, assumptions, and plans.

Daoism emphasizes that success comes most often through a complex set of factors too multifarious to comprehend or even take into consideration. It's not that you should not want good things to happen, but rather that the act of *trying* to bring about your understanding of a good future is as likely to bring misery as to bring happiness. Good outcomes are often unplanned and spontaneous, and we should be open to what happens rather than focusing our energy on trying to make something happen. Daoist stories depict apparent chance bringing about good fortune – people finding something exactly when they were not looking for it or folks saving the day exactly when they stopped trying to play the hero. These stories remind readers that human beings aren't great at making events turn out how they want them to, but this is no reason to despair.

One Daoist parable is about a drunk man who falls from a horse and is not injured. He does not tense his body up to brace himself for the impact, he just literally rolls with it, and his relaxed muscles and joints do not get injured (a trick pro wrestlers use). The implied lesson is that if you stay flexible and roll with things as they happen, you'll be better able to live in the world than if you always think about what you are doing and whether it's working or not. (The story, by the way, is not endorsing drunken horse-riding. Or at least, I'm not endorsing drunken horse-riding. You should always have a designated driver, or at the very least, a sober horse.)

Qui-Gon exemplifies this tendency to stay in the moment and trust in the flow of reality. In some ways, Qui-Gon's actions and non-actions resemble those of a Daoist sage. In fact, the name "Qui-Gon" is likely derived from *qigong*, a set of Chinese practices for aligning the energies of one's mind and body with the natural order. Qui-Gon tells Anakin, "Remember, concentrate on the moment. Feel, do not think. Use your instincts." As the prequel trilogy goes on, we see to what degree Anakin fails to follow this advice.

Everyone else in *TPM* is stressed and worried about things, but not Qui-Gon. So you are being eaten by a fish? Do nothing: "There's always a bigger fish." Jar Jar asks, "Where weesa goin'?" Qui-Gon responds, "Do not worry. The Force will guide us." Their bongo starts to lose power, and Jar Jar exlaims, "Wesa dyin' here!" Another wrong prediction. Qui-Gon calmly replies, "Just relax. We're not in trouble yet."

Cannot get where you are going? No problem, land on Tatooine. Sandstorm coming? Cool, stay with the nearest nine-year-old. Betting everything you have on a child in a death race? This is fine. After Darth Maul arrives on the scene, Anakin asks, "What are we gonna do about it?" Qui-Gon takes a deep breath and says, "We should be patient."

When there seems to be no way off Tatooine, Qui-Gon says, "I'm sure another solution will present itself." This summarizes his whole character. After a Sith assassin comes for the queen, Qui-Gon laughs and counsels patience. Afterward, we see Palpatine, Amidala, and Valorum talking about how "distressed" and "anxious" they are, clear contrasts to Qui-Gon. Unlike almost everyone else in *TPM*, Qui-Gon is not quick to make judgments. When asked whether the queen's idea will work, he does not answer. He often says, "I'm not sure." Even when he thinks Anakin is the "chosen one," when asked about it, he says, "I do not presume …." This starts to change toward the end of the film, but for the most part Qui-Gon remains in the moment, doing non-doing, being mindful, and aligning his will with "the living Force."

The *Zhuangzi* says, "When you let go of the world, you are free of entanglements. Free of entanglements, you are balanced and untilting. Balanced and untilting, you are reborn along with every presence that confronts you."[6] This sounds like Qui-Gon Jinn. He is not chasing a goal so much as allowing every encounter to show him something, acting based on what each changing moment offers to him.

"Now *This* Is Podracing!"

TPM's final victory is not the result of conscious intention. Anakin does not have a plan to fly to the Trade Federation's control ship. He just starts pressing buttons, and things keep working out for him. The Queen has a plan, but it's failing. Meanwhile, Anakin's actions are the opposite of a plan. He's on autopilot, and then when he's not, he's like, "I'll try spinning, that's a good trick." This is not exactly a strategy. After Anakin shoots the torpedoes that destroy the ship, all he can say is "Oops!" Intercut are similar scenes of Jar Jar succeeding through his own seeming incompetence. He keeps accidentally dropping bombs and destroying enemy droids by chance. It's played for laughs, but there are similarities with Daoist stories of eccentrics achieving success without trying for it. Victory comes, not through careful planning or heroic effort, but rather by Anakin being in the moment, acting without acting, just like Qui-Gon told him to do. He's not "doing" anything, and yet everything is done.[7]

Notes

1 For further discussion of Daoist themes in *Star Wars*, see Walter (Ritoku) Robinson, "The Far East of *Star Wars*," in Kevin S. Decker and Jason T. Eberl, eds., Star Wars and Philosophy: More Powerful than You Can Possibly Imagine (Chicago: Open Court, 2005), 29–38.

2 *Daodejing* (or *Tao Te Ching*) is often attributed to the sixth-century BCE philosopher Laozi (or Lao Tzu), though its authorship is debated. *Zhuangzi* is a collection of works by or about the fourth-century BCE philosopher Zhuangzi (or Zhuang Zhou).

3 *TaoTe Ching*, trans. Ursula K. Le Guin and J.P. Seaton (Boulder, CO: Shambhala Publications, 1998), chapter 36.

4 For further discussion of how dynastic changes influenced the development of Chinese philosophy and parallel political changes in *Star Wars*, see Kevin S. Decker. "Dark Times: The End of the Republic and the Beginning of Chinese Philosophy," in Jason T. Eberl and Kevin S. Decker, eds., *The Ultimate Star Wars and Philosophy: You Must Unlearn What You Have Learned* (Malden, MA: Wiley-Blackwell, 2015), 53–64.

5 *Daodejing*, chapter 64, in *Introducing Daoism*, trans. Livia Kohn (University Park, PA: Journal of Buddhist Ethics, 2009), 21.

6 *Zhuangzi: The Complete Writings*, trans. Brook Ziporyn (Indianapolis: Hackett, 2020), 149.

7 *Tao Te Ching*, chapter 48.

2

Bioethics Wars: Fear and Fallacy in *Revenge of the Sith*

Thomas D. Harter

Imagine that the next time you are out in public you come across two people in a fistfight. Stunned and afraid, you watch, but do not intervene. Soon, one of the fighters gains the upper hand. The other attempts a counterattack but fails as the first brutally beats the other. The winner then calmly walks away while the fallen fighter cries for help. Moments later, emergency medical services arrive and begin tending to the beaten fighter, who's barely breathing and bleeding profusely with broken limbs. The fallen fighter is medically stabilized, given pain medication, and transferred to the nearest hospital.

Later, you see a news story about the fight and learn that the fallen fighter was operated on for many hours and survived. The beaten combatant needed both legs and an arm amputated and had to be fitted with prosthetics to regain the ability to move independently. The fighter's lungs were permanently damaged, and so he was given a tracheostomy (a procedure for attaching a mobile respirator) to breathe normally. The fighter also experienced severe throat damage, making it impossible to safely swallow food, meaning he needs a feeding tube to eat.

People are typically grateful for medical technologies used in the treatment of illness or injury. Without knowing any of the context of the case presented above, most readers would be astonished and horrified by the winner's actions – which appear callous or even malicious. And they'd be thankful for the medical providers and the medical technology that saved the victim's life and allowed him to function independently.

Star Wars and Philosophy Strikes Back: This is the Way, First Edition.
Edited by Jason T. Eberl and Kevin S. Decker.

Yet, this is not how movie audiences are expected to feel about the onscreen fight between Obi-Wan Kenobi and Anakin Skywalker in *Revenge of the Sith*. Instead of viewing Obi-Wan, the fight's winner, with horror as he walks away from a mortally wounded Skywalker (who'd become Darth Vader), audiences are led to feel both grateful that Obi-Wan vanquished Skywalker and disappointed that Emperor Palpatine found him in time to allow medical technologies to prosthetically restore Skywalker's body.

Something's amiss. How can it be possible that on twenty-first-century Earth, technology is typically praised for helping people overcome illness or injury, while in *Star Wars* technology and technological innovation are generally treated negatively, as something to be feared rather than praised?[1] In this chapter, we'll explore how Lucas has led *Star Wars* audiences astray into accepting false beliefs and fallacies about the value of technology, particularly in a medical context.

"Fear Is the Path to the Dark Side"

Ethics is the branch of philosophy that addresses questions about how people should live and interact with one another. In its most basic form, ethics is the study of what it means to be good and to act rightly.[2] Bioethics is the study and practice of ethics in a medical context, particularly how we should research, develop, and use medical practices and technologies to help others.[3] An example of a bioethics dilemma: if two Rebel soldiers are wounded in battle but there's only one bacta tank available, who should get it? One person might answer this question by saying the solider who was wounded first should get the tank, while another person might argue that the tank should go to the solider with the worst wounds, or perhaps the solider with the best chance of surviving. Yet another person might argue that the only fair thing to do is randomly pick who the tank should go to.

We must look to *facts* as the essential starting point to answer questions like this. An important fact we know about the *Star Wars* films is that they are George Lucas's interpretative retelling of ancient mythologies that, at their heart, are about the idea that all persons have good and evil traits and that all people can freely choose how to act on them. We also know that Lucas intended that human relationships with technology would be a prominent theme. During a 1999 interview with journalist Bill Moyers, Lucas states, "One [theme] is our relationship to machines, which *are* fearful but also benign and ... they are an extension of the human, not mean in themselves," just as a lightsaber is an extension of its Jedi or Sith wielder.[4] Although Lucas does not tell us what exactly he means by technology being an extension of persons, it's reasonable to assume that what he means is that technology has no *inherent* value, but instead has value only in terms of how it's utilized by persons.

In addition to facts, *context* is important when addressing bioethical questions. Different facts and pieces of information presented from different perspectives can change the assessment or outcome of a bioethical deliberation. Imagine an unmodified, sheathed lightsaber lying on its side. If looked at from either end, it appears circular. If looked at from the top down, it generally appears rectangular. But a lightsaber is neither a circle nor a rectangle, so neither perspective is a fully accurate depiction of the cylindrical shape of a lightsaber. Likewise, narrative stories only show the narrator's perspective but not necessarily the full picture. In *Return of The Jedi* (*ROTJ*), C-3PO captivates the Ewoks with his rendition of the basic plot of *A New Hope* and *The Empire Strikes Back*. The movie-watching audience knows and can verify the truth of C-3PO's summary. The Ewoks, however, know nothing about the battle between the Empire and the Rebellion prior to C-3PO's tale. The story the Ewoks hear is completely one-sided; C-3PO could be lying to them and the Ewoks would not know any better. Storytellers have great power over their audiences and can lead them in any direction they want, truth be damned.

Consider the misleading storytelling around the human relationship with technology in Anakin's final transformation into Darth Vader. Lucas leads the audience to fear this transformation, conveying a perspective about the value of technology that stands contrary to its actual value in a medical context on twenty-first-century Earth.

"What I Told You Was True, from a Certain Point of View"

Points of view matter. *Star Wars* fans know *that* truth all too well. If Lucas's goal was to explore technology as something "fearful ... but also benign," he succeeded but also failed. From his point of view, Anakin's final transformation into Darth Vader is nothing short of horrific. After Anakin is seduced and corrupted by the dark side of the

Force, he's confronted by Obi-Wan on Mustafar. Obi-Wan mortally wounds Anakin by dismembering him with his lightsaber. After telling Anakin how much he loved him and that they were "brothers," Obi-Wan leaves Anakin, screaming in pain, to die on the shore of the lava river. Emperor Palpatine finds and rescues Anakin, who's barely alive. We then see Anakin lying on a metallic table in a dark room being attended to by medical droids. His legs have been replaced with metal prosthetics, his left arm still missing. He remains conscious throughout the ordeal – thrashing his body and screaming in pain as the droids work on him, removing bits of charred flesh. That he remains conscious is an important nuance, as it depicts the medical process as something painful and harmful; the Emperor *wants* Anakin to suffer as part of his final transformation. As the droids complete their work and Vader's now infamous mask is lowered in place, his eyes open wide for a brief second, then narrow with sad resignation to his fate that he is, as Obi-Wan later describes him, "more machine now than man, twisted and evil."

Fear of technological transformation is well communicated in this scene. Technology as something benign is not. Despite Lucas's claim that he wished to show technology as "fearful but … also benign," that is not the message audiences are left with.

The Anakin-to-Vader physical transformation scene is perhaps the starkest example in the entire *Star Wars* canon of the fearful side of technology. But maybe we are not being fair to Lucas. As he noted in the Moyers interview, he wanted to show Vader as a "repulsive," "composite man," who's "lost a lot of his humanity … so there's not much, actually, human left in him."[5] The Anakin-to-Vader transformation was Lucas's way of visually and viscerally showing Vader's transformation from good to evil. So it might be that Vader is the exception rather than the rule. However, throughout the *Star Wars* mythos, technology is rarely shown in a positive light. Rather, technology is something to be questioned, abused (as with the treatment of most droids), discarded, or feared.[6] The Death Star (and its decimation of lush Alderaan), the cyborg body of General Grievous (which raises a question we'll return to at the end of the chapter about using technology to enhance persons), and the Imperial Navy are all examples of Lucas showing technology as fearful, but not benign.[7]

Conversely, what's "natural" and technologically unaugmented is treated as good, pure, or innocent; its loss is grieved. We see this when Obi-Wan misleads Luke about what *really* happened to Anakin. Rather than be forthright with Luke that Anakin *is* Vader, he instead tells him that Vader betrayed and killed Anakin. To Obi-Wan, the fact that Vader is "more machine now than man" is equivalent to Anakin being dead. The Ewoks, another example, are portrayed as simple, innocent creatures who literally live in treehouses. The Jedi wear earth-toned, free-flowing robes, and their entire mythos is about being in balance with the "natural" order – as we see both Obi-Wan and Yoda adapt to their respective desert and swamp climates on Tatooine and Dagobah, while the Empire embraces technology to dominate and rule. Notice too how, after Luke loses his hand fighting Vader and it's replaced with a robotic hand, he hides it beneath a black glove.

"From My Point of View, the Jedi Are Evil"

There are two primary concerns with how Lucas portrays technology in *Star Wars* and specifically regarding the Anakin-to-Vader transformation. First, his perspective is built on the *naturalistic fallacy*. This fallacy is the mistaken belief that because something is "natural," it is necessarily also good. If this belief were true, it would mean that certain states of human existence that occur naturally but are otherwise undesirable are actually "good," such as poor eyesight, poor hearing, headaches, or bacterial infections.

The philosopher David Hume (1711–1776) helps us understand why the naturalistic fallacy is an error in reasoning. Hume argues that it's logically problematic to jump from an "is" statement to an "ought" statement.[8] "Is" statements are empirical; they tell us verifiable facts about the world, for example that Obi-Wan left Anakin to die after their battle on Mustafar. "Ought" statements are value statements about how people should think or act given certain factual statements: Obi-Wan should (or should not) have left Anakin to die after their battle on Mustafar. Because factual statements are value-neutral, giving or attaching value to a factual statement requires showing how the concepts – the fact itself and the value someone gives to the fact – are tied together. The naturalistic fallacy wrongly makes an is–ought connection about what's "natural." As an example, the *fact* that Force-sensitive beings can serve the will of the dark side of the Force does not mean that they *should*. But in *Star Wars*, with few exceptions, what's "natural" is assumed to be good or valuable without clearly explaining why.

Via the naturalistic fallacy, Lucas conveys the false belief that most technology is "unnatural" and so is bad, harmful, or associated with the dark side. There are multiple examples ranging from the use of cloning technology to create an army and to allow Palpatine to survive his pseudo-death in *ROTJ*, to the use of prosthetics to save Anakin's life and finalize his transformation into Darth Vader, to the creation of the Death Star and the Imperial Navy. Rarely does Lucas attempt to display the possibilities of technology as helping the worst-off creatures in the galaxy. Imagine how different *Star Wars* would be if the films tried to show the Rebels using portions of the Death Star plans to create technology capable of growing food crops on Tatooine!

"A Pathway to Many Abilities Some Consider to Be Unnatural"

It should be clear at this point that Lucas's portrayal of technology in *Star Wars* is one-sided and does not map onto twentieth-first-century reality, a context in which it has helped humanity overcome many natural obstacles that threaten the quality and length of many lives. In addition to mass production of clothing, food, and shelter, medical technologies – such as ventilators, feeding tubes, prosthetics, and cardioversion machines to help restore heartbeat – have helped people survive and recover from many potentially fatal events. It may be tempting to say Lucas's portrayal of technology is simply wrong; however, this would be too rash a conclusion.

Lucas is not wrong that technology *can be* fearful, but its value depends in part on how it's intended to be used. Even the use of some medical technologies that can extend life raise questions about whether they should be used in all cases. Many bioethical conflicts center around whether a seriously ill or injured person would want certain medical interventions used to extend their life, given potential trade-offs. Some people are like Darth Vader and need a ventilator to support their breathing for the duration of their lives; but not everyone wants to be connected to a machine in perpetuity.

Lucas's portrayal of technology in *Star Wars* is biased against its true value in societies. However, to assume that because the use of technology is not always negative, it's therefore positive and should be used, for example, to enhance persons – like General Grievous – is also a fallacy, known as the *technological fallacy*. This fallacy, like the naturalistic fallacy, wrongly assumes an is–ought connection between technology and its value. People commit this fallacy when they assume technology is good or must be utilized. While it's possible à la Martin Heidegger (1889–1976) to argue that technology has its own metaphysical reality and so has inherent value (for Heidegger, a negative one) that's independent of how it's used, it's also common to view technology as inherently value-neutral, only having value in relation to its application.[9]

Whether technology should be used to save Anakin's life after his mortal injuries is a different question than whether technology should be used to "enhance" one's natural state of being, as in the case of General Grievous. Without medical technology, both Anakin and Grievous would've died from their respective combat wounds, but whereas the prosthetics of Darth Vader do not improve his abilities – and in fact, hinder his physical movements – Grievous's cybergenic body gives him physical and mental capabilities beyond the natural state of his original, non-enhanced body.

Morally, some will make the argument that people should take opportunities to enhance themselves when they can. After all, we are typically encouraged to enhance ourselves through education, exercise, and healthy diets.[10] However, there are serious concerns and risks with arguing that technology *should be* used to enhance persons. One worry is that technology used to enhance persons may lead to divisions of moral status: the enhanced may view themselves, or be viewed by others, as having superior value over the unenhanced, just as Clone Force 99 (later known as "The Bad Batch") was engineered to be superior to other clone troopers.[11] Even if enhanced persons aren't considered or treated as superior to the unenhanced, there are still concerns that enhancement could result in conflicts of interest between the two groups, resulting in rights of the unenhanced being restricted. The Sith are the embodiment of this concern: they believe that the enhancement of mastering the dark side of the Force gives them a greater standing among all other beings and entitles them to rule the galaxy.

Bringing Balance to the Force?

Lucas's portrayal of technology in *Star Wars* is flawed. Despite claiming that he wanted to show technology as both "fearful … but also benign," he fallaciously presents most technology in a negative light. Yet, Lucas's treatment of technology is not without merit. Embracing technology as inherently valuable is also fallacious. Instead, the value of technology should always be viewed in the context of how it's used.

That Anakin was saved and his body restored after medical intervention is something that typically would be applauded, but how this event is portrayed in *Revenge of the Sith* generates the opposite reaction. Audiences are led to lament Anakin's final transformation into Darth Vader and not condemn Obi-Wan callously leaving Anakin to die on Mustafar.

Perhaps, though, showing Anakin's physical transformation and his need to rely on technology to survive is exactly the point. The Skywalker family – especially Anakin – is prophesied to "bring balance to the Force." That Anakin and Luke are both maimed and need prosthetics shows that technology itself is value-neutral; its moral value depends on specific context. While *Star Wars* is set a long time ago in a galaxy far, far away, context remains important for ethical decisions in our world, where rapidly advancing technology can blur the line between human and machine.

Notes

1 As a branch of philosophy, there is a vast literature on the philosophy of technology, dating back as far as Plato and Aristotle. In this chapter, "technology" broadly refers to any object created by persons that otherwise does not exist in nature and is designed to alter how persons interact with nature. A good introduction to the philosophy of technology is Robert C. Scharff and Val Dusek, eds., *Philosophy of Technology* (Malden, MA: Wiley-Blackwell, 2014).

2 A helpful introduction to the topic of ethics is Peter Singer, ed. A Companion to Ethics (Malden, MA: Wiley-Blackwell, 1993).

3 A good introduction to topics in bioethics is Helga Kuhse, Udo Schühklenk, and Peter Singer, eds., A Companion to Bioethics, 3e (Malden, MA: Wiley-Blackwell, 2015). To learn more about the historical emergence of bioethics, a complete and compelling account is Albert R. Jonsen, *The Birth of Bioethics* (New York: Oxford University Press, 1998).

4 BillMoyers.com Staff, "The Mythology of 'Star Wars' with George Lucas," *BillMoyers.com*, June 18, 1999, at https://billmoyers.com/content/mythology-of-star-wars-george-lucas (accessed November 29, 2021); my emphasis.

5 Ibid.

6 For further discussion of how droids are maltreated in *Star Wars*, see Joshua Jowitt's chapter in this volume (Chapter 16).

7 Perhaps the one example of "benign" technology in *Star Wars* is the Jedi lightsaber. As a piece of technology it is, as Jerold Abrams describes from a Heideggerian perspective, experienced as a "ready-at-hand" – that is, the Jedi lightsaber is not just "an extension of the human," but is a necessary component of a Jedi's *being-in-the-world*; since the Jedi are representative of the philosophical and ethical concepts of "fairness" and "justice," the Jedi lightsaber is the tool by which the Jedi are able to be just and to bring about justice in the universe. It should be noted, however, that Abrams's perspective on technology in *Star Wars* is significantly different from the view I present here. Abrams focuses on persons' metaphysical experiences with technology in relation to being-in-the-world, whereas I am more focused on the disjunction in how technology is valued between the world of *Star Wars* and our current reality. See J.J. Abrams, "A Technological Galaxy: Heidegger and the Philosophy of Technology in *Star Wars*," in Kevin S. Decker and Jason T. Eberl, eds., *Star Wars and Philosophy: More Powerful than You Can Possibly Imagine* (Chicago: Open Court, 2005), 107–119.

8 David Hume, A Treatise of Human Nature, eds. David F. Norton and Mary J. Norton (New York: Oxford University Press, 2000).

9 Again, see Abrams, "A Technological Galaxy" for a Heideggerian account of technology and *Star Wars*.

10 For a concise read about the ethics of enhancement, see S. Chan and J. Harries, "In Support of Human Enhancement," *Studies in Ethics, Law, and Technology* 1 (2007). DOI: 10.2202/1941-6008.1007.

11 Allen Buchanan, "Moral Status and Human Enhancement," *Philosophy and Public Affairs* 37 (2009), 346–381.

3

"A Pathway to Many Abilities Some Consider to Be Unnatural": The Natural Law Ethics of *Star Wars*

Matthew Shea, Joel Archer, and Daniel Banning

According to George Lucas, *Star Wars* is a morality play, a mythological tale of good and evil that's meant to teach timeless lessons about the moral life. The ethical galaxy of *Star Wars* is marked by a conflict between the light side and the dark side of the Force, with the saga's heroes and villains identified by which side they serve. Although the moral messages of *Star Wars* are in some ways simple and commonsensical, the moral system behind the Force is complex and mysterious, lending itself to different interpretations. This chapter shows how the moral framework of *natural law ethics* provides a philosophical foundation for the morality of the Force and helps illuminate *Star Wars'* moral themes.

Natural Law Ethics: A "First Step into a Larger World"

Natural law ethics has ancient roots, encompassing philosophers such as Plato (ca. 427–347 BCE), Aristotle (ca. 384–322 BCE), Cicero (ca. 106–43 BCE), Augustine (354–430 CE), and Thomas Aquinas (1225–1274). The version we'll explore is inspired mainly by Aristotle and Aquinas, the two most influential thinkers in the natural law tradition. According to them, morality is based on human nature and human flourishing, and can be known by natural reason – our built-in

Star Wars and Philosophy Strikes Back: This is the Way, First Edition.
Edited by Jason T. Eberl and Kevin S. Decker.

intellectual capacity for practical reasoning. In short: we don't need a divine lawgiver or a Jedi Council to tell us right from wrong. The purpose of morality is to promote and protect what's good for us: the fulfillment of our nature as human beings. For Aristotle and Aquinas, to be human is to be a *rational animal* with the capacities of intellect (knowing) and will (choosing).[1] According to this view of human nature, creatures who aren't biologically human but have these capacities will count as "human beings" in the sense relevant to natural law ethics because they act as *moral agents*. So maybe Han Solo wasn't simply being sarcastic when he referred to Jabba the Hutt as "a wonderful human being." Characters like Jabba, Chewbacca, and Ahsoka Tano are rational animals and moral agents even though they belong to nonhuman species.

Unpacked a bit more, human beings are essentially intellectual, volitional, social, emotional, and physical organisms. Human flourishing consists in the development and exercise of these natural capacities and the attainment of their corresponding ends. For example, we have intellectual capacities that are aimed at truth, so knowledge is a human good. We have the capacity to make free choices, which is why autonomous agency (especially morally significant choice like that between the light side and dark side) is a human good. We have social powers, and thus personal relationships are good for us, whether they take the form of familial love like that between Anakin and his mother, romantic love like Anakin's and Padmé's, or friendship like that of Anakin and Obi-Wan.[2] We have emotional capacities that enable us to appreciate beauty, which is why aesthetic experiences (like watching a binary sunset) are good for us. We have physical powers aimed at survival and proper physiological functioning, so life and health are human goods.

The natural law, Aquinas says, is "the light of natural reason, whereby we discern what is good and what is evil."[3] It's *natural* because it's based on human nature and knowable by natural reason. It's a *law* because the natural law is equivalent to the moral law, which prescribes how we *ought* to live. The natural law consists of basic moral truths that are objectively and universally true independent of personal opinion, cultural convention, time, and place. So what's right or wrong is the same for bounty hunters in the Outer Rim and senators on Coruscant. Every human being whose rational powers are functioning properly can know basic human goods and basic moral principles, beginning with the supreme first principle of morality: "Good is to be done and pursued, and evil is to be avoided."[4] When

Luke Skywalker asks Yoda, "How am I to know the good side from the bad?" Yoda endorses the idea of natural moral knowledge by replying, "You will *know*." Using reason, we can know that things like knowledge, freedom, friendship, life, and health are good for us, while ignorance, enslavement, loneliness, death, and disease are bad for us. We can also know more specific moral principles that govern how we ought to act, such as: "Do unto others as you would have them do unto you," "Do not murder," "Do not steal," "Help friends in need," "Keep your promises," and "Do or do not; there is no try."

On top of human goods and moral principles, Aristotle and Aquinas stress the importance of moral *virtues*: habits of acting, thinking, feeling, and desiring in morally appropriate ways. Virtues such as practical wisdom, courage, justice, honesty, and benevolence make us good humans beings and are necessary for our flourishing.[5] For instance, an excellent human being (say, Padmé Amidala) is wise and brave. In order to flourish, she must be able to discern which *ends* are really worth pursuing (for example, defending the sovereignty of Naboo against the Trade Federation invaders) and what the best *means* are for achieving them (leading an armed resistance rather than waiting for the Senate to "discuss this invasion in a committee"). She must also have the fortitude to overcome obstacles to flourishing (challenging the Republic's corrupt bureaucracy and risking her life in battle against the droid army). Justice, honesty, and benevolence perfect our nature as social beings and are needed for the sake of social harmony and positive relationships with family, friends, and fellow citizens. By contrast, moral *vices* are obstacles to human fulfillment. An unwise person will be unlikely to pursue what's truly good or to pursue it in an effective way, as when Anakin turns to the dark side in a vain attempt to save Padmé.[6] A coward will be too afraid to pursue or protect what's good when doing so requires risk or sacrifice, like Lando when he initially betrays Han and his friends to the Empire. And someone who's unjust, dishonest, and malevolent will be unlikely to have friends and belong to a peaceful and supportive community. Jabba the Hutt, Boba Fett points out, ruled Tatooine by fear, not respect.

On the natural law approach, what's "natural" in the morally relevant sense is what's good for us given our nature. Moral goodness is natural and beneficial because respecting moral principles and cultivating virtues fulfills human nature and contributes to human flourishing by perfecting our human capacities and enabling us to attain human goods. Moral evil, and having vicious dispositions toward doing evil, is unnatural and harmful because it's contrary to our nature and thwarts our flourishing. In a literal sense, the moral life makes us more *fully human*, whereas an immoral life is *dehumanizing*.

The Morality of the Force: "Twisted by the Dark Side," Saved by the Light

One of the overarching moral messages of *Star Wars* is that the light side fosters human flourishing and the dark side undermines it. Being on the light side is natural and moral because it promotes goods such as life, health, knowledge, friendship, beauty, peace, and inner harmony. Being on the dark side is unnatural and immoral because it undermines those goods and brings evils like death, disease, ignorance, loneliness, ugliness, discord, and internal division.

This message is communicated through the plot, as we see the consequences of characters' good and evil choices. It's also expressed visually. A recurring visual motif is that the light side is humanizing whereas the dark side is dehumanizing. All the major Sith villains experience death, disfigurement, dismemberment, or mechanization as a result of their evil choices. Darth Maul, Count Dooku, Anakin Skywalker, and Sheev Palpatine are abandoned, betrayed, or killed by their fellow Sith. Maul's eyes exhibit the yellow color characteristic of the dark side, and Anakin's eyes become yellow after he turns to the dark side and commits mass murder in *Revenge of the Sith* (*ROTS*). Palpatine is physically deformed by the use of his own Sith lightning in the same film. Anakin and Dooku both lose hands. Maul is cut in half in *The Phantom Menace* and ends up with mechanical legs in *The Clone Wars*. Most dramatically of all, shortly after Anakin becomes Darth Vader, he's dismembered, physically scarred, critically injured, permanently dependent on technology, and completely hidden within an armored suit, to the point where he is, as Obi-Wan Kenobi puts it, "more machine now than man." These are all examples of characters losing their humanity and undermining their own flourishing by their immoral choices.[7]

The light side, by comparison, is humanizing and beneficial. Virtuous characters use the Force to attain goods in extraordinary ways, and the Force enhances their human capacities so they can perform their natural functions even better. For example, in the Mortis story arc from *The Clone Wars* ("Altar of Mortis"), the mysterious character known as The Daughter uses the Force to transfer her life energy to the deceased Ahsoka, bringing her back to life. In the episode of *The Mandalorian* titled "The Reckoning," Grogu uses Force healing to cure Greef Karga's poisonous wound and prevent his death. In *ROTS*, it's revealed that Qui-Gon Jinn's spirit was able to survive his physical death, allowing him to experience eternal life; he later teaches other Jedi to do the same. The Jedi abilities of Force meditation and foresight (seeing the future) give them special kinds of knowledge. The Force augments their physical powers, giving them enhanced reflexes, speed, strength, dexterity, and jumping ability. In *The Empire Strikes Back* (*TESB*), Luke and Leia are able to communicate telepathically via the Force. The Force also gives Jedi the ability to "see" things non-visually by "reaching out with their feelings." Kanan Jarrus from *Rebels* and Chirrut Îmwe from *Rogue One*, for instance, have this special kind of perception even when physically blind.

Now, there are apparent counterexamples of Jedi and other virtuous characters who are dismembered or dehumanized, which may seem to count against the natural law interpretation of *Star Wars'* visual imagery. For instance, Anakin hasn't yet turned to the dark side in *Attack of the Clones* (*AOTC*), but he's dismembered by Dooku. Luke's hand is severed by Darth Vader in *TESB*. Mace Windu is dismembered by Anakin when he attempts to assassinate Palpatine in *ROTS*. Saw Gerrera, one of the founders of the Rebel Alliance, is shown in *Rogue One* to have suffered extensive physical damage that's left him partly mechanized and dependent on artificial technology, reminiscent of Vader. These aren't real counterexamples, though, because in each case the character's dehumanization is the result of a morally bad choice. Anakin attacks Dooku in a spirit of pride, recklessness, hate, and aggression. Luke exhibits arrogance, impatience, impetuousness, and foolishness when he rushes to confront Vader against the better judgment of Yoda and Obi-Wan. Windu is attacked by Anakin because he tries to execute vigilante justice on Palpatine, taking the law into his own hands and usurping the rightful authority of the judicial system (which, as Anakin warns him, is "not the Jedi way"). Gerrera's injuries come after he commits acts of violent terrorism against the Empire that harm innocent people in the spirit of "the end justifies the means." All of these actions are immoral according to natural law theory and further illustrate the dehumanizing and destructive effects of evil.

Natural law theory can also explain one of the central moral themes in *Star Wars*: *redemption*. After Anakin turns to the dark side and becomes Vader, some of his closest friends, including Obi-Wan and

Yoda, believe that he's "gone" and beyond saving. Padmé and Luke, however, maintain that "there's still good in him" and hold out hope that Anakin can come back to the light. At the end of *Return of the Jedi*, Anakin is redeemed by the love of his son.[8] As Luke is about to be killed by the Emperor, the good in Anakin is finally awakened and he sacrifices his life to save his son, thereby returning to the light side and fulfilling his destiny as the Chosen One who brings balance to the Force.

The lesson here is that no person – not even Darth Vader – is beyond saving; everyone always has some goodness in him or her that allows for the possibility of moral and spiritual redemption. Aquinas maintains that the natural law can't be completely "abolished from the heart of man." He argues that vice and evil can cloud the mind and distort the will so that we fail to know specific moral principles and to make correct moral judgments in particular cases. But the "[most] general principles [of] the natural law, in the abstract, can nowise be blotted out from men's hearts."[9] Aquinas is referring to the knowledge of fundamental human goods, the supreme moral principle to "do good and avoid evil," and some basic moral norms like "Don't murder," "Tell the truth," and "Treat others fairly." All people, no matter how wicked their character or how many horrible things they've done, still have some natural knowledge of good and evil and some natural desire for the good. Some deep recess of the human soul is always aware of and aimed at the good. Aquinas helps us see why Padmé and Luke are right to think there's still good in Anakin, despite how "twisted and evil" he'd become, and why Anakin is redeemable in the end.

Jedi and Sith Ethics: "Similar in Almost Every Way"?

Natural law theory also explains the moral perspectives of the Jedi and the Sith. Their rival moral codes display conflicting views of human nature and human flourishing (keeping in mind that "human" means *rational animal* rather than *Homo sapiens*). During his conversation with Anakin at the opera in *ROTS*, Palpatine says that "The dark side of the Force is a pathway to many abilities some consider to be unnatural," and that "Good is a point of view." The implication is that the Jedi and Sith disagree about what's natural to human beings, and consequently what's good and evil.

To start, they have fundamentally different conceptions of human nature. The Jedi see human persons as *spiritual* beings who are capable of mystical union with the Force and with other living entities. As Yoda tells Luke, "Luminous beings are we, not this crude matter." The Sith see us as nothing but *material* beings, which is evident in their attempt to create and extend life through midi-chlorian manipulation, cloning, and technological apparatus, as opposed to the spiritual immortality experienced by some Jedi. For the Jedi, human beings are *relational* by nature, existing as members of the interconnected and interdependent community of all living things, united through the Force. For the Sith, human beings are *atomistic individuals*, existing independently and self-sufficiently. Even the closest relationship in the life of a Sith – between master and apprentice – is marked by ruthless individualism, for a central tenet of the "Rule of Two" is that the apprentice tries to kill the master. The Jedi see human beings as naturally *altruistic* and motivated to help others. As Anakin puts it to Palpatine, "The Jedi are selfless. They only care about others." Relatedly, a defining human trait is the *will to serve*. The Sith see human beings as *egoistic* and motivated by self-interest. For them, the defining human trait is the *will to power*. This is why Palpatine tells Anakin that "The Sith and the Jedi are similar in almost every way, including their quest for greater power."

A central characteristic of the Jedi is that they respect the natural order and act in accordance with nature. The Sith revolt against nature and violate the natural order. According to George Lucas, to be a Jedi is to "accept the natural course of things. Anakin's inability to follow this basic guideline is at the core of his turn to the dark side."[10] The contrast is most apparent in the ways the Jedi and Sith approach the beginning and end of life. The Jedi respect the natural generation of life, whereas Darth Plagueis and Darth Sidious manipulate midi-chlorians to create life "artificially."[11] The Jedi accept their mortality as part of what it means to be a finite being. As Yoda instructs Anakin, "Death is a natural part of life. Rejoice for those around you who transform into the Force." Plagueis and Sidious obsessively quest for immortality in an attempt to "cheat death." Anakin's fall to the dark side is motivated by his refusal to accept the fact that his wife Padmé is a mortal being and that he's not omnipotent, that he lacks power over her life and death – his failure to acknowledge the true nature of things. This tragic vice is foreshadowed in *AOTC* when, after murdering the Tuskens who abducted his mother, Anakin is despondent at his inability to save her. Padmé tells him, "You're not all-powerful," and he replies, "Well, I *should* be. Some day I will be ... I will even learn to stop people from dying."

The Jedi and the Sith also have diametrically opposed moral codes. The Jedi Code mandates selflessness, compassion, love, benevolence, honesty and truthfulness, humility, peace, justice, respecting the freedom of others (aside from the occasional mind trick), detachment, and the ability to let go.[12] As Yoda again instructs Anakin, "Train yourself to let go of everything you fear to lose." They strive to conform their individual wills to the will of the Force. For the Jedi, selflessness is the supreme virtue and service is the highest good. Anakin summarizes the Jedi ethos when he tells Padmé that "Compassion, which I would define as unconditional love, is central to a Jedi's life." The Sith Code, by contrast, mandates power, passion, hate, anger, aggression, strength, malevolence, dishonesty and deception, conflict, and control of others. Typical Sith character traits are selfishness, pride, fear, jealousy, wrath, greed, and possessiveness. They seek to exert their own will and conform everything else to it. For the Sith, selfishness is the supreme virtue and power is the greatest good. Palpatine's devilish scream – "Power! Unlimited power!" – is a fitting expression of this view.

There are other significant points of contrast. One is that the Jedi strive for rational control over their emotions for the sake of a stable commitment to their duties and responsibilities, but the Sith advocate giving in to their passions for the sake of greater power.[13] Another is that the Jedi have symbiotic relationships with all living things based on respect for life and the balance of the natural order, whereas the Sith practice dominance, exploitation, and destruction of living things and the natural world to serve their own interests.[14] The Jedi Code also forbids revenge and the use of violence against the innocent, accepting violence only as a last-resort means of defense. As Yoda tells Luke, "A Jedi uses the Force for knowledge and defense, never for attack." The Sith condone vengeance and indiscriminate violence against the innocent whenever their ends require it. This difference comes out after Anakin kills Dooku and says regretfully, "He was an unarmed prisoner. I shouldn't have done that; it's not the Jedi way." Palpatine replies, "It is only natural. He cut off your arm. You wanted revenge." Of course, Palpatine's view of what's "natural" indicates that the conflicting moralities of the Jedi and the Sith stem from opposing views of human nature.

Our sketch of the moral doctrines of the Jedi and the Sith illustrates the stark differences in their beliefs about the natural moral law.

Although we haven't examined the complete set of human goods, moral principles, and virtues, we can conclude that the moral framework of *Star Wars* is aligned with the natural law tradition stemming from Aristotle and Aquinas. On virtually all points, the Jedi understanding of human nature and the human good more closely conforms to the natural law, which explains why they're the moral heroes of *Star Wars*.[15]

Notes

1 See Aristotle, *Metaphysics* VII. 12, *Politics* I. 2, and *Nicomachean Ethics* I. 7; and Thomas Aquinas, *On Being and Essence*, chapters 1–3.

2 For a discussion of friendship as a natural good in *Star Wars*, see James Okapal's chapter in this volume (Chapter 30).

3 Thomas Aquinas, *Summa theologiae*, Part I–II, Question 91, Article 2, trans. Fathers of the English Dominican Province, at https://www.newadvent.org/summa.

4 Ibid., Part I–II, Question 94, Article 2.

5 For more on virtue ethics in *Star Wars*, see Judith Barad, "The Aspiring Jedi's Handbook of Virtue," in Kevin S. Decker and Jason T. Eberl, eds., *Star Wars and Philosophy: More Powerful than You Can Possibly Imagine* (Chicago: Open Court, 2005), 57–68.

6 For a moral analysis of Anakin's fall, see Jason T. Eberl, "'Know the Dark Side': A Theodicy of the Force," in Jason T. Eberl and Kevin S. Decker, eds., *The Ultimate Star Wars and Philosophy: You Must Unlearn What You Have Learned* (Malden, MA: Wiley-Blackwell, 2015), 100–114.

7 Our way of speaking in this section might raise the concern that natural law theory implies that human beings who are disabled, physically disfigured, or dependent on artificial technology are thereby less than fully human or worse off as a result. But natural law ethics doesn't carry these problematic implications, and our analysis of *Star Wars'* visual imagery shouldn't be interpreted in that way. According to natural law theory, all human beings – regardless of ability, appearance, age, size, level of development, degree of flourishing, etc. – are equally fully human and have equal intrinsic value because they all possess the same human nature (they're all rational animals). Moreover, a natural law conception of human flourishing need not see disability, disfigurement, or technological dependence as intrinsically bad things that make a person worse off. For a natural law account that rejects a negative understanding of disability, see Matthew Shea, "The Quality of Life is Not Strained: Disability, Human Nature, Well-Being, and Relationships," *Kennedy Institute of Ethics Journal* 29.4 (2019), 333–366.

8 For further discussion of redemptive love in *Star Wars,* see Charles Taliaferro and Annika Taylor Beck, "'Like My Father Before Me': Loss and Redemption of Fatherhood in *Star Wars*," in Jason T. Eberl and Kevin S. Decker, eds., The Ultimate Star Wars and Philosophy: You Must Unlearn What You Have Learned (Malden, MA: Wiley-Blackwell, 2015), 117–126.

9 Aquinas, *Summa theologiae*, Part I–II, Question 94, Article 6.

10 George Lucas interview with Sci-Fi Online (2005), available at http://www.sci-fi-online.com/Interview/05-11-01_GeorgeLucas.htm.

11 See James Luceno, Darth Plagueis (New York: Del Rey, 2012).

12 Although not all Jedi perfectly embody these virtues, as when Obi-Wan lies to Luke about his father. See Shanti Fader, "'A Certain Point of View': Lying Jedi, Honest Sith, and the Viewers Who Love Them," in Kevin S. Decker and Jason T. Eberl, eds., *Star Wars and Philosophy: More Powerful than You Can Possibly Imagine* (Chicago: Open Court, 2005), 192–204.

13 For elucidation of the Jedi's Stoic philosophy, see Matt Hummel, "'You Are Asking Me to be Rational': Stoic Philosophy and the Jedi Order," in Jason T. Eberl and Kevin S. Decker, eds., The Ultimate Star Wars and Philosophy: You Must Unlearn What You Have Learned (Malden, MA: Wiley-Blackwell, 2015), 20–30.

14 For more on the Jedi's ecological ethics, see Elizabeth F. Cooke, "'Be Mindful of the *Living* Force': Environmental Ethics in *Star Wars*," in Kevin S. Decker and Jason T. Eberl, eds., *Star Wars and Philosophy: More Powerful than You Can Possibly Imagine* (Chicago: Open Court, 2005), 80–92.

15 Many thanks to the editors of this book, Masters Jason Eberl and Kevin Decker, for their advice and feedback throughout the writing process. Thanks also to series editor William Irwin, as well as Ben Richardson, Cam Richardson, Erica Ridderman, and William Shea, for their helpful comments on various drafts of this chapter.

4

Mothers, Daughters, Rebels: Women's Bodies in *Star Wars*

Aikaterini-Maria Lakka

A fierce politician who advocates peaceful negotiations yet is ready to defend herself and her loved ones when necessary, Padmé Amidala could be described as a feminist figure, at least in the first two prequel films, where she addresses the galactic Senate, forms an alliance with the Gungans, and brandishes a blaster. *Revenge of the Sith* (*ROTS*) tells a different tale. The plot revolving around Padmé's pregnancy and political career parallels Anakin's turn to the dark side, but it gets less screen time than it was initially supposed to in the theatrical cut. In his introduction to the deleted scenes of Padmé's involvement with the nascent Rebel Alliance, George Lucas comments that it was with "deep regret" that he had to let this whole subplot go, but he wanted Anakin's fall from grace to be the film's focus. Feminist criticisms of *ROTS* have pointed out that her character was thereby reduced to the stereotypical role of the mother, her function limited to giving birth to the twins[1] and naming them.[2]

This chapter will examine Padmé's portrayal in *ROTS* through feminist philosophy, looking into the ways her character changed over the prequel trilogy. In order to explore how Padmé's pregnancy influenced her storyline, we'll employ feminist theories that study motherhood in regard to both the pregnant individual and social structures. Afterwards, we'll delve into the abusive nature of Padmé's relationship with Anakin, discussing how his anger and jealously contributed to her death.[3]

Star Wars and Philosophy Strikes Back: This is the Way, First Edition.
Edited by Jason T. Eberl and Kevin S. Decker.

"I'm a Senator": Padmé's Journey in the Prequels

ROTS brings Anakin Skywalker's character arc full circle, putting together all the missing pieces of the Darth Vader puzzle. Fans finally got to experience the young, promising Jedi's fall from grace in a spectacle that explored how Anakin, manipulated by Palpatine, surrendered to the dark side of the Force and became the infamous man behind the obsidian mask. It's no wonder that *ROTS* is considered the best of the prequels, since all the figures of the classical drama are here: the tragic hero, torn between his morally questionable quest for power and his duty to the Jedi Order; the corrupt politician planning to turn a democracy into an empire; the mentor who failed to instill the Jedi way in his former apprentice; and the love interest who dies in childbirth. The movie ends with Darth Vader having completely given in to his anger and despair caused by Padmé's death, unaware that his children, Luke and Leia, are safely hidden.

In *Return of the Jedi*, Leia tells Luke that she remembers their mother. "She was very beautiful, kind, but sad," she claims, implying that Darth Vader's partner was in hiding with Leia and her adoptive family on Alderaan. *ROTS* tells a completely different story, with Padmé dying moments after giving birth to the twins. Fans have provided their own interpretations of why Leia remembers Padmé, but the questions surrounding Padmé's death do not stop there.[4] Did she die of a broken heart? Had the medical robot, who informed Obi-Wan, Yoda, and Bail Organa that "medically" she was "completely healthy," failed to run the tests that might've diagnosed a brain injury caused by Anakin's violence? It's worth noting that *ROTS*'s novelization and the comic book version both describe a more violent sequence, presumably based on an earlier version of the script, in which Anakin not only Force-chokes Padmé but then dashes her against the wall.[5] Or did Palpatine transfer Padmé's lifeforce to Darth Vader to save him, just as Ben Solo transferred his lifeforce to save Rey in *The Rise of Skywalker* (*TROS*)? This theory is supported by the sequence alternating between the twins' birth and Anakin's transformation.[6]

For any female or femme *Star Wars* fan, Padmé's destiny seems to be a big disappointment, and rightfully so. As Jeanne Cavelos notes, instead of becoming "a greater adversary to Palpatine," a politician capable of revealing his authoritarian plans and protecting the Republic, Padmé is shown spending time alone in her luxurious apartment, worrying solely about Anakin, and revealing a passive side incoherent with her portrayal in the previous two movies.[7] Of course, her professed love for Anakin since *Attack of the Clones* (*AOTC*) is already difficult to understand. The young Jedi had already expressed some worrisome (and meme-worthy) opinions favoring dictatorship that Padmé diminishes by laughing them off. After he murders a group of Tusken Raiders, Anakin projects his own superiority complex – presumably trying to forget he was once a slave himself – by exclaiming, "They're like animals, and I slaughtered them like animals!" Instead of walking out on him, Padmé comforts him, failing to abandon him even after he proclaims his vision of complete power and declaring that he'll save the ones he loves from dying, defying the natural course of life.[8]

Anakin's fear of death and loss is completely antithetical to Yoda's mindset in *Return of the Jedi* (*ROTJ*), where, moments before dying, he peacefully tells Luke that death "is the way of things. The way of the Force." Not heeding the wisdom of his first teacher, Qui-Gon Jinn, Anakin never manages to mindfully ponder the present moment, nor accept the way of the Force when it's contrary to his wishes.[9] In *ROTS*, Padmé becomes the object of his fixation with immortality, something that only adds to her passive portrayal throughout the movie. Not only is she depicted as the reason Anakin joins the dark side, but she's unable to convince him to return to the light, and, at the end, dies, her last words being about him and not about her newborn twins: "Obi-Wan, there's good in him." Although her final lines mirror Luke's belief that there's still good in Darth Vader in *ROTJ*, they are contrary to her independent attitude in the previous two movies when she repeatedly tells Anakin that they do not need each other and that she's perfectly capable of continuing to be her own person.

A Tale of Fathers and Sons, but Someone Has to Bear Them First

In the home video extra features and documentaries for *ROTS*, Palpatine actor Ian McDiarmid observes how the *Star Wars* movies tell the tale of two generations of male heroes: "If you wanted a subtitle for these movies, it could be 'Fathers and Sons.'" Palpatine and Obi-Wan function as father figures for Anakin throughout his temptations to the dark side. Luke's journey echoes that of Oedipus – who killed his father, then married his mother – enduring the consequences of the nemesis to his hubris when he decides to confront

Vader too soon in *The Empire Strikes Back*. However, unlike Oedipus, Luke's ignorance does not get him in more trouble than this; it is Vader himself who's committed the most serious acts of hubris. The fact that Luke must ultimately face his father reflects the influence of Joseph Campbell's book *The Hero with a Thousand Faces* (1949) on George Lucas.

Padmé's role in *ROTS* shows the ways in which *Star Wars* focuses primarily on fathers and sons. She's a senator in title only, her political voice limited to a handful of lines, the fiercest of which is her observation: "So this is how liberty dies. With thunderous applause." If it were not for Palpatine's pivotal role in Anakin's story, even this scene would seem out of context, since Padmé spends almost the entire movie inside her apartment, crying or worrying over Anakin. One of her worries is especially troubling: "This baby will change our lives," she says to Anakin. "I doubt the Queen will continue to allow me to serve in the Senate. And if the Council discovers you're the father, you'll be expelled." And while we can easily understand how Anakin could risk expulsion from the Order for secretly marrying and having kids, it's Padmé's mention of the Queen of Naboo that strikes a nerve. Why would she be forced out of her political career for becoming a mother? Has the *Star Wars* galaxy failed to create welfare benefits for working moms at a time when many of the movies' fans have access to paid parental leave?

In a seminal work of twentieth-century feminism, *The Second Sex*, Simone de Beauvoir (1908–1986) discusses how women in literary and mythological traditions are represented as either "devilish" or "angelic," two opposite poles both linked to motherhood.[10] More specifically, Beauvoir studies how women are thought to have a good side, flowing from motherhood, and a bad one, related to sexuality: the Mother is "devoted," whereas the Mistress is "perfidious."[11] According to the patriarchal narratives Beauvoir studies, a woman is good so long as she decides to become a mother and to concentrate on that; the sexual act should not serve as a source of pleasure, but only as a means to pregnancy. Since a cisgender woman is expected to be able to bear children, she's automatically "related to *nature*, she incarnates it," her growing belly being a parallel to the spring blossoms.[12] Beauvoir mentions how a woman, at least up until her time, was usually expected – in literature and in life – to "give up all personal transcendence and confine herself to furthering that of her male."[13] Her existence was, therefore, reduced to childbearing and playing the role of caretaker within a community.

Influenced by Beauvoir's works and by Marxism, Silvia Federici observes how women's unpaid labor at home has contributed to the accumulation of wealth for men in modern capitalist societies, as well as to gender-based discrimination against women in the workforce.[14] Even though Padmé is quite privileged, living among the most privileged beings of the galaxy and having a protocol droid tending to her every need, in *ROTS* she incarnates the stereotype of the pregnant woman gradually being transformed into a stay-at-home mom. Almost every time we see her, with a few exceptions including her Senate service, Padmé is inside her luxurious apartment with C-3PO as her only company. Her handmaiden from *AOTC*, Dormé, is nowhere to be seen. Has her salary been cut due to war expenses? Or has Anakin's jealousy forced her to isolate herself from her friends and family?

In the deleted scenes for *ROTS*, Padmé is seen in the Senate, actively campaigning for the Petition of the 2000 and participating, along with Mom Mothma, another strong female character we do not get to see in *ROTS*'s theatrical cut, in the creation of the Rebel Alliance. When she finally presents the Petition to Palpatine, Anakin silently observes, without supporting her cause, and Padmé seems annoyed. This reaction is quite different from the reactions she has in the first half of the theatrical cut, where her role is strictly connected to Anakin seeking help from Palpatine.

Her passiveness could also be stressed, according to Diana Dominguez, because she gives birth to the twins in "a supreme form of martyrdom" but also out "of selfishness," since she dies of a broken heart, not caring enough to raise her children.[15] However, even if we accept that Padmé did die of a broken heart, it's not at all certain that her will to raise her children would have sufficed for her to survive and be medically healthy. Considering her death "selfish" or "selfless" does not really bring anything to the table other than a criticism, echoing the (false and potentially dangerous) conviction that an individual has complete power over their body and health. In the case of a woman dying in childbirth, such criticism could also take the form of "mom-shaming." Many patriarchal narratives would certainly see in Padmé's death a form of martyrdom, or a self-sacrifice; after all, the Christian canon promises immediate entry to Heaven to any baptized woman who sacrifices herself in childbirth in order for her newborn(s) to survive.[16]

Padmé's stereotypical representation as simply a mother-to-be throughout *ROTS* is highlighted through the transformation her body undergoes and her fashion choices, notably different than in the previous films. Padmé's blue nightgown in particular reveals that she spends more time at home than anywhere else. Feminist philosophers might see Padmé's body in *ROTS* fitting into a patriarchal narrative that links childbirth to the rebirth of nature every spring. By the end of the film, her task has been completed, and, like the fallen autumn leaves, she does not serve any further purpose. She dies, leaving audiences wondering how Leia could've ever remembered her. Judith Butler, in her book *Gender Trouble* (1990), studies the mother's separation from the girl-child. Relying on the work of feminist Julia Kristeva, Butler says that the moment a woman gives birth she becomes her own mother, performing a specific role within a continuity of childbearing. Butler observes that the separation between the mother and the girl-child "is never fully completed," resulting in melancholy for both.[17] Since Padmé's dead, we can only guess that Leia has sensed through the Force this very melancholy of separation, her own burden of becoming a woman within a patriarchal society.

"It Seems, in Your Anger, You Killed Her"

"You're not all-powerful, Ani," Padmé warns in *AOTC*, while Anakin is mourning his mother's death. "Someday I will be," he replies, eyes glazed with anger, fists clenched, mouth trembling. "I will be the most powerful Jedi ever. I promise you. I will even learn to stop people from dying." Soon he realizes how un-Jedi-like his behavior is and rushes to blame another for his anger: "It's all Obi-Wan's fault! He's jealous! He's holding me back!" It's not the first time Anakin's anger management issues become physical and certainly not the last. Overall, his behavior could easily be called "abusive." Again, Lucas may have been inspired by mythological and literary tradition: rage has been one of the predominant themes in storytelling ever since the *Iliad*, where Achilles's anger drives the plot and changes the course of events for both armies fighting the 10-year war. In Shakespeare's *Othello*, the titular character, blinded by his anger and jealousy, chokes his wife, Desdemona, to death after accusing her of adultery.

Anakin also chokes Padmé using the Force. His violent act probably puts her life in danger, making it necessary for the medical robots to rush to induce the delivery of the twins. Like Othello,

Anakin accuses Padmé of adultery, since he believes she's having an affair with Obi-Wan, or at the very least has been colluding with him. This is specifically implied in his question "Because of Obi-Wan?" when Padmé says she cannot follow him down the path he's chosen. In Anakin's mind, his wife seems like a possession that his former mentor took away from him. Anakin's jealously is not restricted to Obi-Wan. In *The Clone Wars* Anakin believes Padmé is cheating on him with her ex-boyfriend, Clovis.[18] He asks her to step down as senator in the episode "An Old Friend" before beating Clovis in "Rise of Clovis."

In *ROTS*, Anakin seems irritated when he senses that Obi-Wan has been to Padmé's apartment: visions of her dying in childbirth and Obi-Wan being there for her flood his mind. "Obi-Wan's been here, has not he?" he asks, not in a casual fashion, but as if interrogating his wife. Padmé responds by caressing him, attempting to ease his irritation with physical contact, before stressing that Obi-Wan is worried about him. At this point, Padmé's logical take on things could've helped Anakin realize that part of the problem stems from himself, his anger management issues and irrational jealousy. By the time Padmé confronts him on Mustafar, he's become a mass murderer who cannot be talked back into reason. Instead of admitting his crimes, Anakin tries to manipulate Padmé into believing that Obi-Wan is jealous of their relationship. Like elsewhere, Padmé repeats that the only thing she needs is his love, but he insists, "Love cannot save you, Padmé. Only my new powers can do that." Anakin becomes more and more delusional, ignoring Padmé's words and refusing to engage in dialogue. Once more his authoritarian opinions take the lead when he asks her to rule the galaxy with him, so that they can "make things the way we want them to be." When he becomes aware of Obi-Wan's presence, he uses the Force to choke Padmé, calling her a liar, and leaving her unconscious.

The scenes on Mustafar illustrate the abusiveness in Anakin and Padmé's relationship. Anakin constantly directs his anger against her, is controlling, and is not open to honest, equal communication, despite her best efforts. Padmé's left feeling responsible for his anger and violence and constantly tries to console him, apologizing for everything, and assuming the caregiver role that patriarchal societies have traditionally assigned to women.[19] Beauvoir describes heterosexual marriage within the patriarchy as a form of "imperialism" that the husband imposes on the wife. He demands to be admired, viewing every small step of hers that smacks of independence as an act of rebellion that must be suppressed.[20]

Maybe Palpatine does not lie after all when he tells Darth Vader, "It seems, in your anger, you killed her." In the original trilogy, the Force choke was Vader's favorite way to kill off anyone who disappointed him, disobeyed his orders, or whose lack of faith he found disturbing. Maybe Padmé held on just long enough for the twins to be born, then succumbed to her injuries. Padmé's death could be a feminicide – the murder not just of a woman, but of a woman *as a woman*, the result of an abusive patriarchal relationship, of a husband's anger and his need for absolute power.

A New Hope? Inclusive Representation in the Galaxy

Padmé's story in *ROTS*'s theatrical cut is marked primarily by her abusive relationship with Anakin, whose anger is often directed against her. When she becomes pregnant, the story focuses more on her stereotypical role as a mother-to-be and less on her heroic deeds that contribute to the creation of the Rebel Alliance. Had the deleted scenes where she discusses the need to resist Palpatine and his authoritarian turn with the nascent Rebel leaders been included in the theatrical cut, we'd be speaking of a quite different film with quite different character development.

Nowadays, the #MeToo movement stresses the need for inclusive representation in the film industry, and the *Star Wars* saga is no exception. Since *ROTS*, the sequel trilogy has introduced a female protagonist, Rey, whose storyline does not revolve around her love interests (at least not until the very end of *TROS*). Ahsoka Tano has become a fan favorite as a formidable Jedi turned rogue warrior for justice. Rose Tico persuaded Finn to go with her on a mission to save the Resistance, and if not for Jyn Erso's dedication and fierceness Luke Skywalker could never have destroyed the Death Star. The various television series and anthology movies have introduced the possibility for more female, femme, and queer characters, as well as for more BIPOC (Black, Indigenous, and People of Color) representation.[21] At the end of the day, the galaxy is vast enough for us to enjoy stories about all these diverse kinds of people, not just those about the Skywalker family.

Notes

1 See, for example, Jeanne Cavelos, "Stop Her, She's Got a Gun! How the Rebel Princess and the Virgin Queen Became Marginalized and Powerless in George Lucas's Fairy Tale," in David Brin and Matthew Woodring Stover, eds., *Star Wars on Trial* (Dallas: Benbella Books, 2006), 305–327; Veronica A. Wilson, "Seduced by the Dark Side of the Force: Gender, Sexuality, and Moral Agency in George Lucas's *Star Wars* Universe," in Carl Silvio and Tony M. Vinci, eds., *Culture, Identities, and Technology in the Star Wars Films: Essays on the Two Trilogies* (Jefferson, NC: McFarland, 2007), 134–152; and Carolyn Cocca, *Superwomen: Gender, Power, and Representation* (New York: Bloomsbury, 2016), 101.

2 Megen de Bruin-Mole, "Space Bitches, Witches, and Kick-Ass Princesses *Star Wars* and Popular Feminism," in Sean Guynes and Dan Hassler-Forest, eds., *Star Wars and the History of Transmedia Storytelling* (Amsterdam: Amsterdam University Press, 2017), 230.

3 For another feminist perspective on Padmé's pregnancy, see Cole Bowman, "Pregnant Padmé and Slave Leia: *Star Wars*' Female Role Models," in Jason T. Eberl and Kevin S. Decker, eds., *The Ultimate Star Wars and Philosophy: You Must Unlearn What You Have Learned* (Malden, MA: Wiley-Blackwell, 2015), 161–171.

4 There have been many theories all over the Internet on why Leia remembers Padmé, ranging from her Force sensitivity to Sabé having joined forces with the Rebel Alliance and being present in Leia's upbringing. See for example Eirenical's post: http://eirenical17.wordpress.com/tag/and-the-whole-eyes-openeye-closed-force-using-thing-is-actually-pretty-cool (accessed January 6, 2022); and Thomas Bacon's analysis on Screen Rant: https://screenrant.com/star-wars-leia-remember-padme-why-book (accessed January 6, 2022).

5 See the analysis on *Padawanlost*: https://padawanlost.tumblr.com/post/173031258845/i-have-a-morbid-question-to-ask-you-what-is-the (accessed January 6, 2022).

6 For a more in-depth analysis of this theory, see C.J. Hawkings's piece on *Fansided*: https://dorksideoftheforce.com/2019/07/08/star-wars-theory-palpatine-padme-death (accessed January 6, 2022).

7 Cavelos, "Stop her, She's Got a Gun!," 318.

8 Ibid., 320.

9 For further discussion of Qui-Gon's example as a portrayal of Daoism, see Russell Johnson's chapter in this volume (Chapter 1).

10 Simone de Beauvoir, *The Second Sex*, trans. H.M. Parshley (London: Jonathan Cape, 1953), 206–207.

11 Ibid., 206.

12 Ibid., 256.

13 Ibid., 256.

14 Silvia Federici, *Caliban and the Witch: Women, the Body, and Primitive Accumulation* (Williamsburg, NY: Autonomedia, 2004), 94–95.
15 Diana Dominguez, "Feminism and the Force: Empowerment and Disillusionment in a Galaxy Far, Far Away," in Silvio and Vinci, *Culture, Identities, and Technology*, 123.
16 Beauvoir, *The Second Sex*, 141.
17 Judith Butler, *Gender Trouble: Feminism and the Subversion of Identity* (New York: Routledge, 1999), 107.
18 Cocca, *Superwomen*, 101.
19 Cocca, *Superwomen*, 110; Federici, *Caliban and the Witch*, 80.
20 Beauvoir, *The Second Sex*, 450–451.
21 For further discussion of representation in *The Force Awakens* and other latter-day *Star Wars* incarnations, see Edwardo Pérez's chapter in this volume (Chapter 26).

Part II

CLONE WARS, REBELS, AND *THE BAD BATCH*

5

Order 66: The Fragility of Moral Autonomy in *The Clone Wars*

Timothy Challans

LAMA SU: They are totally obedient, taking any order without question. We modified their genetic structure to make them less independent than the original host.
OBI-WAN: And who was the original host?
LAMA SU: A bounty hunter called Jango Fett.

– *Attack of the Clones*

In one of the most stunning *Star Wars* story lines, the Republic's clone troopers turn on and kill their Jedi generals upon receiving – personally from Darth Sidious – the message, "Execute Order 66." Everything changes after this moment: the Clone Wars come to an end, the Republic becomes the Empire, Supreme Chancellor Palpatine becomes Emperor, and the clone troopers of the former Grand Army of the Republic become Imperial stormtroopers. The nexus of plot lines surrounding the origin of Order 66 in *Attack of the Clones* and *Revenge of the Sith* is simple, settled, and cut-and-dried: "Conceived, born, and raised simply to serve the Empire – essentially 'programmed' to obey orders such as Order 66 to kill their Jedi generals with no reason given – they were essentially conscripted soldiers with no choice in the matter."[1]

However, animated series such as *The Clone Wars*, *The Bad Batch*, and *Rebels*, novels such as *Order 66*, and comics such as *Star Wars: Republic* more deeply explore and explain Order 66. We find out that biochips, sometimes referred to as "inhibitor chips," have been implanted in the clones' brains; in some stories, it seems that the chips force the clones to follow the order. Some troopers didn't follow the

Star Wars and Philosophy Strikes Back: This is the Way, First Edition.
Edited by Jason T. Eberl and Kevin S. Decker.

order because they'd had their chips removed. A few others questioned the order or even resisted and disobeyed it even though their chips were activated. These story elements raise many questions: How do these chips work? Are they forcing or inhibiting action? What exactly are the "inhibitor chips" inhibiting? Do they lie dormant until activation, or do they have an inhibiting function until activation? Did the clones' personalities change completely, or did they not change at all? While wrestling with the different explanations and interpretations of Order 66 and its significance, we'll explore answers to these questions.

We begin by recognizing a tension between two competing ideals when the Kaminoans created the clones. The Republic needed clone troopers who were highly disciplined to work as a unit, yet also had enough independence of thought to develop highly specialized expertise and competence across a range of tactical and strategic dimensions. This need for both discipline and independence creates a paradox between the competing operative "behavioral" qualities of obedience and autonomy. *Moral autonomy*, independent moral judgment, is a requirement of a highly trained military force, yet the capacity for independent thinking entailed by moral autonomy is an impediment to obedience. The clones' inhibitor chip degrades or destroys their capacity for independent thought, testifying to the fragility of moral autonomy.

Bred to Obey

> And then he realized something important. These were clone troopers sitting around him now – bred to war, bred to discipline, bred to obey without question the orders of the powers that paid for their services. But though their faceplates were expressionless, minute perturbations in the Force told Anakin that these five were reacting to the impending attack like regular troopers, troopers who sweat, were afraid, who could imagine their own deaths.[2]

The Republic apparently faces many challenges as they turn to the Kaminoans to clone an army that can successfully fight the Separatist droid army. The Separatist leaders have nearly perfect control over their battle droids because they're machines. Machines can malfunction, but they otherwise follow orders perfectly according to their programming. One challenge for the clone army is that they're humans and not programmable like droids. Even so, there's a long human history, on Earth at least, of organizations and institutions working to homogenize and make people programmable. Michel Foucault (1926–1984) examines this historical development in his book *Discipline and Punish*, where he studies efforts to develop obedient soldiers as *projects of docility*, leading to the development of *docile bodies*. These projects had as their principal aim

> an increase of the mastery of each individual over his own body ... at the formation of a relation that in the mechanism itself makes it more obedient as it becomes more useful, and conversely ... The human body was entering a machinery of power that explores it, breaks it down and rearranges it. A "political anatomy," which was also a "mechanics of power," was being born; it defined how one may have a hold over others' bodies, not only so that they may do what one wishes, but so that they may operate as one wishes, with the techniques, the speed and the efficiency that one determines. Thus discipline produces subjected and practiced bodies, "docile" bodies.[3]

Complemented by Philip Zimbardo's Stanford Prison experiments on situational power and obedience,[4] we learn from Stanley Milgram's experiments that most people follow orders, even when the compliance brings about the appearance of harm or even death.[5] As a result, Milgram considers obedience to be our default state. Nevertheless, he observes that a small number of independent people question or disobey orders from an authority. Milgram explains that proportionally few people can maintain *autonomous* action when navigating personal, social, and especially authoritative influences and pressures, while most people succumb to *agentic* action, acting as someone else's agent, or as Darth Sidious puts it, "through the agency of my Galactic Empire."[6] One would expect that Jango Fett's independent nature as the clone's host would genetically transmit a trait of independence, which would then need to be inhibited. Even though they were clones, they were not identical: their physical attributes, aptitudes, and personalities varied. They preferred names to numbers, and they differentiated themselves as individuals with various hair styles, tattoos, and uniform markings. It appears the Chancellor reserved the activation of the inhibitor chip for the issuance of Order 66. What did the Kaminoans do to reinforce obedience before the use of the chip? Good old-fashioned punishment. Foucault details the historical program to instill obedience, whether it be in the prison, the school, or the army, "The least act of disobedience is punished and the best way of avoiding serious offences is to punish the most minor offences very seriously."[7] The Kaminoan program is resemblant:

> The Kaminoans were proud of their low rate of *aberrance*. They had a behavioral norm for clones, and any clone who didn't fit it – any clone who didn't have the sense or self-control to keep his opinions to himself – was classed as deviant, and *reconditioned*. They were full of euphemisms, the Kaminoans; it was the language of purity and cleansing. But it was destruction – of will, of hope, and even of life.[8]

Yet aberrance resulting from independence was common among the earlier batches of clones. One of these earlier batches, Omega Squad, received Order 66, and one of its Republic Commandos, Darman, "hardly knew where to start. He'd been sure he'd misremembered the contingency orders, and that Order 66 was the command code for shutting down the banking system to avert an enemy computer attack, but it was wishful thinking. It was desperate thinking."[9] He and his squad weren't with any Jedi when he got the order. Unknown to the Jedi Council, he was discreetly married to Jedi Knight and General Etain Tur-Mukan, and she was also not with them at the time. He acknowledges to himself that he has no problem with the order, but he doesn't want to kill his wife; his squad mates reassure Darman that they'll help him to protect her from other clones gunning for Jedi. Darman, a crack commando who's both obedient and competent, continues his reflection:

> An order was an order. And orders had to be followed, or else society fell apart. It wasn't blind obedience, [Sergeant] Skirata told his commandos, but a conscious suppression of individual choice that every soldier made in a democracy. The soldier was the instrument of the state, not its master, and the state was the citizens. The citizens made their choice of civil government, and that government tasked the army. The army couldn't pick and choose which lawful orders it obeyed. An army that took those decisions upon itself undermined democracy, and ended up overthrowing the government.[10]

Sergeant Kal Skirata, one of the Mandalorian trainers for the clones, had adopted Darman into his family. Skirata had also specifically adopted the six Null ARC troopers who survived genetic modification, the very first batch of clones made from Jango Fett's DNA. The Kaminoans wanted to exterminate these Null troopers because of their excessive aggressiveness, willfulness, and disobedience, but Sergeant Skirata, supported by Jango Fett, convinced the Kaminoans that he would adopt them and complete their training. The Kaminoans started putting organic inhibitor chips into the clones after this "failure" of the first prototype batch. The earlier batches of commando troopers after the prototypes – such as the Commandos (Captain Rex) and the Bad Batch, or Clone Force 99, still had plenty of independence, but clones' independence waned in later batches.[11]

Absolute Power

> The writings I have collected in this volume appear in their original forms. Many are fragments of what once were longer works, but the preservation of what remains is less important than the recognition of how they led to my new vision of the Sith Order. The following three books – *The Weakness of Inferiors*, *The Book of Anger*, and *The Manipulation of Life* – present how I achieved absolute power, how I shall maintain it through the agency of my Galactic Empire, and how I will reshape the galaxy throughout the ages to come.[12]

How did the galaxy change so drastically all at once? The Chancellor, in fashioning his grand conspiracy, controlled (almost) everything: the war (both sides), the political and diplomatic organizations, the economic centers of power, and even criminal elements such as the Bounty Hunters' Guild. With control of the Holonet, he also fought an effective information war, and his propaganda campaign was a necessary feature toward facilitating the efficacy of Order 66.

> Order 66: In the event of Jedi officers acting against the interests of the Republic, and after receiving specific orders verified as coming directly from the Supreme Commander (Chancellor), Grand Army of the Republic (GAR) commanders will remove those officers by lethal force, and command of the GAR will revert to the Supreme Commander (Chancellor) until a new command structure is established.[13]

Order 66 was always a major part of the Chancellor's conspiracy. How did he envision killing thousands of Jedi across the galaxy? While the overt purpose of the clone army was to fight the Separatist droid army, the covert purpose was to kill the Jedi. In *Attack of the Clones*, Jango tells Obi-Wan that he was recruited by a man named

Tyrannus, and we see minutes later how formidable Jango is in their fight before they leave Kamino. Jango was a Mandalorian, and they had a long history of developing and perfecting armaments and tactics that could defeat Jedi in battle. Also, Jango was known as the *Jedi killer*. Who better to recruit to provide genetic material for the clones as well as to oversee their training? Order 66 required legitimacy, however, or at least legitimacy's appearance, for the clone army to perform the stunningly radical act of turning on and killing their generals, especially given the bond of camaraderie they had after years of fighting together. Chancellor Palpatine was leading a comprehensive grand conspiracy. He ran an effective information operation to hide his actual conspiracy by creating a cover story framing the Jedi as traitors intent on bringing down the Chancellor and destroying the Republic. Commander Bacara offers an obedient clone's perspective on receiving the order:

> I hesitated for a moment when I received Order Sixty-six – because the last thing I expected was a Jedi coup. Did I feel betrayed? You bet I did. I thought of all my men who'd died under Ki-Adi-Mundi's command, and if I'd known then that he and his buddies were gearing up to do the Separatists' work for them and overthrow the government, I'd have shot him as a traitor a lot earlier. He betrayed the trust of every one of us.[14]

The tactic of encouraging a *conspiracy theory* originates with those in power trying to discredit explanations for remarkable events that differ from their own preferred narrative. On our own world,

> The *conspiracy theory* label took form and gained meaning over a period of several years (or longer) in the context of efforts by the CIA, one of the world's leading experts in psychological warfare, to deflect accusations that officials at the highest levels of American government were complicit in Kennedy's murder.[15]

Back in the Star Wars universe, it's safe to infer that explanations of political events that would implicate the Chancellor in a plot to rule the galaxy would be considered a conspiracy theory, and any such accusations could result in charges of treason. Feeding the propaganda was Mace Windu and other Jedi masters' attempt to arrest the Chancellor. When that failed, the Chancellor was able to substantiate his narrative by claiming that the Jedi committed treason. In the minds of many of the clone troopers, the Jedi became treasonous when they got Order 66. This campaign made it even harder for the clones to challenge the order's legitimacy or substance. Yet there were some clone troopers who maintained their independence of mind and moral autonomy.

Moral Autonomy

> Captain Rex: I used to believe that being a good soldier meant doing everything they told you. That's how they engineered us. But we're not droids. We're not programmed. You have to learn to make your own decisions.[16]

Captain Rex talks to his troopers here about making their own decisions while facing their mutinous and potentially treasonous choice of confronting and arresting their general in the Battle of Umbara. Their general is actually the traitorous, cruel, deceitful, yet extremely powerful Jedi, Master Pong Krell. When Clone Troopers Fives and Jesse disobey a direct order from Master Krell, resulting in them facing a firing squad, Fives's last words reinforce his independence of thought and moral autonomy:

> Wait! This is wrong. And we all know it. The general is making a mistake, and he needs to be called on it. No clone should have to go out this way! We are loyal soldiers. We follow orders, but we are not a bunch of unthinking droids! We are men. We must be trusted to make the right decisions, especially when the orders we are given are wrong.[17]

The firing squad shoots high, missing their targets. Clone Trooper Tup also demonstrates moral autonomy later in the episode when stunning Master Krell with his blaster, allowing his team to capture the Jedi traitor.[18] Later, in another battle under another general, Tup – in an obviously confused mental state – mumbles "good soldiers follow orders" and surprisingly kills General Tiplar.[19] In the following episode, "Conspiracy," we learn that his inhibitor chip activated early, but also that Count Dooku provided the technology of the chip to the Kaminoans, saying that "the chip is a safeguard against betrayal from rogue Jedi."[20]

It takes more than discipline to make a soldier, especially an elite soldier. It also takes the development of a high level of skill and competence. In fact, military organizations in two different galaxies proved wrong the claim that obedience and competence reinforce each other, as Foucault describes our historical idea of the connection between discipline and punishment, that "the mechanism itself makes it more obedient as it becomes more useful, and conversely."[21] Two far, far away examples demonstrate the lack of correlation between obedience and competence. First, the Emperor replaced the clone troopers with stormtroopers after Order 66. The Empire's leaders thought the clones were becoming less useful due to their rapid aging, but they also found that recruiting humans led to a force that was much more compliant and obedient (though we've known since *A New Hope* that stormtroopers couldn't shoot and were generally incompetent). Second, consider two American elite units that operated very differently in the aftermath of the downing of an American helicopter in Mogadishu, captured in both a book and a film entitled *Blackhawk Down*. One unit (Rangers) was highly trained yet emphasized obedience and cohesive compliance while deemphasizing independence of thought and action. The other unit (Delta Force) was more highly trained and specialized yet emphasized independent thought and action, even at the expense of obedience and cohesion.

> The Delta soldiers were able to function autonomously, cut off, without orders from higher or assistance from others. The Rangers nearly fell apart in this chaotic environment, precisely because of their extreme cohesion and attendant dependence upon each other.[22]

The clones' moral autonomy was indeed quite fragile upon hearing the order. It takes autonomy to make a competent soldier, especially an elite clone trooper. And it takes moral autonomy for that competent soldier to act morally. Thousands of clones killed thousands of Jedi after Order 66, and we know that only a handful of clone troopers questioned or outright resisted the order. Despite the typical clones' perspective on the "legitimacy" of Order 66 – its source being the Supreme Commander and its justification being to "remove those officers (the traitorous Jedi) by lethal force" – many viewers cringe at the immorality of the clone troopers unquestioningly killing their generals. Captain Rex is one of the few clone troopers who, with Ahsoka's help, refrains from killing any Jedi. Rex, though, was an exception who maintained his independence and autonomy, and clearly struggled with moral issues throughout *The Clone Wars*, *The Bad Batch*, and *Rebels* series, which makes him one of the most well-developed and admired characters, perhaps the exemplar of moral autonomy in *The Clone Wars*.

Notes

1 Charles C. Camosy, "Chasing Kevin Smith: Was It Immoral for the Rebel Alliance to Destroy Death Star II?" in Jason T. Eberl and Kevin S. Decker, eds., *The Ultimate Star Wars and Philosophy: You Must Unlearn What You Have Learned* (Malden, MA: Wiley-Blackwell, 2015), 75.
2 David Sherman and Dan Cragg, *Jedi Trial: A Clone Wars Novel* (New York: Ballantine Books, 2004), 260.
3 Michel Foucault, *Discipline and Punish: The Birth of the Prison*, trans. Alan Sheridan (New York: Vintage Books, 1977), 137.
4 Philip Zimbardo, *The Lucifer Effect: Understanding How Good People Turn Evil* (New York: Random House, 2007).
5 Stanley Milgram, *Obedience to Authority* (New York: Harper & Row, 1974).
6 Daniel Wallace (as Darth Sidious), *The Book of Sith: Secrets from the Dark Side* (San Francisco: Chronicle Books, 2012), 145.
7 Foucault, *Discipline and Punish*, 294.
8 Karen Traviss, *Order 66:A Star Wars Legends Republic Commando Novel* (New York: Ballantine Books, 2008), 331.
9 Ibid., 436.
10 Ibid., 441.
11 Ibid.
12 Daniel Wallace (as Darth Sidious), *The Book of Sith: Secrets from the Dark Side*, 145.
13 Traviss, *Order* 66, 436.
14 Ibid., 459.
15 Lance deHaven-Smith, *Conspiracy Theories in America* (Austin: University of Texas Press, 2013), 25.
16 "The Carnage of Krell," *The Clone Wars*, Season 4, Episode 10.
17 Ibid.
18 Ibid.
19 "The Unknown," *The Clone Wars*, Season 6, Episode 1.
20 "Conspiracy," *The Clone Wars*, Season 6, Episode 2.
21 Foucault, *Discipline and Punish*, 137.
22 Timothy Challans, *Awakening Warrior: Revolution in the Ethics of Warfare* (Albany: SUNY Press, 2007), 170.

6

"Corporations Do Not Rule Us!": The Separatist Freedom Movement and the Struggle for Justice

Mohammed Shakibnia

In *Star Wars* many of our favorite characters have struggled in the face of social and political crises. *The Clone Wars* in particular shows the impacts of a major crisis on vulnerable communities, drawing our attention to those people rendered invisible by conflict as well as those caught in its crosshairs. As we'll see, the *people's-led* Separatist movement was justified as an effort to bring about self-determination, freedom, and justice for marginalized planets that did not feel represented by the Republic. The same spirit of resistance of the Separatist movement can also be found in the citizens of the Republic itself. Both of these movements are similar to our real-world people's-led efforts for justice, such as Black Lives Matter (BLM) and the fight for better living conditions. *The Clone Wars* depicts the dangers and costs of endless militarism and highlights problems with the Jedi. Indeed, these factors, key to the Republic's downfall, are relevant in our world today where we must remain vigilant to prevent democracy from transitioning into an evil empire.

In the past few years, we have faced numerous crises and challenges. From the onset of the COVID-19 pandemic to movements centered on combating racial injustice and climate change, there has been a lot of concern, fear, and uncertainty. We've seen some of the largest social movements and uprisings in modern history centered on the pursuit of racial justice with the rise of the BLM movement. Alongside this, we have seen a new rise of class-consciousness, with

Star Wars and Philosophy Strikes Back: This is the Way, First Edition.
Edited by Jason T. Eberl and Kevin S. Decker.

many people angered at their stagnating wages while the profits of corporations balloon. In response, there's been a reinvigorated movement of direct action, one calling for better working and living conditions through strikes, protests, and boycotts demanding treatment with dignity and respect. The episodes in *The Clone Wars* are pertinent in relation to the events we are witnessing today, giving us helpful tools to understand them.

"My Allegiance Is to the Republic, to Democracy!"

Noam Chomsky and Cornel West help us make this connection to contemporary political issues. Chomsky underscores the need for progressive policies to solve issues like economic, social, and racial inequality.[1] He highlights how the pandemic, in particular, has deeply exposed the pernicious impacts of social and economic inequality. Chomsky's analysis of the US government is helpful because of similarities to the Republic before its eventual demise. Both benefit the wealthy and powerful rather than represent the interests of everyday people in a truly democratic way. Chomsky argues that we must move to a more free and just society, where there is "production for need rather than production for profit," and where working people control their own lives.[2]

Cornel West discusses the ways democratic traditions and values are under threat in the US, highlighting three dogmas that seriously threaten democratic sensibilities: free-market fundamentalism, aggressive militarism, and escalating authoritarianism. The first glorifies market-driven, for-profit forces.[3] Rather than being challenged for unethical business practices, manipulation, and worker-mistreatment, corporations are protected by political elites. The result is an obscene amount of wealth inequality, threatening the democratic distribution of resources, power, and opportunity for ordinary people.

The second dogma comes in the form of unilateral military interventions, armed occupations, and imperialism. Most recently, these forces have played out in the Middle East post-9/11 with the expansion of the War on Terror, leading to devastating consequences for the people of Iraq and Afghanistan.[4] Aggressive militarism also manifests through policies like the War on Drugs and the martial policing and criminalization of poor communities of color. In West's third dogma, fear of the "Other" and potential, hidden enemies has justified civil liberties and rights being curtailed.[5] He cites how 9/11 allowed authoritarian sensibilities to take over through imperialistic acts from the Bush administration through the PATRIOT Act.

West's lens in examining these dogmas is the Socratic tradition: the commitment to questioning, reevaluating, and critiquing institutions of authority. He describes it as fearless speech (*parrhesia* in the original Greek) that is not afraid to make those in power uncomfortable. The Socratic tradition acknowledges that unpopularity follows from exposing abuses of power and structures that oppress the most vulnerable in our society. West also believes we should learn from Rev. Dr. Martin Luther King, Jr. and the Civil Rights Movement, which focused on the intersections of racial, social, and economic justice in the US and overseas. King's thoughts about racial discrimination, class struggle, and imperialism are interconnected, and these themes are also applicable to the Republic in *The Clone Wars*.

From Senator Halle Burtoni to Halliburton

The dangers of the power of for-profit and corporate interests are a central message in *The Clone Wars*. The show highlights the sinister nature of *Star Wars'* military–industrial complex, which rakes in money at the expense of people's lives. In the episode "Heroes on Both Sides," the Republic Senate debates whether to invest in more clone soldiers, a move that would raise tensions and escalate the war. Alongside the provision for more clone troopers, the senators propose to deregulate the banking system to finance military costs. When Padmé calls for the Senate to oppose the bill, those who sponsored the legislation are enraged and senators from the Trade Federation, the Techno Union, and the Banking Clan plot to push their corruption through. A representative from the Banking Clan remarks, "That legislation would have meant billions for us!" Corporations that fund war benefit the most and their interests were prioritized in the Republic rather than a peaceful, humanitarian resolution.

Connections are also made clear with the military–industrial complex in the US. It's no coincidence that Senator *Halle Burtoni*, from Kamino, who strongly supports banking deregulation and creating more clones, is named after the US multinational corporation Halliburton.[6] During both wars in Afghanistan and Iraq, Halliburton was the prime recipient of Pentagon contracts, which included coordinating support functions for troops, setting up military bases, and maintaining military equipment.[7] By 2008, the company had received over *$30 billion* for its involvement in the wars. Vice President Dick Cheney was well-connected with Halliburton, having served as CEO until 2001. Accounting for the profits of the top five weapons companies during the War on Terror, there are clear benefactors as the value of defense stocks is now ten times greater than before 9/11.[8]

This illustrates the "revolving door" of influence in American politics and the suspect relationship between the defense industry and government officials. West would certainly criticize the pursuit of militarism by corporate interests, whether Halle Burtoni or Cheney. Under the dogma of free-market fundamentalism, the Commerce Guild, Banking Clan, and Techno Union are elevated for their "magical powers of salvation" rather than put under democratic scrutiny.[9] West asks how the leaders in the Black freedom struggle, like Dr. King, would ask us to reevaluate our prioritization of militarism. King criticized US involvement in the Vietnam War, pointing to how resources being used to drop bombs and create a larger military are antithetical to a democratic experiment with the aim of providing opportunity to all.[10] King tied the struggles of Black people in America to unjust foreign wars abroad, making connections between the ways empire, race, and class operated. King recognized how the injustices of ongoing wars are motivated by "immense profits from overseas investments," themselves part of the "giant triplets of racism, extreme materialism, and militarism" that needed to be changed with a radical revolution of values.[11]

In "Heroes on Both Sides," we get a glimpse of the Separatist Parliament, which is notably filled with a majority of nonhuman species, and its motivations for resisting the Republic. Communications between Padmé and Separatist Senator Mina Bonteri open up the possibility of peace negotiations. A Separatist leader remarks how their institution is a "*true democracy*," and how, unlike in the Republic, "corporations do not rule us." These factors are added to what they see as a human supremacist institution that does not give nonhumans leadership in key military positions, along with an exploitative system that does not give adequate voice to Outer Rim planets. Yet, the overwhelming majority offers a peaceful resolution to finally end the conflict.[12]

The Separatists were justified in their movement for self-determination and more dignified conditions of life. The Republic, on the other hand, did not accept these articles of secession, instead painting the Separatists as insubordinate "anarchists" counterposed to the Republic as an institution trying to bring "law and order."[13]

The Separatists also saw the Jedi, in their role as peacekeepers, as carrying out missions primarily focused on the core worlds, leaving the more endangered Outer Rim worlds without attention. Even though bad actors like Count Dooku and the corporate alliance co-opted the Separatist movement and sabotaged attempts at reconciliation, we see that in the heart of this people's effort, self-determination and democracy were their goals.

"Not the Jedi Way"

One of the main lessons from *The Clone Wars* is about how the Jedi Order compromised their values by entering the conflict. The Jedi were known as paragons of virtue, justice, and compassion, but they failed to live up to their reputation as the war raged on. The people of the Republic grew angry with the Jedi for their preoccupation with an endless war that only further militarized the Republic and led to the expansion of the clone army. In the episode arc featuring the expulsion of Anakin's Padawan Ahsoka Tano from the Jedi Order and her decision not to return after her name had been cleared, we see the discontent of the people on Coruscant toward the Jedi war efforts.[14]

In the *Clone Wars* episode "Sabotage," the end of the war is near, and the Republic's increasing militarization foreshadows its transition to the Empire. With Admiral Tarkin in command, the Republic becomes more ruthless in carrying out the war effort. Following the Jedi Temple bombing, the council assigns Ahsoka and Anakin to investigate. When they interview potential suspects, Ahsoka notices how the employees of the Jedi Temple are living. In the underbelly of Coruscant, beneath the luxurious skyscrapers, they visit the home of Jackar Bowmani, a working-class Abyssin, who worked in the Temple as a munitions expert and was killed in the blast. Jackar lived in degrading conditions: his residence is full of debris, fading paint, toxic fumes, and mold. As they walk toward the entrance of Bowmani's home, Anakin remarks, "This is not the nicest place … ." and Ahsoka replies, "*I would've thought working for the Jedi paid better.*"

In the eyes of people like Jackar, the Jedi were respected figures who were supposed to make people feel safe and secure. We learn how Jackar worked tooth and nail to get the Jedi Temple job, a competitive achievement because of the prestige of working for the Order. His living conditions pose the question, if the Jedi paid their employees this way, how did the rest of the people on Coruscant itself live? Why was there so much money for bombers, tanks, and clone soldiers, while so many Republic citizens lived in squalor and catastrophic conditions? When Ahsoka talks to Letta Turmond, in "The Jedi Who Knew Too Much," she reveals that the plot against the Jedi, which Jackar had unluckily been at the center of, was motivated by the fact that the Jedi as an institution had changed. Letta tells her, "The Jedi have become warmongers. *They've become military weapons*. And they are killing when they should be keeping the peace."

In light of Chomsky's and West's work, we can see the way social elites such as the Jedi and the Republic's politicians lose touch with the people, appearing to put the needs of the many in the rear-view mirror. If Chomsky were analyzing this situation, he'd point to the failures of the Republic and Jedi in not taking care of the people they are supposed to represent and protect. He'd warn that if people continue living under these kinds of conditions, they'll become disillusioned, feeling betrayed and rightfully angry with their leadership, which could lead to a charismatic, insidious, and authoritarian figure – like Palpatine – seizing power and destroying democracy itself.

Observing a parallel trend in the US, Chomsky would point to the increase of wealth inequality: over the past several decades, unfettered capitalism (which he attributes to neoliberal economic policies) has allowed an estimated $47 trillion to be upwardly distributed to the wealthiest Americans away from the working and middle classes.[15] This pattern is tied to the stagnation of wages for the past 40 years, while the cost of living has continuously climbed. The legacies of trickle-down economics, deregulation, corporate bailouts, and attacks on bargaining power have become central to a political system that puts the material interests of the ruling class above everyday people. Chomsky would note that Jackar's living situation is not so different from many struggling today, portraying the plight of the impoverished and disempowered.

The COVID-19 pandemic is for us what the height of the war is to *The Clone Wars*: legacies of gross inequality have been laid bare for all to see. The economic repercussions of the pandemic disclose America's tiered class system: the poor, often disproportionately people of color, work the most dangerous jobs, putting themselves at high risk on the front lines.[16] Dangers are compounded by a privatized health-care system that supplies profits to insurance companies while tens of millions of Americans remain uninsured or underinsured during a pandemic. Black and Latino communities are disproportionately impacted by COVID-19 and inadequate health care access, leading to a higher proportion of deaths.[17] Moreover, there's the severe impact of structural inequality on a global scale, with poorer nations facing major vaccine shortages while wealthier Western countries have an abundance of vaccines – leading to the emergence of dangerous variants that puts the world at risk.[18]

There is a problem when the powerful remain indifferent to the pain of so many for so long. Chomsky identifies the fault in state capitalist *systems*, not the personal failings of individuals. Change must come by reimagining who's properly served by government and policy. Chomsky has advocated for public policies that uplift everyone and provide opportunities that improve the standard of living, involving a redistribution of not just wealth, but *power*. He affirms that economic rights are human rights, including universally accessible education, health care, adequate housing, strengthening of organized labor, and jobs that provide a living wage with purpose.[19] This type of reimagined society can prevent democratic sensibilities from eroding.[20] By establishing a culture that brings along everyone, people will be collectively invested in the *common good* and public institutions that will foster solidarity, compassion, and care. Such a culture would also mitigate the power of authoritarian, reactionary, and demagogic movements that thrive on a mantra of division. President Donald Trump was able to use the conditions caused by 40 years of class war waged on working people to successfully gain power and galvanize his base with divide-and-conquer style politics. With his scapegoating of immigrants, Muslims, BLM protestors, and the "Other" as being responsible for their struggles, many saw Trump as a solution to their disillusionment with US democracy and the political process. While in power, he was most successful doing the bidding of the ultra-wealthy, consigning millions of American workers to more inequality and further calcifying the power of corporate tyrannies.[21]

Despite these serious challenges, there's been an uprising of social movements, notably the resurgence of BLM protests in the summer of 2020. Estimated to be the largest social mobilization in US history, the protests addressed the brutality of the US criminal justice system, from disproportionately high numbers of police killings of unarmed Black men, women, and children, to mass incarceration and the criminalization of behavior in poor communities and communities of color. Protests also called for getting to the root of the conditions that cause crime, such as a severe lack of economic opportunities and the racial wealth gap. Instead of treating crime with punitive measures and militarized policing, we are called to reinvest resources in areas that would substantially improve people's lives. The protest movement transcended borders, sparking the global outrage of multi-racial coalitions who mobilized to take a stand against racial injustice and demanded an immediate reckoning with institutions embedded in white supremacy.

In the *Clone Wars* episode "Sabotage," we also witness social movements critical of injustices and focused on ending the war. Protestors mobilize directly outside the Jedi Temple, chanting "No more clones! Stop the violence! End the war!" as Republic gunships and clone troopers with riot gear surround them. The violence had been brought home to Coruscant by an attack, and Republic citizens were frightened and outraged at the Jedi's role in the war. This concern is acknowledged by Mace Windu when he, Yoda, Ahsoka, and Anakin discuss the potential motives of the suspect responsible for the Temple bombing: Jackar Bowmani's wife, Letta Turmond. Windu says, "I think we can guess her motives easily enough. Public opinion is swaying against the Jedi, that is becoming clear. This war is becoming less and less popular every day it persists." In the episode "Sacrifice," Yoda also reflects on the futility and injustice resulting from the Jedi entering the war. When Mace Windu asks for his insights on how the Jedi can win the conflict, Yoda replies: "no longer certain that one ever does win a war, I am. For in fighting the battles, the bloodshed, already lost we have."

"We Were Trained to Be Keepers of the Peace, not Soldiers"

When I imagine an alternative path that could've saved the galaxy from falling into the evils of imperialism, I imagine a Jedi Order that confronted the Senate for its corruption and mockery of the democratic process. I think of a Jedi Order that became invested in the needs of the people, helping them resolve conflicts diplomatically and using resources to protect them from the social violence of poverty and despair when their elected representatives failed to do so.[22] I think of the conditions on Separatist-aligned planets and how they felt that the Republic did not uphold their interests. In our world, the BLM movement is doing what the Jedi should've done, raising class consciousness through direct action aimed at a revitalization of democracy.

Ahsoka's experiences building relationships with everyday people, like Trace and Rafa Martez, open her eyes to how far the Jedi and the Republic have fallen from what they are supposed to be. She says, "In my life, when you find people who need your help, you help them, no matter what." She also proclaims, "It's every citizen's duty to challenge their leaders, to keep them honest, and hold them accountable if they are not." These are the values and principles that made her the person she is, a person who walked away from the Jedi Order. They should also be the governing philosophies of our political and social institutions. It's what being the guardians of peace and justice requires.

Notes

1 Noam Chomsky, *The Precipice: Neoliberalism, the Pandemic, and the Urgent Need for Social Change*. Interviews by C.J. Polychroniou (Chicago: Haymarket Books, 2021).

2 Stan Cox, "Noam Chomsky Talks Climate and Racial Justice," *Yes Magazine*, November 9, 2021, at http://www.yesmagazine.org/environment/2021/11/09/noam-chomsky-stan-cox-climate.

3 Cornel West, *Democracy Matters: Winning the Fight Against Imperialism* (New York: Penguin Books, 2004), 4.

4 Ibid., 10.

5 Ibid., 6.

6 Fans and scholars have pointed out the ways *Star Wars* critiques neoliberalism and is connected to US politics, including the parallels between Halle Burtoni, Halliburton, and Cheney. For example, see Jason Ward, "Star Wars & Neoliberalism: Lucasfilm's Critique of Free Market Capitalism," *Making Star Wars*, August 6, 2013, at http://makingstarwars.net/2013/08/star-wars-neoliberalism; Hello Greedo, "A War Profiteering Star Wars Senator Named 'Halle Burtoni' in Star Wars CMON George This Is Obviously a Jab at Vice President Cheney's Connection to the No-Bid-Contract War-Profiteering Company Halliburton! Keep Your Commentary Out of My Star Wars, George Lucas!" *Twitter*, August 17, 2019, 9:45 a.m., at http://twitter.com/hellogreedo/status/1162767387634163712?lang=en.

7 William Hartung, "US Empire Is Lining the Pockets of Defense Contractors," *Jacobin*, September 30, 2021, at https://www.jacobinmag.com/author/william-hartung.

8 Jon Schwarz, "$10,000 When Afghanistan War Began Now Worth $100,000," *The Intercept*, August 16, 2021, at https://theintercept.com/2021/08/16/afghanistan-war-defense-stocks.

9 West, Democracy Matters, 3.

10 Ibid., 57–58.

11 Martin Luther King, Jr., "Beyond Vietnam – A Time to Break Silence, Delivered 4 April 1967, Riverside Church, New York City," *American Rhetoric*, at http://www.americanrhetoric.com/speeches/mlkatimetobreaksilence.htm.

12 Mohammed Shakibnia, "What the Clone Wars Can Teach Us about Racial, Social, and Economic Justice," *Eleven-ThirtyEight*, February 4, 2019, at http://eleven-thirtyeight.com/2019/02/what-the-clone-wars-can-teach-us-about-racial-social-and-economic-justice.

13 Pablo Hidalgo, *Star Wars Propaganda: A History of Persuasive Art in the Galaxy* (New York: Harper Design, 2016), 25.

14 The systemic injustice surrounding Ahsoka's treatment in this arc is also discussed in James and Mona Rocha's chapter in this volume (Chapter 9).

15 Chomsky, *The Precipice*, 327.

16 Nick Hanauer and David M. Rolf, "The Top 1% of Americans Have Taken $50 Trillion From the Bottom 90% – And That's Made the U.S. Less Secure," *Time*, September 14, 2020, at http://time.com/5888024/50-trillion-income-inequality-america.

17 Andre M. Perry, Ariel Gelrud Shiro, Anthony Barr, and Carl Romer, "Amid the Pandemic, Black and Latino Men Have Experienced the Largest Drop in Life Expectancy," *The Brookings Institution*, October 11, 2021, at http://www.brookings.edu/research/amid-the-pandemic-black-and-latino-men-have-experienced-the-largest-drop-in-life-expectancy.

18 Stephanie Nebehay and Josephine Mason, "WHO Warns against Vaccine Hoarding as Poorer Countries Go Without," *Reuters*, December 9, 2021, at http://www.reuters.com/business/healthcare-pharmaceuticals/who-warns-against-vaccine-hoarding-poor-countries-go-without-2021-12-09.

19 Chomsky, *The Precipice*, 183, 298–299.

20 For further analysis of how *Star Wars* depicts the erosion of democracy into tyranny, see Kevin S. Decker, "By Any Means Necessary: Tyranny, Democracy, Republic and Empire," in Kevin S. Decker and Jason T. Eberl, eds., *Star Wars and Philosophy: More Powerful than You Can Possibly Imagine* (Chicago: Open Court, 2005), 168–180.

21 Tim Dickinson, "How Trump Took the Middle Class to the Cleaners," *Rolling Stone*, October 26, 2020, at http://www.rollingstone.com/politics/politics-features/trump-covid-response-economy-jobs-taxes-inequality-1080345.

22 In the "Legends" novel series *Fate of the Jedi*, the New Jedi Order strives to preserve its moral independence from the political machinations of the New Republic.

7

"No One Rescues Droids": *Rebels* on Race and Racism

Steve Bein

In the *Rebels* episode "Stealth Strike," Kanan, Ezra, Rex, and Chopper rescue Commander Sato and his crew from the clutches of the Empire. It's Chopper who saves the day, by rigging an Imperial cruiser to use its gravity well projectors to destroy itself and the rest of its detachment. Without him, the Imperials would only have expanded their collection of high-value prisoners. How does Commander Sato thank the heroic droid for his efforts? "Gentlemen, my crew and I owe you our gratitude. All three of you." Not four. *Three.*

Chopper occupies an uncomfortable moral position in *Rebels*, as do so many droids in the *Star Wars* canon. Many are highly intelligent, with unique personalities that aren't merely a function of their programming (surely no engineer would *choose* to build a droid as temperamental as Chopper or as persnickety as AP-5!). Hera treats Chopper like a crewmate, and Sabine is nice to him sometimes, but everyone else on the *Ghost* abuses him. He's the linchpin of so many of their plans, he saves their lives time and time again, yet his crew constantly treats him like a second-class citizen. What gives?

The truth is, Chopper's mistreatment is business as usual in that galaxy far, far away. Virtually everyone seems to snub droids this way, ever since their first appearance in *A New Hope*. Is everyone just racist against droids? Is that even a thing, if the "race" you're prejudiced against is mechanical, not biological? And just what is racism, anyway? Some say it lives in our heads, a set of beliefs sometimes expressed in words and actions. Others say it's not merely psychological but also structural, expressed through social institutions like school systems, courts, police departments, and so on. Droids certainly aren't a

Star Wars and Philosophy Strikes Back: This is the Way, First Edition.
Edited by Jason T. Eberl and Kevin S. Decker.

stand-in for any group of human beings – they are in fact property, as humans should never be – but we may still ask important questions by proxy.[1] If there's such a thing as anti-droid racism, does it exist in individual minds or in institutions? What does this imply for confronting real racism? We have questions. *Rebels* can suggest answers.

"Luminous Beings Are We, Not This Crude Matter!"

The "organics" of the *Star Wars* universe – those sentient species made of flesh and blood – seem to have relationships with droids similar to the kind many of us have with our laptops and smartphones. We rarely thank them for a job well done, and we vent our frustration at them when they do something unexpected. But there's a world of difference between the Siri and Alexa of our backwater planet and the astromech and protocol droids of *Star Wars*. Siri and Alexa are mindless apps, not at all like Chopper. We needn't understand a single word of binary to know his mind. Through tone, body language, and action, we see him express thoughts and opinions that are clearly his own.

Philosophers call beings who exhibit traits like self-awareness, independent thought, and unique preferences *persons*. Questions of personhood are a philosophical Sarlacc pit: once you jump in, it's not so easy to get back out (though perhaps a flamethrower could help). For instance, when does personhood start, and when does it end? Does a fetus count? How developed does it have to be to count? Can you lose personhood to brain injury or severe mental illness? Does the latter question reflect a social prejudice against people with mental disabilities? These aren't easy questions to answer. Then there's an even bigger philosophical question, more relevant to an interstellar saga: which species count as persons?

For a lot of humans, the initial, intuitive response is that only humans count. Yet many scientists, legislators, and activists argue that certain nonhuman species – namely, cetaceans, great apes, and elephants – deserve some of the rights and protections of personhood that previously belonged only to *Homo sapiens*.[2] But as *Star Wars* fans know, organics don't have to be *humans* to be *persons*.

Consider Hondo Ohnaka. Ezra likes him, Hera hates him, and *everyone* knows he'll choose profit over conscience at a moment's notice. That last bit strongly suggests he's a full-fledged person. A cornered Loth-cat might bite you, but it can't *betray* you like Hondo can. It just does what frightened cats do. To betray you, it needs to have some understanding of how morality works, and maybe even how having a *self* works. One way Hondo betrays people is to leave loopholes in his promises, knowing Future Hondo can wriggle through them. His ethics are twisted, but they're there.

So we can call Hondo a *nonhuman person*, and some people put chimps and dolphins in the same category. But what about droids? Immanuel Kant (1724–1804) offers a litmus test. Any being capable of making moral decisions ("acting according to his own conceptions of laws," as he puts it) is a moral person, to be treated with dignity and not to be used like a tool.[3] So Hondo the Weequay counts, and so does Chopper the droid. Perhaps not all droids are sophisticated enough to engage in moral reasoning – we've never seen a GNK power droid debate whether it should supply power to smugglers or just law-abiding citizens – but Chopper demonstrates that ability repeatedly. First and foremost, he joins the budding Rebellion against the Empire. That's a moral decision right there. And in the tellingly titled "The Forgotten Droid," he and AP-5 engage in a debate about moral duty and free will. Clearly Chopper passes Kant's test. He's a person, therefore abusing him is immoral.[4]

The utilitarian Peter Singer disagrees with Kant on many things, but he agrees that Chopper deserves the moral respect worthy of a person. If Chopper is capable of expressing *preferences* – for example, wanting to replace his jury-rigged leg with a better one (the plot device that drives "The Forgotten Droid") – then, Singer says, the rest of us ought to respect those preferences, just as they ought to respect yours or mine.[5]

Chopper's crewmates treat him more like a piece of equipment than a fellow person, but that alone doesn't prove they're *racist* against droids. We'd need to see how they treat other droids they encounter. But there lurks an even bigger question: Is racism against droids even possible? Even if they're people, are they a *race* of people?

On the Origin of Races (and Species)

Colloquially, it's easy to refer to Kanan, Hera, and Zeb as members of different *races*, where what we really mean is different *species*. Kanan is racially ambiguous, but there's no doubt he's human.[6] Like humans, other species exhibit different skin tones – Hera is green, her dad is orange – but whether they're different *races* is an open question.

That's because the whole concept of race is a relatively recent invention, and contrary to popular belief, it has nothing to do with the color of your skin.

Many people assume that if race is visible in the body, then it must exist in the body: not just your skin, but also the shape of your eyes or nose or lips, the flatness or kinkiness of your hair, and so on. But as Charles W. Mills (1951–2021) observes, this is nonsensical:

> Consider me an example of the contingency and arbitrariness of race. [...] I'm a light brown-skinned Jamaican-American with mixed European and African ancestry. And that means that in the U.S. I count as a black guy. [...] But suppose I were to go home to Jamaica tomorrow. There [...] I am seen as a "brown man," and if I were to describe myself as black, Jamaicans would respond with bewilderment and murmurs that I had been in the U.S. too long.[7]

If you think the hyperdrive is crazy transportation, how about this: a Black man takes his seat on a plane in Chicago, but when the plane lands in Kingston, it's a Brown man who gets out of that very same seat. Why? Because in Jamaican history, the prevailing "racial rules" established not a Black/white divide but a Black/Brown/white divide.[8]

Physiologically, Mills is the same passenger. Nothing about his body has changed. But racially, he's Black or Brown depending on where he's standing. In fact, if we dabble in some philosophical sci-fi, he can be white too:

> A staple of science fiction is an alternate universe where, because some pivotal event turns out differently, the resulting world is radically divergent from the one familiar to us. [...] Imagine an alternate universe where, during the Dark Ages, black Africans sail north, link up with the Moors in Spain and the forces of Islam in the East, and overrun and conquer Europe, establishing a racial dictatorship where dark people rule. In such a world, whites – the conquered race of "savages" – would be seen as the inferiors. So the one-drop rule could be applied in reverse, since white blood is what would stigmatize you. In this alternate universe, I would be socially categorized as a white guy.[9]

It's enough to make your head spin like Chopper's. If the same person can be Black *and* Brown *and* white, depending on the social or historical context, then his race has nothing to do with his biology. But if it's not in the body, where is it?

"It Surrounds Us and Penetrates Us"

Mills says race is a *social construct*, not a biological fact. That doesn't mean it's not real, though. It just means it's not real in the way that blood types or allergies are real. Social constructs – things that exist because societies create them – include things like money, empires, and rebellions, things so real that people are willing to die (or kill) for them.

Hera and her father, Cham, are different *colors*, but whether they're different *races* depends entirely on whether Twi'lek culture constructed the concept of race. It's not clear whether the humans of *Star Wars* ever invented it.[10] (We have so little evidence to judge by! Prior to *Rebels*, virtually everyone in the galaxy was white.[11]) But they and other intelligent species have certainly invented an analogue to racism: the second-class citizenship of droids. If race isn't located within biology, then there's no reason you can't be racist to beings who aren't biological. And the maltreatment of droids certainly resembles what we'd recognize as racism. Consider the conversation between Zeb and Captain Rex at the beginning of "The Last Battle" about the legions of battle droids Rex used to fight:

REX: We used to call them clankers.
ZEB: Clankers. [Chuckles.] I like that. How many of those do you think you blasted?
REX: Oh, I don't know. Probably thousands. Tens of thousands.

How flippant they are! Zeb chuckles at the thought of destroying battle droids by the thousands, and Rex thinks it's no big deal. That's okay *if* battle droids are nothing but mindless machines. In that case, Rex was just doing his job. But what if they're not mindless? What if they have opinions and desires of their own? In short, what if a battle droid is a person? If so, then "clanker" sounds more like a racist slur and Rex looks more like a war criminal than a hero.

"Never Underestimate a Droid"

Before we condemn Rex and Zeb, we need to recognize two crucial differences between droids and humans. First, not all droids are created equal. Some (like astromech and inventory droids) satisfy the criteria for personhood, while others (like mouse droids) have rudimentary data-brains built for rote, repetitive tasks. Battle droids are arguably in the latter camp; they were added to the *Star Wars* mythos not as characters but as cannon fodder and comic relief. They're totally expendable – the clones before there were clones – so Rex is probably in the clear.

Second, droids are property. Some of them resent that fact, and a few – well, just three so far – take a stand for droid liberation.[12] There's also the occasional organic like Hera Syndulla, who doesn't think of droids as mere equipment. In "Hera's Heroes," she says she *saved* Chopper from a crashed Y-Wing, where others might have said *salvaged*. She's the only one who consistently treats him with a modicum of respect. But even Hera doesn't always think of him as an equal – at least, not equal enough to consider him a friend. The first time she and Kanan meet AP-5 ("The Forgotten Droid"), they're stunned to hear him stand up for Chopper:

AP-5: I am Chopper's friend.
KANAN: Friend?!?
HERA: Chopper doesn't *have* any friends.

The plainest way to read Kanan and Hera's response is to say they know Chopper well – well enough to know he's such a pain in the ass to be around that no one who meets him wants to be his friend. But note the subtext in this conversation: even Kanan and Hera don't think of themselves as Chopper's friends. They sometimes use the word *family* to describe the crew of the *Ghost*, but Chopper? At best he's the family member nobody likes. At worst, he's a piece of equipment.

But this isn't racism yet. Racism isn't an interaction, it's a widespread pattern of interactions. Thus, if anti-droid racism exists, it must be in many places at once and it has to persist over time. Which is exactly what we see in *Star Wars*, right from the beginning. "We don't serve their kind here," says Wuher, proprietor of the cantina in *A New Hope*. He's even got a droid detector at the door, to warn him if "their kind" set foot in his bar while he's not looking. Does Obi-Wan, our noble Jedi Knight, challenge this injustice? Does Luke? No. "Why don't you wait out by the speeder?" Luke says. "We don't want any trouble."

Worse yet, Threepio doesn't even resent it. Keep in mind that he, Artoo, and Luke already know the Empire is looking for them. Stormtroopers have put a cordon around Mos Eisley, and squads of them scour the city in search of these two droids. Yet Threepio – the worrywart whose most defining character trait is avoiding risk – doesn't object. He simply says, "I heartily agree with you, sir," and heads out into danger. Why?

AP-5 knows: it's racism. In this case, it's *internalized racism*: here, as in so many other scenes, Threepio's dialogue suggests he sees himself as subservient, unequal. We see the same with AP-5 in "The Forgotten Droid." When he learns Hera rescued Chopper, he says, "Rescue? No one rescues droids." He's not merely reporting facts; he's taking his own expendability for granted. Not all droids do, of course. Chopper certainly doesn't, and I like to think Artoo leaves the cantina whistling a long beep-boop-beep of protest that's drowned out by the band. But we can hardly blame AP-5 for feeling hopeless. Where you see droids in *Star Wars*, you see second-class citizenship.

"Everything's under Control, Situation Normal"

What can all this tell us way out here, far beyond the Outer Rim, where the best we can do in the droid department is a phone that can fake being smart? Let's start with "We don't serve their kind here" and unpack what it really means.

The first way to explain the cantina scene is to think of racism as a set of *beliefs*. Beliefs belong to individual people, who act on them in different ways and who (presumably) could be talked out of those beliefs if they were open-minded enough to consider counterarguments and counterevidence to their position. So if a group of people on Tatooine decided racism is stupid and they wanted to rid their world of it forever, the most straightforward solution would be to just do philosophy: demonstrate the faulty reasoning underlying racist beliefs so that reasonable people dump those beliefs in the nearest trash compactor.[13] It's a strategy that should work just as well in Minneapolis or London as Mos Eisley or Lothal.

The second explanation says racism resides not merely in personal beliefs but also in social institutions – school systems, government agencies, economic policies, and so on. This is the core of *critical race theory*, which is suffering from a PR problem lately. Its opponents call it a radical new political movement, but it's none of those things. It's not new; it's of the same vintage as *Star Wars*, dating back to the late 1970s. It's not a political movement; it's an academic one, a movement of wonky nerds in law schools and university departments like Philosophy and Sociology. It's not even all that radical; its critics usually agree with it once you explain what it actually is. At its core it just says racism is much too big to be propelled by personal beliefs alone.

Think about the cantina. The fact that anyone even sells droid detectors already points to widespread social prejudice. The Mos Eisley city council could've banned those machines, but didn't (if they were illegal, surely Wuher would keep his hidden, not right by the front door). The sentence "We don't serve their kind" tells us even more about droids' social status. Wuher didn't say "*I* don't want them in *my* bar." No, he belongs to an empowered "we" who gives or denies rights to "their kind." Plus, how did the droids get there in the first place? If Threepio and Artoo are persons, then they weren't *scavenged* by Jawas, they were *kidnapped* (which, by the way, explains the restraining bolts placed on them). Subsequently they were sold into servitude, not to some evil Sith Lord but to an ordinary family of moisture farmers.

Owen Lars doesn't buy droids as a conscious expression of his racist beliefs about them. He buys them because they're for sale, in a political system that has legalized putting price tags on them, in an economy where it's normal to pay for droids instead of paying droids for their labor. Similarly, according to critical race theory, the reason Black Americans are imprisoned five times more often than white Americans isn't because each and every judge acts on their own racist beliefs.[14] Sure, there must be some racist judges out there, but judges don't have the power to create a nationwide trend that spans generations. To do that, they'd need a say in who gets arrested and which suspects get charged with what. They'd have to pre-screen lawyers and jurors, weeding out those whose racist beliefs aren't strong enough. And they'd have to do this not just in their own courtrooms, but across thousands of them, for more than a century.

A racist judge who wanted to pack prisons with people of color would have to pull off the greatest Jedi mind trick of all time – *if* racism was a matter of personal belief. Or, consider the more straightforward explanation: racism isn't just in your head. It lives in overlapping systems of control. It's built into law schools and police academies, courthouses and prisons, as well as Empires and Rebel Alliances. To use Han Solo's phrase, it's situation normal.

That's why critical race theory upsets certain people. It points out who wins and who loses in situation normal. If I'm winning the game, I don't want to learn it's been rigged in my favor. Fixing the rules so others have a shot at winning might not feel fair to me; to people in power, equality feels like oppression.

You're Our Only Hope

A final question: Who cares? Why should Chopper care *why* Ezra insults him? Maybe the kid consciously chose to believe droids are lesser beings, or maybe his belief is just a trickle-down effect of Lothalian politics. What's the difference?

In the moment, maybe not much. Chopper's feelings are hurt either way. But if we actually want to *solve* racism, the difference is bigger than a Death Star. To change personal beliefs, we engage in philosophical dialogue. To change entire social institutions, it'll take concerted political effort, and that means effort from *you*. We all have to pitch in. As Mills puts it, "[I]n the same way society created [race], society will have to dismantle it. It won't go away by pretending it doesn't exist because social structures will continue to reproduce that race-based privilege and disadvantage."[15] Critical race theory isn't about the past, or about making anyone feel guilty about what their ancestors did. The theory acknowledges that we today aren't the ones who built this system. But the system is fully armed and operational, and we can keep it running or we can do the hard work of deconstructing it.

That means seeing a country plagued by racism the same way we'd see a malfunctioning droid. There's no reason we can't love the droid *and* recognize it needs repair. In fact, loving it may well *require* repairing its malfunctions. Personal beliefs are like oil leaking from a bad motivator: They're not the heart of the problem. Yucky, yes. In need of cleanup, yes. But the motivator itself – the motor that's pushing society in the wrong direction – is what we need to take apart, reexamine, and replace.

Notes

1 For an argument that droids, too, shouldn't be treated as property in *Star Wars*, see Joshua Jowitt's chapter in this volume (Chapter 16).

2 For a philosophical overview, see Paola Cavalieri, *The Animal Question: Why Nonhuman Animals Deserve Rights* (Oxford: Oxford University Press, 2002). For overviews of the science, regarding cetaceans see https://us.whales.org/whale-culture/scientific-evidence-for-whale-and-dolphin-rights, and regarding apes see Wolfgang Scharmann, "The Great Ape Project: Human Rights for the Great Anthropoid Apes," *ALTEX* 17 (2000), 221–224 [German]: https://www.altex.org/index.php/altex/article/view/1388/1384. For a short history of successful litigation on

behalf of elephants and chimpanzees, see https://www.nonhumanrights.org/progress.

3 See Immanuel Kant, *Groundwork for the Metaphysics of Morals* (Indianapolis: Hackett, 1993), 23. By the way, treating Hondo with dignity doesn't mean giving him a free pass! Kant says that for us to respect Hondo's dignity as a person, we have to hold him accountable for his actions – something we don't have to do with Loth-cats. See Claudia Blöser, "Degrees of Responsibility in Kant's Practical Philosophy," *Kantian Review* 20 (2015), 183–209.

4 It's worth noting – especially in discussing race and racism – that Kant didn't believe all humans could pass this test. Small children clearly have to grow into it, and it's hard to identify a bright line between little rule-follower and grownup moral decision-maker. Some adults might lack full moral agency too, due to certain kinds of cognitive dysfunction. But Kant's most egregious position is that only white people have full moral agency. He said Asians were capable of following moral rules but not of actually doing moral philosophy. Africans were another rung down, unwilling to follow rules but capable of being beaten or trained into compliance. Native Americans were lower still, not even capable of being educated. So we can draw a distinction between "Kant's standard" (which is clearly racist) and "the Kantian standard" (which, *when applied fairly*, will identify adults of every race as having full moral personhood). For a quick overview of Kant's racism, see Charles W. Mills, *The Racial Contract* (Ithaca: Cornell University Press, 1997), 70–71. For a deeper dive, see Emmanuel Eze, "The Color of Reason: The Idea of 'Race' in Kant's Anthropology," in Katherine Faull, ed., *Anthropology and the German Enlightenment* (Lewisburg, PA: Bucknell University Press, 1995), 196–237.

5 Singer's utilitarianism is called preference utilitarianism, and it says an action is morally right to the extent that it fulfills as many personal preferences as possible, for all parties involved, and an action is wrong to the extent that it thwarts these preferences. This is a modified version of classical utilitarianism, which measures right and wrong in terms of whether an action maximizes overall pleasure and minimizes overall pain. See Peter Singer, *Practical Ethics* (Cambridge: Cambridge University Press, 2011), 13.

6 In fact, all the human leads in *Rebels* are of mixed racial heritage, according to Lucasfilm's Pablo Hidalgo. See Mia Moretti, "Rebels, Kanan Jarrus, and the Race Factor," February 24, 2014, at http://eleven-thirtyeight.com/2014/02/rebels-kanan-jarrus-and-the-race-factor.

7 Charles W. Mills, "White Being/Black Being: Metaphysics of Race," in Kerry James Marshall, ed., *One True Thing: Meditations on Black Aesthetics* (Chicago: Museum of Contemporary Art, 2003), 8.

8 Yes, I find the majuscules distracting too. Capitalizing "Black" and "Brown" but not "white" is a complex choice, even for people who write about this stuff professionally. The *Columbia Journalism Review*

provides us an excellent case study. For an argument to capitalize either all of them or none of them, see Merrill Perlman, "Black and White: Why Capitalization Matters," June 23, 2015, at https://www.cjr.org/analysis/language_corner_1.php . For a later argument reversing the journal's position, see Mike Laws, "Why We Capitalize 'Black' (andNot'White')," June16,2020,athttps://www.cjr.org/analysis/capital-b-black-styleguide.php.

9 Mills, "White Being/Black Being," 8. The "one-drop rule" is the umbrella term for a set of laws in American history that legally defined people as Black, based not on their parents' (or grandparents' or great-grandparents') race, but on having even one Black ancestor at any point in their lineage. These lawmakers must not have noticed that these laws made them Black too, along with every human being ever born, since *Homo sapiens* itself is originally an African species.

10 Timothy Zahn's novels *Specter of the Past* and *Vision of the Future* give us only a hint: Imperials routinely refer to the New Republic as being run by "aliens and alien-lovers." That's surely an allusion to racist lingo in the United States, but we'd need more details to know if this gets us all the way to racism. However, it's definitely a commitment to *speciesism* (the belief that one species is superior to others).

11 Actor, director, and *Star Wars* nerd Kevin Smith aptly pointed this out through the critical eye of his character Hooper X in the film *Chasing Amy* – the same Kevin Smith, of course, who declared the Rebels to be "terrorists" in his film *Clerks*. For a rebuttal to the latter, see Charles C. Camosy, "Chasing Kevin Smith: Was It Immoral For the Rebel Alliance to Destroy Death Star II?" in Jason T. Eberl and Kevin S. Decker, eds., *The Ultimate Star Wars and Philosophy: You Must Unlearn What You Have Learned* (Malden, MA: Wiley-Blackwell, 2015), 67–78.

12 The three droids are *Solo*'s L3-37 (discussed in Jowitt's chapter, see n. 1) and the little-known 0-0-0 and BT-1, heroes of the mini-comic "The Misadventures of Triple Zero and Beetee" (*Darth Vader*, #20, Marvel Comics, 2015).

13 For explication of the faulty reasoning underlying racism, in addition to the sources already cited, see Joseph W. Long, "The Logical Mistake of Racism," *Philosophy in the Contemporary World* 8 (2001), 47–51.

14 For a nifty interactive infographic, see "Incarceration in Real Numbers," at https://mkorostoff.github.io/incarceration-in-real-numbers. For a more detailed analysis, see the Fair Trials white paper, "The Disappearing Trial: Towards A Rights-Based Approach to Trial Waiver Systems," (Fair Trials, 2017), especially 9–17, at https://www.fairtrials.org/app/uploads/2022/01/The-Disappearing-Trial-report.pdf.

15 Mills, "White Being/Black Being," 9.

8

Individuality and Identity: Are Clones Literally a "Band (or Batch) of Brothers"?

Patricia L. Brace

YODA: (*asking the three troopers to remove their helmets*) Your faces I wish to see.
THIRE: There's not much to look at here, sir. We all share the same face.
YODA: Deceive you, eyes can. In the Force, very different each one of you are.

Star Wars: The Clone Wars 2008 / Cary Silver

In the first episode of *The Clone Wars*, "Ambush," Jedi General Yoda is on a mission with three of the thousands of clone troopers created from the DNA of bounty hunter Jango Fett. As trooper Thire reminds Yoda, to most people, they're copies of the same template, physically identical, with the same mission written into their code: to serve, fight, and die, if necessary, for the Grand Army of the Republic. Under Republic law the clones are considered property of the state, bred by Kaminoans. They are, in effect, slaves, trained for a single purpose. Their individuality is tempered by genetic manipulation and conditioning; yet, as Master Yoda recognizes, cloning can't duplicate the entirety of a human being. Like natural-born identical multiple children (twins, triplets, etc.), a clone's sense of self depends on both nature *and* nurture. Their "father" provided the genetic material, but the artificial womb jar, accelerated growth rate, and other alterations give them a very different life experience from a natural-born child. Raised and trained in "batches," the clones come to see one another as *brothers*, adding a layer of familial loyalty to their military code of honor.

Star Wars and Philosophy Strikes Back: This is the Way, First Edition.
Edited by Jason T. Eberl and Kevin S. Decker.

Can the Fett clones be considered unique individuals even though they're all created from the DNA of a single person? Is human DNA all it takes to make one a person? Is the self simply the mind or the body or a combination of the two? If law specifies that only a naturally born person has rights, protections, privileges, responsibilities, and liabilities, can the artificially created Fett clones be considered persons? Are they non-person slaves since they're "owned" by the Republic? What happens when the war for which they were bred ends? Do their owners have the right to dispose of them? The concepts of *personhood* and *personal identity* provide a basis for examining these questions.

One way to discuss personal identity is by distinguishing between *specific* and *numerical* types of similar things. Aristotle (384–322 BCE), in his *Topics, Book I*, states:

> It seems that things numerically one are called the same by everyone with the greatest degree of agreement. But this too is apt to be rendered in more than one sense; its most literal and primary use is found whenever the sameness is rendered by a *name or definition*, as when a cloak is said to be the same as a doublet, or a two-footed terrestrial animal is said to be the same as a man; a second sense is when it is rendered by a *property*, as when what can acquire knowledge is called the same as a man, and what naturally travels upward the same as fire; while a third use is found when it is rendered *in reference to some accident*, as when the creature who is sitting, or who is musical, is called the same as Socrates. For all these are meant to signify numerical *unity*.[1]

The Star Wars clones are all of the same *kind* but differ in number – that is, in a line-up of clones, each is counted as a separate thing. Each is a cloned being, originating from the DNA of Jango Fett, but as soon as they start to differentiate and develop individual personality traits, they cannot be seen as the *same* being.

"Very Different, Each One of You Are"

For John Locke (1632–1704) a person is a thinking self, rational and self-aware.[2] Personal identity is based on *memories*: if you can recall an event, you experienced it; if you have no memory of something, it didn't happen – at least not *to you*. While the Fett clones may share the same physical form – except for the genetically modified "Bad Batch" group, female clone Omega, and the too rapidly aged, mutated

Clone 99 – as soon as they leave their maturation chambers, they start creating their own individual memories. Even the unaltered clone Boba Fett, raised by Jango as his son, isn't an exact duplicate because he doesn't share his father's unique life experiences. They're all different people, despite sharing a face.

We follow several clones' stories through the seasons of *The Clone Wars* series. Two of these are CT-5555 (known as "Fives") and CT-1409 (known as "Echo"), both originally members of cadet training squad Domino. We follow them from their start on Kamino. In their first appearance in the episode "Clone Cadets," we are introduced to the clone training methods instituted by the tough bounty hunters and their more understanding Jedi supervisor. We watch them bond with their squad, and in subsequent episodes, see them rise to the occasion bravely and face the deaths of their brothers. The two remaining, Fives and Echo, are promoted to be ARC troopers and become trusted and respected soldiers, accompanying Generals Obi-Wan Kenobi and Anakin Skywalker on their missions. With each subsequent appearance they make new choices, adding to their individual memories, and so growing as individuals. This also allows us as the audience to see them as such, and we find ourselves rooting for them. Fives is given a tragic character arc when he discovers the Emperor's plot to use the clone control chips to execute Order 66, resulting in his death in season six's "Orders." Since we have followed his journey to that point, we mourn him, just as his comrades do. We see him as a person.

When Echo appeared to be killed in a shuttle explosion in season three's "Counterattack," Fives had been thought the sole survivor of the original Domino squad. Four seasons later Echo is discovered alive but altered. His damaged limbs have been replaced with cybernetic implants and he has been forced by the unscrupulous Techno Union to plot counterattacks against the Republic forces. He no longer shares the full human physicality of the rest of the clones. His body is "more machine than man," as he is later described by Bad Batcher Crosshair, but his mind is intact, including his memories of clone brotherhood and loyalty to the Republic that the Techno Union had suppressed by placing him in cryostasis. When he's freed, he retains all the plans and schematics of the Separatists, and his nifty new robot arm lets him access info-ports just like an R2 unit. The combination of old and new knowledge allows him to heroically save the day on their next mission. As the last of his squad, and because he has been so physically altered, he worries that he doesn't fit in with the "Regs" anymore. Captain Rex realizes this and encourages him to find a new purpose by joining the Bad Batchers. This shows how the personal experiences of the clones builds their memories and individuality, even giving them agency, to some extent, to choose their fate.

No Place Like Home

Some of the ways in which the individuality of each clone comes out are found in the alterations they make to their alphanumeric designations, uniforms, and living environments. In *The Bad Batch*, Experimental Clone Force 99 consists of deliberately genetically manipulated mutated clones "Hunter," "Crosshair," "Tech," and "Wrecker." The original group is completed by Echo, who, as we saw, was turned into a cybernetic slave by the Separatists. In *The Bad Batch*'s first episode, "Aftermath," Omega, a young girl working for the Kaminoans, comes to evaluate them. She tours their quarters, and the differences she observes reveal things about each of them. In general, their barracks are more lived-in and have more personal effects than any of the clone living spaces on Kamino. Crosshair, the gray-haired sharpshooter, has droid anatomy targets and boxes of weapons. He is very thin, has a gunsight crosshair tattoo over his right eye and likes to chew on toothpicks. On the left side of the space is Crosshair's neat and tidy bunk (the Latin word for left is "sinister," foreshadowing Crosshair's coming defection to fight for the Empire).

In opposition to Crosshair's bunk is the personal space of Wrecker. Taller than the others by at least a foot and hugely muscular, he is their Hulk. His copious scars and missing eye on his left side show that he is a survivor. A childlike strongman, Wrecker has soft-looking blankets and plushies, including his favorite, Lula, a handmade Tooka cat, as well as some hand grenades and weights for lifting. Also on the right is the team leader Sergeant Hunter's bunk; he's their strategist and tracker. Hunter can sense electromagnetic fields, allowing him to map planetary terrain correctly. He wears his dark hair long and held back from his half-tattooed face by a red bandana. His area is sparse, with the squad's skull logo and three service medals as the only decorations. Omega finds a photo of the squad in his go-bag, but otherwise Hunter seems to have few personal possessions.

Tech's area is next on the right, exploding outwards from his bunk. The balding clone wears goggles that enhance his vision and give him data about the environment. He's drawn diagrams of his inventions on the walls and spread his work out onto the flat surfaces all around the room, sharing or barging in on everyone else's space. The fifth and newest member of the team, Echo, has joined the squad by choice because of his cybernetic enhancements. Since the quarters were designed for only four residents, he must settle for a hammock. Crosshair distrusts him; his sniper rifle is aimed directly at Echo's corner.[3]

The individuality shown in their living spaces and personal appearances help differentiate them from one another. Another example of this, first-generation clone officer Captain Rex, worked directly with Jedi Generals Kenobi and Skywalker and had their respect and loyalty. He wears a blonde buzzcut and has rank and regimental colors, as well as symbols and additional uniform pieces: a blue pauldron and a kama.[4] His helmet has hash marks and "jaig-eyes" on the front, symbolic of a shriek-hawk, a sigil awarded for bravery in traditional Mandalorian warrior culture and adopted by the clone troopers.[5] He is easily recognizable in each appearance and provides the viewer with a thread through all three of the animated series: *The Clone Wars*, *Rebels*, and *The Bad Batch*.[6]

Frankfurt's Concept of a Person

In his important article "Freedom of the Will and the Concept of a Person," Harry G. Frankfurt explains that what makes humans unique according to his concept of personhood is their "capacity for reflective self-evaluation."[7] What is this capacity? According to Frankfurt, animals and humans both act by consulting what he calls *first-order desires*: "desires to do or not to do one thing or another." Only humans, though, have *second-order desires*, which are desires about first-order desires. "Besides wanting and choosing and being moved to do this or that, men may also want to have (or not to have) certain desires and motives. They are capable of wanting to be different, in their preferences and purposes, from what they are."[8] This reflective self-evaluation may move a person to want to make "a certain desire to be his will," strengthening the second-order desires into "second-order volitions."[9]

Frankfurt recognizes that there may be some humans who don't meet his criteria for personhood:

> I shall use the term "wanton" to refer to agents who have first-order desires but who are not persons because, whether or not they have

> desires of the second order, they have no second-order volitions. ... The essential characteristic of a wanton is that he does not care about his will. ... The class of wantons includes all nonhuman animals that have desires and all very young children. Perhaps it also includes some adult human beings as well.[10]

Wrecker is a Bad Batch clone who sometimes seems to act without reflective self-evaluation, even when the opportunity to reflect is present and the situation warrants it. Genetically mutated to have greater height and strength than the others, he often "Hulks" his way into situations like a wrecking ball; obviously, this can be both tremendously helpful and horribly destructive. Wrecker is childlike, generally happy, and bonds most easily with Omega when she joins the crew. He is also the only one of the group in whom the inhibitor chip becomes active before they can remove it. He almost kills Omega while under the chip's control, but upon its removal he is remorseful. He seems to want to be better and make better choices, but often falls short.

The scarring on his face and scalp indicates that at some point he had a terrible head injury. If he had a traumatic brain injury, that could account for his inability to always think things through and might make him one of Frankfurt's "wantons."

In both *The Clone Wars* and *The Bad Batch*, we meet clones who have gone beyond their initial genetic manipulation. As Frankfurt states in his discussion of second-order desires, "They are capable of wanting to be different, in their preferences and purposes, from what they are." In the *Clone Wars* episode "The Deserter," Captain Rex and his squad meet up with Cut Lawquane, a clone who became a farmer with a wife and children. When his entire squad is killed, he can hear the wounded being executed all around him and so he runs. As he explains to Rex, "I like to think I'm merely exercising my freedom to choose: to choose not to kill for a living." When Rex counters by reminding him that he took an oath and has a duty to the Republic, Cut says his duty is to his family. He also tells the captain that although they are clones, they are still individuals. After all, why does he go by his name instead of his assigned clone trooper number? Cut's ability to escape his destiny as a soldier gives the other clones who encounter him pause. What will become of *them* after the war is over? If they survive, will they have any choice, or will they be the equivalent of slaves, owned by the Grand Army of the Republic, serving it for the rest of their lives?

After disobeying Order 66, the new Bad Batch (minus Crosshair and with the addition of Omega) revisit the Lawquane farm in "Cut and Run," looking for safe haven from the Empire. When Echo asks if they can trust a deserter like Cut to help them, Tech reminds him, dryly, "We're all deserters now." Cut echoes this in his advice to Hunter: "Put being a soldier behind you and make a new life for yourself."

Freedom of Action and Freedom of Will

In "Shattered," the penultimate episode of *The Clone Wars*, Captain Rex offers his mixed feelings about the end of the war, telling Ahsoka Tano that if it hadn't been for the Republic's need for many troops quickly, he and the rest of the clones would never have existed. Her response is that "perhaps some good had come of it [the war]" and that she couldn't have asked for a better friend. This shows their bond and is of course ironic since a moment later, Order 66 is initiated.

The activation of the Fett clones' inhibitor chips with Order 66 represents the intention of the Empire to deprive all the chipped clones of their freedom of action and will. The order to kill the Jedi, their commanders and friends from the start of the war, is a horrible betrayal of both the Jedi and the clones. After a moment of hesitation, Captain Rex and the other troopers' determination to carry out the directive is chilling. The very efficiency that made them such good soldiers now makes them excellent assassins. It is especially poignant to see the 501 troopers, with their helmets painted to honor Ahsoka by mimicking her orange and white facial markings, trying to kill her.

Rex's hands shake as he pleads to the former Jedi Ahsoka Tano: "Fives! Find him. *Fives*." Clearly, he tried to fight the compulsion that Order 66 put upon him and help her but was unable to do so.[11] According to Frankfurt, this means Rex never lost his free will:

> But suppose that someone, without being aware of it, has in fact lost or been deprived of his freedom of action. Even though he is no longer free to do what he wants to do, his will may remain as free as it was before. Despite the fact that he is not free to translate his desires into actions or to act according to the determinations of his will, he may still form those desires and make those determinations as freely as if his freedom of action had not been impaired.[12]

When his chip is removed by Ahsoka, Rex is free to reconcile his actions and second-order desires, but he never lost his "personhood," as defined by Frankfurt, even when under the influence of Order 66.

Those who were not affected by the Order, such as Clone Force 99, Echo, and Omega, decide to leave Imperial-controlled space, but are pursued by a new squad made up of the best of the new, non-clone elites and led by the turncoat Batcher, Crosshair.

"Good Soldiers Follow Orders"

In fact, it may be Crosshair's betrayal that best exemplifies Frankfurt's idea of second-order volitions. All along in the first season of *The Bad Batch*, the viewers and the other clones have been assuming that Crosshair is still under the influence of his enhanced inhibitor chip, intent on carrying out Order 66 and whatever commands his Imperial overlords give him. In the season finale, when he reveals that he had it removed long ago, all are shocked.[13]

The fact that we see his choice to align with the Empire as immoral because it is evil doesn't mean that it cannot be a second-order volition. Frankfurt states, "It may not be from the point of view of morality that the person evaluates his first-order desires.... Second-order volitions express evaluations only in the sense that they are preferences. There is no essential restriction on the kind of basis, if any, upon which they are formed."[14] Crosshair wants to be on the winning side, so he throws in his lot with the Emperor. As an individual, he has every right to do so. Master Yoda was right when he said that each of the clones was different from all the others. As Frankfurt states, "Suppose, however, that he enjoys both freedom of action and freedom of the will. Then he is not only free to do what he wants to do; he is also free to want what he wants to want."[15] This means that he decides, of his own free will, to remain with and support the Empire and not his former band or batch of brothers. And even if we disagree with his decision, we can now see that this is his right – as a *person*.

Notes

1 W.A. Pickard-Cambridge, "Topics," in *Complete Works of Aristotle, Volume 1: The Revised Oxford Translation*, ed. Jonathan Barnes (Princeton: Princeton University Press, 1984), 167–277; my emphasis.

2 John Locke, *An Essay Concerning Human Understanding*, 27e (London: T. Tegg and Son, 1836).

3 See Jennifer Roy, "*Star Wars*: How the Bad Batch's Quarters Reveal Insights into Their Personalities," http://CBR.com, May 14, 2021, at https://www.cbr.com/star-wars-bad-batch-quarters-reveal-personalities.

4 A pauldron is like a shoulder pad attached to the collar of a uniform. Color can indicate rank: https://starwars.fandom.com/wiki/Pauldron. A kama is a leather half kilt worn originally by Mandalorian warriors to help protect their legs from the downdraft of their jetpacks. It was adopted by the ARC clone troopers and could indicate rank: https://starwars.fandom.com/wiki/Kama/Legends.

5 "Rendered as a stylized pair of shriek-hawk eyes, jaig were a mark of honor that select Mandalorian clan chieftains elected to bestow on warriors in recognition of their bravery." Since some of their trainers were Mandalorian, the clones adopted this tradition: https://starwars.fandom.com/wiki/Jaig_eyes.

6 Captain Rex was so popular that Dave Filoni, producer/writer/director of the animated *Star Wars* series, agreed with fans who posited that the white-bearded rebel commander in the Battle of Endor in *Return of the Jedi* is Rex. Peter Sciretta, "A 'Star Wars' Animated Character Might've Appeared in a Live-Action Star Wars Movie?" slashfilm.com, March 30, 2016,athttps://www.slashfilm.com/543496/captain-rex-in-return-of-the-jedi/?utm_campaign=clip.

7 Harry G. Frankfurt, "Freedom of the Will and the Concept of a Person," *The Journal of Philosophy* 68 (1971), 5–20.

8 Ibid., 6–7.

9 Ibid., 10.

10 Ibid., 11.

11 Rex took Fives's conspiracy theory seriously enough to file a report that was buried by the Empire. Ahsoka finds it when she follows up Rex's clue and figures out how to capture and help him.

12 Frankfurt, "Freedom of the Will...," 15.

13 Ironically his chip removal was probably after his head injury battling against his former friends in "Battle Scars."

14 Frankfurt, "Freedom of the Will...," 13.

15 Ibid., 17.

9

The Failure of Jedi Ethics: The Jedi Betrayal of Ahsoka

James Rocha and Mona Rocha

When the Jedi betrayed Ahsoka Tano, it established beyond any doubt that the Jedi aren't as morally superior as they may wish to believe. This betrayal occurred when the Jedi Council, over objections from Anakin Skywalker and Obi-Wan Kenobi, handed Ahsoka to Republic authorities while ignoring the possibility that she was innocent. The fact that the Jedi relented to the demands of Admiral Tarkin instead of supporting one of their own is just one example of the serious moral predicaments of the Jedi during the Clone Wars.[1] Of course, the very authority that the Jedi respect during this period is under the leadership – unbeknownst to them – of the Sith Lord Darth Sidious. In siding with him, the Jedi are supporting the creation of an evil Empire that will eventually murder almost all of them. By looking at one moment, prior to Order 66, when the Jedi betrayed Ahsoka Tano, we get a glimpse into the larger moral failures of Jedi ethics.

We must celebrate Ahsoka for leaving the Jedi in such dark times. In doing so, she prioritizes justice over blind faith in an authority that happened to be evil. Ahsoka recognizes that obtaining her autonomy means she could *not* follow the orders of persons who insist on being called "master." Jedi ethics are flawed because they submit to the demands of *hierarchy*. Hierarchy in its many forms – whether on the job, in government, or even within a *Star Wars* fan club – makes demands due to its very nature. People above you in a hierarchy expect you'll listen to them just because they are above you. We cannot avoid hierarchy: like the Force, it's all around us. But morality requires us to follow our duty regardless of what so-called superior figures demand. That means that when something morally significant

Star Wars and Philosophy Strikes Back: This is the Way, First Edition.
Edited by Jason T. Eberl and Kevin S. Decker.

is at stake, we should not blindly follow hierarchy, but rather must make sure we check the dictates of moral duty. The Jedi ignore this lesson. They serve the Senate, and thereby Chancellor Sheev Palpatine. At key moments when morality would tell the Jedi to proceed more cautiously, they instead give in to the demands of power that come from higher up in the hierarchy.

The Jedi *claim* to have an impartial system of ethics based on their advanced ability to rise above their feelings, but rising above your feelings is not enough to be impartial. Impartiality also demands that the Jedi ignore their place in larger hierarchical systems, such as their relation to the Senate, or, in one powerful interpretation of what the Senate *actually is*, Chancellor Palpatine.

Disappointing Jedi at a Place So Sacred

Like the droid Russo-ISC in *The Clone Wars* episode "Sabotage," we must begin by analyzing the crime scene. When the Jedi Temple is bombed, suspicions immediately turn toward the possibility of a Jedi culprit. While Ahsoka initially doubts a Jedi could've been responsible, Anakin explains, "Not every Jedi agrees with this war." We later see the family and friends of workers in the Temple protesting the war and the violence they associate with the Jedi. While the Jedi present themselves as "keepers of the peace," they are also generals leading a galaxy-wide war, bringing violence and destruction to pretty much every planet they visit.

Initially, it appears that Letta Turmond bombed the Temple by feeding explosive nano-droids to her husband, Jackar Bowmani, who had access to the Temple as a munitions expert. Tarkin convinces Anakin and Ahsoka that it makes perfect sense for Letta's trial to be held under military jurisdiction, arguing that clone soldiers died in the bombing; an attack on the Jedi is an attack on the Senate; and the suspect wasn't a Jedi. It's troubling that the Jedi go along with this plan: as Ahsoka argues, it should've been handled as a Jedi matter. Regardless, Letta is arrested by the Republic military and Ahsoka's objections are swept aside. The Jedi give up their responsibility to investigate much too easily, simply letting Tarkin take over. The Jedi are agents of the Senate, and Tarkin speaks on behalf of the Senate; in other words, they are merely adhering to their place in the hierarchy.

As Tarkin further adds, "The Chancellor feels very strongly that the Jedi be removed from as many military matters as possible.

You yourselves said that you're peacekeepers, not soldiers" ("The Jedi Who Knew Too Much"). In acquiescing, the Jedi are merely playing their roles in the matter, but not as peacekeepers. The Jedi cannot claim to be peacekeepers if they so easily defer to the military authority on important moral matters. This blind acceptance of hierarchy becomes even more problematic when Ahsoka is later charged.

Trusting Ventress

One way in which reliance on hierarchy can cause moral trouble is when it's allowed to overtake other moral values. This arc in *The Clone Wars* showcases various questions of trust. As we transition from the Jedi turning over Letta, who did confess, we see the Jedi continuing to prioritize the demands of hierarchy even when they imperil their relationship of trust with one of their own, Ahsoka Tano.

Ahsoka is the only person in the room when Letta's murdered in "The Jedi Who Knew Too Much." Ahsoka is quickly accused not only of being the murderer, but also of being the mastermind behind the Temple bombing. Consequently, in "To Catch a Jedi," the Jedi Council struggle to maintain trust in Ahsoka as the evidence seems to build against her. Even Anakin must confront his trust in Ahsoka when she insists on running. She sees no reason to trust the Jedi Council, other than perhaps Anakin, when the evidence is stacked against her. Unfortunately, Anakin *orders* her to go back to the Jedi Council instead. In this moment, Anakin is still fully trusting the Council. Ahsoka, though, is right that the Council does not deserve her trust. Ahsoka disobeys her master's order and looks for someone she can fully trust. These are strange times when Asajj Ventress is the most trustworthy person around!

Annette Baier (1929–2012) explains that trust can be quite confusing, as it's partially rational, but also based on feelings.[2] Extending trust is rational in the sense that evidence can go a long way to help determine who ought and ought not to be trusted. But at some point, the demands of trust must go beyond what the evidence shows. When you trust someone, you count on them to do something they have not yet done, or not to do something they should not. At the point when evidence cannot tell you what'll happen, trust is determined by your feelings.

Ahsoka trusts Ventress not to betray her, but does not trust the Jedi Council. Ahsoka cannot be *certain* what others will do, but knows that the Jedi Council members are rule-followers, even when those rules come from questionable sources like Palpatine or Tarkin. Yet, Ahsoka cannot be sure the Jedi would actually betray her. Trust concerns the unknown, and you cannot rationally be certain about what's unknown. You must listen to your feelings, and Ahsoka clearly does not feel good about the Jedi Council.

Since you cannot know what will happen when you trust others, you are *vulnerable* to what might happen from trusting them.[3] Ahsoka feels safer opening herself to Ventress, of all people, rather than the Jedi Council. She's right to do so, based, in large part, on the evidence that Ventress knows the feeling of betrayal from the Battle of Sullust. There, her own master, Count Dooku, turned on her. In agreeing to help, Ventress makes herself vulnerable by trusting Ahsoka, which later gets her in trouble – trust is never a guarantee.[4] The Jedi Council, on the other hand, prove themselves unworthy of Ahsoka's trust, as they end up turning her over.

The Not So Precious Jedi Order

The Jedi Council places more value on playing their part in hierarchical political and military systems than trusting one of their own. Once Anakin catches Ahsoka and brings her before the Jedi Council in "The Wrong Jedi," it becomes clear that the Council will not give Ahsoka a fair chance. Mace Windu and Yoda make clear that they have already decided, along with the majority of the Council, to expel Ahsoka from the Order and hand her over to the military authorities, just as they'd done with Letta before. Ahsoka's innocent, of course, which is *obvious* to anyone who's been paying attention during the Clone Wars. How are the illustrious members of the Jedi Council so easily duped, both by Barriss Offee, the actual culprit, and by Darth Sidious?

The answer lies in their repudiation of their feelings. The Jedi's claim to ethical *impartiality* is due in large part to their denial of their feelings. Yet, feelings can be guides to what's ethically important. Fear and anger – to name two feelings the Jedi attempt to rise above – can be essential warning signs to potential moral quandaries. Fear tells Ahsoka to flee because she's afraid the Jedi Council will betray her, and the feeling leads her well in this regard. Anakin's anger at the Council's betrayal of Ahsoka motivates his pursuit of the real killer, whom he eventually finds.

Eventually, however, Anakin's anger creates a wee bit of a problem for the galaxy, but only because he loses control over his anger. Our emotions definitely make our moral problems worse when we let them take us over. But when we treat our emotions as *guides* to what's morally important, we can constructively rely on them. Yet, we cannot allow our emotions to be decisive, as we should always strive to act according to *reasons* regardless of what our emotions try to compel us to do. Ahsoka feels trusting toward Ventress, even though Ventress is a fairly evil person. But Ahsoka also plans around her trust by offering to help Ventress get a pardon and warning her not to kill when they fight the clones. Thus, feelings aren't the main problem for acting ethically. It's certainly true that we have to *limit* our feelings in the pursuit of impartiality and only listen to them as *guides*. Yet, merely constraining feelings in these ways does not ensure someone will be morally good.

Another key step to impartiality is found in recognizing that moral duties must be prioritized over hierarchical demands. When the Jedi hand over Ahsoka to Tarkin, they reduce the morally ambiguous situation to the fact that it's their job to serve the Senate, as represented by Tarkin. Tarkin wants to put Ahsoka on trial because he believes that the Jedi have a biased attachment to Ahsoka. But the Jedi *should* be biased and provide Ahsoka a trial within the system she consensually joined. The Jedi, however, prioritize their place within the larger system of the Republic, instead of trusting the person they know. It's always a challenge, and sometimes dangerous, to deny requests and orders from within a hierarchical system. If the Jedi were to refuse Tarkin's demand for Ahsoka, this could cause significant tension between them and the Senate.

The Jedi default to the system because they accept their social position within the hierarchy. Iris Marion Young (1949–2006) argues that we all inhabit a variety of social positions or roles that define our relationships to each other in society. These positions often constrain what we do, but they also provide us opportunities.[5] Positions and factors include not only race, gender, and sexuality, but also our career choices, hobbies, political positions, religions, and so on. The Jedi play key roles not only in the greater galactic society, but also in the war that Palpatine is secretly orchestrating. The Jedi could refuse to accept what the hierarchy demands of them, but doing so would require them to abandon their social roles.

It's because the Jedi embrace their honored social positions that they are so easily manipulated. Hierarchy, by its very nature, sends *demands*, typically without reasons, downward. We must do our jobs, and in doing our jobs, it's necessary that we tell ourselves that those above us know what they are doing when they direct us in a questionable way. Of course, those higher up rarely have to prove themselves to those below. It would feel natural to the Jedi to follow orders in their social roles supporting the Senate and serving the Chancellor. And when morality is involved, it's much easier to simply assume the hierarchy is not abusing us than to check things out for ourselves. But, it is worth noting that this approach results in lazy thinking and could lead to trouble down the road. And in this case, the Jedi simply follow Palpatine's lead and accept Tarkin's demands, instead of doing their own work to figure out what's really morally required of them.

Learning to Disobey from the Best

Ahsoka, starting in "The Wrong Jedi," walks a different path – a path we can now identify as one of *moral autonomy*.[6] An agent has moral autonomy when she ensures that she makes moral decisions for herself – and does not merely defer to the authority of others. Moral autonomy also requires that she acts according to her best judgment of what moral duty requires of her. The idea of moral autonomy is historically rooted in the thinking of Immanuel Kant (1724–1804), who felt one of the main challenges of moral theory was to explain why moral duty has a stronger claim on us than anything else. Kant's answer is that moral duty derives from our ability to reason about our intentions and actions. So when morality tells you what to do, it's really you (your reason) telling yourself what to do. When you accept the moral law, you have autonomy because you are following rules that you are giving to yourself. On the other hand, when you follow interests that aren't derived from reason, like the commands of others, then you are acting *heteronomously*, which is the opposite of acting autonomously.[7]

The Jedi partially forego their moral autonomy by merely following direction from the Chancellor and the Senate, especially in matters of violence where so much is morally at stake. This moral forfeiture would be a problem even if the Chancellor did not turn out to be a Sith Lord. When you let others make morally significant decisions on your behalf, you just cannot be sure they aren't Sith Lords. So you should never hand over your moral decision-making to *anyone*.

Ahsoka walks away from the Jedi Order, but she does not say she's leaving because the Order betrayed her. She does not seem to blame them at all. Instead, as Ahsoka explains to Anakin, "I have to sort this out on my own, without the Council, and without you." In other words, the violence, the war, and the killing in which the Jedi are wrapped up presents a set of serious moral problems. If they are justified in their actions, then they are fine. If they are not justified, then the Jedi are seriously bad people. And, as Luke Skywalker laments in *The Last Jedi*, the Jedi aren't justified in what they do during the Clone Wars.

Ahsoka realizes she has to make her own decisions about grave moral matters, such as fighting in a war that serves an increasingly autocratic hierarchy. Hence, she only chooses violence when she can confirm for herself that it's absolutely justified – as when she confronts Imperial magistrate Morgan Elsbeth on Corvus in *The Mandalorian* episode "The Jedi." Ahsoka walks away from the Jedi Order, but in doing so, she walks toward her own moral autonomy.

Do Not Ask Him to Be Rational

Though this is Ahsoka's story, it's not hers alone. Ahsoka's growth coincides with Anakin's fall. Anakin shares Ahsoka's concerns, but he falls into heteronomy by putting his concern for Padmé above more important considerations and by pledging himself to Sidious's dark side teachings instead of asserting his own moral autonomy.

As Anakin tells Ahsoka in "The Wrong Jedi," "More than you realize, I understand wanting to walk away from the Order." Anakin also does not feel the Jedi Council is as wise and perfect as they may seem. A significant part of Anakin's realization occurs the moment he comprehends Ahsoka's hearing is a mere formality. The Council wasn't giving Ahsoka a fair chance, and Anakin cannot help but be disappointed. Anakin's anger guides him to track down Ventress and later the real killer, Barriss Offee. But he does not limit his anger and instead uses Darth Vader's signature move, the Force choke. It may not be the first time Anakin has used that dark side move, but its use signifies that Anakin's starting to turn. It also signifies that Anakin's turn to the dark side is motivated by his unconstrained love for three women: his familial love for his mother, his romantic love for his wife, and his brotherly love for Ahsoka.[8]

So why does Anakin not end up gaining autonomy, as Ahsoka does? Although Anakin is growing disappointed with the Jedi, he still reaches out for the comfort of a role within the hierarchy. Anakin does not reject social positions that conflict with his moral autonomy, but merely seeks a different but similar social position. Anakin pushes Ahsoka to trust the system. And even though Anakin's disappointed with the Council, he fully expects and hopes for Ahsoka's return to the Order. While Anakin sees the imperfections of the Jedi Council, he still needs the ease of having moral decisions made for him from up high. Anakin seeks a passive social position, which he finds at the side of Palpatine, as in our final view of him at the end of *Revenge of the Sith*.

Notes

1 For further discussion of the Jedi's troubling moral entanglements in the Clone Wars, see Mohammed Shakibnia's chapter in this volume (Chapter 6).

2 Annette C. Baier, "Two Lectures on 'Trust,'" in *Tanner Lectures on Human Values*, vol. 13 (Salt Lake City: University of Utah Press, 1991), 137–142.

3 Ibid., 113, 137.

4 Ibid., 110.

5 Iris Marion Young, *Responsibility for Justice* (Oxford: Oxford University Press, 2011), 55–59.

6 For one example of an account of moral autonomy, see Onora O'Neill, *Autonomy and Trust in Bioethics* (Cambridge: Cambridge University Press, 2002), 83–95.

7 Immanuel Kant, *Practical Philosophy*, trans. and ed. Mary J. Gregor (Cambridge: Cambridge University Press, 1996), 83–93.

8 For more on how Anakin's "inordinate" love leads to his moral downfall, see Jason T. Eberl, "'Know the Dark Side': A Theodicy of the Force," in Jason T. Eberl and Kevin S. Decker, eds., *The Ultimate Star Wars and Philosophy: You Must Unlearn What You Have Learned* (Malden, MA: Wiley-Blackwell, 2015), 100–114.

10

Of Graffiti and Kalikoris

Daniel P. Malloy

In *Star Wars: Rebels*, Sabine Wren's paintings are more than mere decoration that she slaps onto whatever surface happens to be available, and the Syndulla family's Kalikori is hardly some trinket, as it's passed down generations in memory of a long dead ancestor. Sabine's paintings and the Syndulla's Kalikori have a peculiar quality that we only find in works of art, and yet they don't seem to fit traditional accounts of art in terms of representation, expression, or institutional recognition. Neither Sabine's graffiti nor the Kalikori is representational; collaborative works like the Kalikori are difficult to classify as "expressive"; and both works are excluded from the institutions of the *Star Wars* artworld. So, according to these accounts, Sabine's graffiti and the Kalikoris are not art. And yet they are.

Sabine's Masterpiece

Sabine is a painter, but she doesn't confine her work to canvases or walls. She'll paint seemingly anything – walls are her favorite surface, but she also paints on droids, speeders, her armor, Rukh, and a dizzying array of stormtrooper helmets. Her indiscriminate choice of media is one of the things that makes it difficult to decide whether her work is art. The fate of the TIE fighter that Ezra and Zeb steal in the episode "Fighter Flight" can help illustrate the problem. When Zeb and Ezra steal the TIE, it's a fairly standard piece of Imperial hardware, fast and maneuverable, lightly armed with no shields or hyperdrive. It looks a bit like an eyeball with wings, and its exterior is standard Imperial grey.

Star Wars and Philosophy Strikes Back: This is the Way, First Edition.
Edited by Jason T. Eberl and Kevin S. Decker.

Enter Sabine. Once she's done with the TIE, it's been transformed. Its capabilities as a fighter remain intact, but with the addition of Sabine's unique touches, it's now a work of art, a Sabine Wren original. Gone is the drab Imperial grey, replaced by patterns of yellow, orange, red, and black with Sabine's signature check pattern mixed in. An inert hunk of matter, a weapon of war, designed and built to bring death and destruction, has seemingly become a work of art, with the application of a few well-chosen and well-placed layers of paint.

For comparison, consider Chopper. Chopper spends most of his time in his accustomed orange-and-white coloring, but Sabine sometimes has to paint him. Chopper swaps his orange-and-white for Imperial black or Mining Guild yellow, but *these* paint jobs aren't works of art. They're disguises; decorations added to fool the enemy. There's a difference between the TIE fighter's new paint job and Chopper's, but what, really, is the difference?

"I Paint What I See"

Apart from her love of painting Chopper, Sabine seems to enjoy depicting her crewmates in her work. She paints a fight between Zeb and Ezra in their room ("Fighter Flight"), Kanan and Rex in their shuttle ("Stealth Strike"), and, of course, a mural of the entire *Ghost* crew in the tower on Lothal ("Family Reunion – and Farewell"). Her portraits hint at the oldest notion of what art is: *representation*.

According to the representational account, a work of art must represent other things. This is most obvious in visual arts like Sabine's paintings. A portrait represents the person without being the person. Beyond her portraits, many of Sabine's other paintings are representative. Her preferred graffiti tag is a stylized representation of a phoenix. Stylized representations of Loth-cats and Loth-wolves are also common subjects of her paintings. If we're asking what makes art unique, the idea that it represents things without being them has an appeal. One expectation we have of art is that it'll point us to other things without being them. Sabine's portraits of Ezra and Zeb or Kanan and Rex remind us of those people, but aren't to be confused with the people themselves.

According to this view about how art represents other things, the difference between a Sabine Wren original work and one of her paint jobs on Chopper is that Chopper's various disguises have functions *beyond just representation*. The point of a work of art is to point beyond itself to something else – to draw attention not to the artwork but to what it represents. Of course, maps do this without being art, but if something doesn't represent something else it can't be art. Chopper's paint jobs, on the other hand, are meant to fool others. The point isn't for people to think how much the ornery little droid looks like an Imperial astromech; it's for people to think that he *is* an Imperial astromech.

"Forget the Explosion. Look at the Color"

The intention and ability to "fool the eye" for purposes unrelated to art explains another difference between Sabine's works of art and Chopper's disguises. When Sabine disguises Chopper, the work is picture perfect. Chopper may give away the game with his behavior, but no one would ever guess that he wasn't an Imperial droid based on looks. On the other hand, Sabine's paintings are less accurate representations of their subjects. Sabine's art has many fine qualities, but its stylizations certainly don't *copy* the things they represent. Even her portraits are stylized and abstracted to the point of unrecognizability. When Grand Admiral Thrawn asks Colonel Yularen to identify a sample of Sabine's work, Yularen can only come up with "a beast of some kind" ("Through Imperial Eyes"). His reaction is typical of the dismissive attitude of Imperials, but it's also the best Yularen can do, not being familiar with the animal – a Loth-cat – represented in Sabine's piece. Someone who's never encountered a Loth-cat would have no chance of identifying one based on Sabine's work.

This doesn't mean that Sabine's paintings aren't art, or not good art. It means that not all art is representative. *Visual* arts like painting and sculpture lend support to representation theories because they tend to depict things. But they don't have to; abstract paintings and sculptures aren't necessarily representative of anything. The same holds of other arts that are often representative, like drama and poetry. Other arts like music, dancing, and architecture are mostly not representative, even if they sometimes can be.

A defender of a representation theory might argue that all arts are imitative, but their representation isn't the kind of one-to-one correlation between the image and the subject of a painting or sculpture. A musician, for example, might try to represent birdsong or thunderstorms, but they may also be trying to depict the rhythms of life or the beats of a story. Just as a painter can try to represent something that isn't visual, a musician can try to represent things that aren't sounds. For example, Agent Kallus interprets one of Sabine's phoenix tags as "a symbol of their commitment to victory" ("An Inside Man"). But the more abstract the objects of representation become, the less distinctive and useful representation theories of art seem to be. Much abstract art loses its "art-like" quality and becomes more and more a specific system of signs accessible only to a very few who can interpret them. If we take representational theories of art to this extreme, then *anything* that represents another thing becomes art – including people's names, social security numbers, charcoal rubbings, maps, photocopies, and grocery lists.

"Family History as Living Art"

Understanding representation more broadly leads to a second type of theory of art: *expression theories*. According to an expression account, art communicates in ways that go beyond signs and resemblances. Just as the *Ghost* crew hijack an Imperial communications center to send a message of rebellion to like-minded Imperial subjects ("Call to Action"), Sabine applies her paints to walls (and armor and vehicles and droids and people) to express ideas or feelings to an audience.

This account has the intuitive appeal that what's essential about art is its expressive nature. To return to Sabine's masterpiece, the difference between the Imperial grey of the TIE fighter and Sabine's work of art isn't just that Sabine's piece is more colorful, it's also more expressive. By making one of the symbols of the buttoned-down Empire into a work of eye-catching art, Sabine communicates her feelings about the Empire itself in terms of a contrast: where they're drab and grey, she's bright and colorful.

This theory offers us a much better way of understanding the other prominent piece of art in *Rebels*: the Syndulla family Kalikori. The Kalikori is a traditional piece of Twi'lek art, passed down the generations within a family. Each generation adds something to the Kalikori to express something about their lives and their place in the Syndulla legacy. After Kanan's death, Hera adds a piece to the Kalikori to honor him. The Kalikori is plainly not imitative or representative – no one could say that it resembles the Syndulla family except in the most abstract way. But the Kalikori just as plainly expresses a Twi'lek tradition and the Syndulla family's place in it. By adding to it, each succeeding generation expresses their connection to both the family and the tradition.

On the other hand, the uniformity of the Empire, from the grey ships to the white stormtrooper armor to the red Imperial guards, is also expressive. It all makes manifest the Imperial determination to impose order on the galaxy. But that sort of expression doesn't qualify to define Imperial designs as art. In order to be art, an object must express something – an idea, a feeling, a moment in time – often something that's unique to its creator. This is one of the core differences between expression and representation theories: in a representation theory of art, what makes something art is what it contains, while expression theories place the emphasis on the creator. Any literate person can put words on a page, but only a poet or author can create.

"It's Art. Everything Has a Meaning"

This emphasis on the uniqueness of the artist and the act of creation, however, creates its own weakness in expression theories, one shown by the example of the Kalikori. The Kalikori is the work of many hands. A number of artists have contributed to it over the generations. This presents a problem. It isn't clear how we should understand this collaboration as an expression, or how many artists, separated by generations, can create a single expressive work. More specifically, we have a problem about how the whole of the work relates to its various parts. The whole of the Kalikori is an expression of Twi'lek tradition and of the Syndulla family, but the individual parts are supposed to express something from their different makers. Hera adds a piece to honor Kanan, but if, three or four generations down the line, the Kalikori is still being worked on but no one remembers Kanan, that expression would seem to have lost its meaning and thus its status as art.

A defender of expression theories could say that this sort of detailed information isn't necessary to recognize something as art. We don't need to know what an artist or a group of artists is trying to express in order to say that their work is art. We just have to know that they were trying to express something. We don't need to know who created a particular work to know that it's art. The cave paintings of Lothal, for example, are too ancient for anyone to know who painted them, but we can still say that they are works of art.

The problem with this response is that without knowing something about the artist behind a particular work, we really can't say that this work carries expressions of any sort. We know the Kalikori expresses something, even if we don't know exactly what it is, because we're familiar with the tradition in which it participates. The cave paintings, on the other hand, *may* carry expressions from their creators, and so they're works of art: they could be expressions of gratitude for success in a hunt, or parts of a long-forgotten religious ceremony, or appreciations of the beauty of Lothal's indigenous wildlife. But they could also be the doodles of a bored cave dweller on a rainy day. In that case, they wouldn't be art according to expression theories. Without context, we have no way of knowing.

Art Appreciation with Grand Admiral Thrawn

Yet Thrawn seems to be an expert in just that sort of context. He studies art, appreciates it, and even collects it. He seems to have an uncanny ability to recognize art, and he can pick out an original Sabine Wren from hundreds of similar graffiti tags. While other Imperials ignore the Kalikori in the Syndulla house, dismissing it as "Some primitive, native trinket," Thrawn instantly grasps its significance and infers the identity of its would-be thief ("Hera's Heroes"). What seem like unimportant pieces of trash to others are valuable works of art in the eyes of the Grand Admiral.

This may be because of Thrawn's unique interests or his talent for predicting the actions of his opponents from knowledge of their cultures. But there's also another possibility: perhaps Thrawn is so good at spotting works of art because his appreciation *makes them art*. It's not that Thrawn can transform just anything into a work of art by saying that it is. Instead, Thrawn is a representative of something larger than himself – something philosophers of art call the "artworld." Just as Thrawn has authority aboard his Star Destroyer *Chimaera* because he's a representative of the Empire, his declaration that a piece of work is art carries weight because he represents the artworld.

The parallels between the artworld and the Empire are limited. Who is or is not a representative of the Empire is clearly defined and rigidly regimented. Whose view takes precedence in the event of a disagreement is determined by a known set of rules and regulations. The artworld is far less defined. When Lando Calrissian and Alrich Wren evaluate Sabine's work, they're also acting as representatives of the artworld. To a lesser extent, so is Ezra when he says her work is good. There are no set rules about who can or can't be part of the artworld, or whose opinion is more important than that of others. We do have some broad guidelines. For example, in "Idiot's Array," Sabine explains to Ezra that his evaluation of her art isn't as important as Lando's because, while they both say it's good, only Lando knows why. Lando has broader knowledge of art than Ezra and more skill in articulating what makes a piece of art good or bad. His knowledge lends his views more weight as a representative of the artworld.

According to this *institutional theory* of art, what makes a particular object a work of art is a kind of collective decision on the part of the artworld. The artworld includes artists, critics, museum curators, collectors, and everyday art appreciators as well. So there's nothing inherent in a given object that makes it art, nor is there anything that sets apart the works of some creators as art. Anything, created by anyone, could be art if the artworld agreed.

Not Merely Trophies

That *anything* could be a work of art and that *anyone* could be part of the artworld are common criticisms of the institutional theory. Its broadness doesn't give us any clear guideline to distinguish what *is* art from what *isn't*. However, Sabine's work and the Syndulla Kalikori present us with a more interesting problem. There's only one place where we see one of Sabine's pieces and the Kalikori together: in Thrawn's office. Thrawn has collected the pieces to understand and honor his foes and to preserve what he can of the worlds he destroys for the Empire. He's trying to preserve and display pieces he's identified as works of art. The problem is, in doing so he isn't simply preserving the works, he's changing them.

Thrawn displays one of Sabine's signature phoenix graffiti tags painted on a piece of retaining wall. Describing it, Thrawn notes Sabine's technique, her line work, and her choice of color. But what seems to escape him is that the piece isn't just the paint, but where she chose to put it. Sabine could easily confine her art to canvases or some other medium, but she chooses to paint on nearly anything, including on Thrawn's own bodyguard/assassin Rukh. The medium and context are as important to the work of art as the aspects Thrawn appreciates. By removing the retaining wall and displaying it in his office, Thrawn destroys the piece.

The Syndulla Kalikori is a more dramatic example of this problem. Recall that the Kalikori isn't a finished work: it's a *living* work, designed to be added to by subsequent generations. Further, it's not for public display: the Kalikori is of little to no value, even to other Twi'lek families. But perhaps the Kalikori is finished, as Thrawn says ("Jedi Night"). If the last member of the family dies, then the Kalikori is done. That raises the question of what should happen to the Kalikori when the family is gone. Thrawn's solution is to preserve and display the piece, hoping to learn as much as he can about it from Hera before she dies. But that leaves aside the question of what Twi'lek tradition – the context for the Kalikori's meaning – would do with it. Other Twi'lek families have probably died off while maintaining Kalikoris. We don't know what happened to the pieces in these cases. It may be that when Hera tells Thrawn, "If I knew you'd take it, I would've smashed it when I had the chance," she's respecting tradition ("Hera's Heroes"). When the family dies, the Kalikori dies. We don't know, but Thrawn doesn't either.

Institutional theories confront two possibilities in the face of Sabine's street art and the Syndulla folk art. They can restrict the artworld to certain sorts of figures and institutions, like Thrawn and his collection, or they can recognize wider institutions including graffiti and folk traditions. In the first case, recognizing street art and folk art means removing it from its context, rendering it inert and impotent, stripping it of its meaning and power. In the second case, institutional theories give up their power to determine what is and isn't art – there seems to be no limit to what might be included in the artworld, and so what might count as art.

Something's Missing

The three kinds of theories of art presented here – representation theories, expression theories, and institutional theories – each have difficulties dealing with Sabine Wren's street art and the Syndulla family's folk art. For some reason or other, each theory leads us to conclude that Sabine's graffiti and Hera's Kalikori both are and are not works of art, an impossible outcome.

The basic problem that each type of theory faces is that it tries to define art – a complex phenomenon if ever there was one – by a single feature of a potential artwork. Representation theories are concerned only with the content of a work of art. Expression theories focus on the creation of art. And institutional theories lead us to look at the context in which a work of art is made and presented. Each theory touches on something important to art, but they also ignore other important factors.

Art is a complex social and psychological phenomenon, depending in equal parts on the intentions and talents of the artist and its reception by audiences in the broader social world. It exists only within a context of various traditions, but at the same time it can challenge and overturn those traditions. To get at what makes things art, a philosophical theory has to encompass all these things while still acknowledging the uniqueness of individual works. The Syndulla Kalikori may be part of a Twi'lek tradition, but it's a part like no other. It only makes sense within the tradition, but its loss would do irreparable harm to the tradition.

The examples in this chapter come from a galaxy far, far away, but equally problematic examples can be found here on Earth. So our search must continue. It's usually easy to recognize art when we see it, but good philosophers won't be content until they know *why* something like a Kalikori or graffiti counts as art.

11

A Long Time Ago? Time and Time Travel in *Star Wars*

Philipp Berghofer

Prophetic visions of the future feature prominently in our favorite space opera. Luke has them, like his father before him. The Skywalker saga is basically the story of Anakin being unable to let go, willing to do anything to prevent his prophetic visions from becoming true. The tragedy, of course, is that the very actions he undertakes to save his beloved Padmé lead to her demise. Are the events in the *Star Wars* universe set in stone – that is, deterministic – or could Anakin have chosen different actions that would lead to his living with Padmé happily ever after? Can *we* change the future or is our fate set in stone? Is the future real, just as past and present appear to be? Is time travel logically possible? Can we change the past? While questions like these are debated in contemporary metaphysics, they are also raised by the *Rebels* episode "A World Between Worlds." Here, time travel is finally introduced into the *Star Wars* lore – a surprise, to be sure, but a welcome one.

But, beware! Do not underestimate the menacing paradoxes of time travel!

The Tragedy of Anakin Skywalker

Anakin loves Padmé, and the thought of losing her is unbearable to him. In *Revenge of the Sith*, Anakin is plagued by visions of the future, of his beloved dying. He cannot accept this fate; this future must be prevented at all costs. To do so Anakin is willing to pursue "a pathway to many abilities some consider to be unnatural." The fact that

Star Wars and Philosophy Strikes Back: This is the Way, First Edition.
Edited by Jason T. Eberl and Kevin S. Decker.

his crusade for power, intended to save Padmé, turns out to cause her demise is *the* defining element of the tragedy of Anakin Skywalker. As we'll see, these events pose challenges to thinking about time, determinism, and free will.[1]

Jedi Master Luke Skywalker's later life is shaped by a similar tragedy. Foreseeing all the horrors that'll be caused by Ben Solo, Luke ignites his lightsaber. Ben's realization that his uncle is on the verge of murdering him is *the* crucial factor by which he justifies his later wrongdoings.

This idea that the future is set in stone and that our attempts to prevent future horrors actually cause these horrors is common in storytelling. In Greek mythology, Oedipus becomes aware of the prophecy that he will kill his father and marry his mother. In *Harry Potter*, Voldemort learns of a prophecy that a child will be born who will become his nemesis.[2] In *Star Wars*, Anakin has prophetic visions of Padmé's death that echo visions he'd previously had of his mother's death, which he was unable to prevent in *Attack of the Clones*. Such stories seem to imply that while we can *cause* future events to occur, we cannot *change* what must occur.

Similarly, many time travel stories are based on the idea that we can cause *past* events but cannot change them. In *The Terminator*, the eponymous cyborg travels back in time to kill Sarah Connor so that her son, John, is never born and thus cannot become the leader of the human resistance. However, the Terminator's actions cause Kyle Reese to be sent back in time to save Sarah; he makes love with her and she gives birth to John.[3] In *The Prisoner of Azkaban*, Harry Potter and his friends mistakenly believe that an innocent hippogriff has been killed. They travel back in time to prevent this death, but it turns out that the hippogriff never has been killed and that its death had already been prevented by the actions of the time traveling friends.

Time travel stories in which the past is changed are in danger of being inconsistent or plagued by paradoxes. Imagine that it's possible to travel back in time and you kill your grandfather before he was conceived. You've just undermined your own existence! But if you have never existed, then you have never traveled back in time to kill your grandfather. So you live only if you do not live? Paradox!

We do not have to invoke fancy examples of undermining your own existence to see that changing the past leads to logical problems. Imagine that George Lucas travels back in time and makes some changes to *A New Hope* (*ANH*) so that, in the cantina scene of the 1977 original cut, Han does not shoot first. Lucas has changed the past. But this means that "Han shot first" is both true and not true in 1977! Many philosophers believe that time travel to the past that does not change the past is logically possible.[4] Whether it's possible or not in our world, let us proceed as if time travel is possible and has actually happened in *Star Wars*.

Ezra Bridger – Time Traveler

It's the year 0 BBY (Before the Battle of Yavin) and, perhaps, Ezra Bridger's most desperate hour. His Jedi mentor and friend, Kanan Jarrus, has just died, and Ezra's about to enter the Jedi Temple on his homeworld, Lothal. A painting of the Mortis gods serves as a portal. Ezra manages to open the portal and arrives at the "World Between Worlds," a plane within the Force beyond space and time, binding all moments in time together.[5] There are a vast number of portals that allow travel through space and time, but this one is a "pathway between all time and space" and "he who controls it controls the universe."

Shortly after entering the World Between Worlds, Ezra finds a portal in which he sees Ahsoka Tano dueling Darth Vader. This event happened in 3 BBY. We see Ahsoka fighting bravely but about to be slain by her former master when Ezra reaches into the portal, grabs Ahsoka, and pulls her through, saving her life. Was Ahsoka originally slain by her former master and then Ezra changed her fate? Is this event best understood as Ezra *changing* the past or merely *causing* an event in the past? Ezra believes that changing the past is possible. After saving Ahsoka, he wishes to save his recently killed mentor, Kanan. He tells Ahsoka, "If I can change your fate, I can change his." However, it's far from clear that changing the past is logically possible. At the moment Ezra is about to save Ahsoka, he believes that he knows this fact: "In the year 3 BBY Ahsoka was slain by Darth Vader." Yet when he saves her, that statement cannot be a fact. Could a statement be both true and false? This would be a logical contradiction!

Maybe by entering the portal, Ezra created an alternate timeline: in one timeline Ahsoka was killed and in the other Ahsoka lives! There's no consensus on whether this form of intervention in history should even be understood as an instance of changing the past at all. As seen on screen, the fates of Ahsoka and Kanan are very different. We see Kanan die on screen in the *Rebels* episode "Jedi Night." We never see Ahsoka die in her duel with Vader two seasons earlier in "Twilight of the Apprentice." So, our story may be similar to the hippogriff story in *Harry Potter*. Harry and his friends believe the hippogriff to be dead. However, the hippogriff never died, having already been saved by the time travelers – without them changing the past! Similarly, Ezra may have believed Ahsoka to be dead, but in truth she never died, having been saved by the actions of time traveling Ezra. But what about Kanan?

Saving Kanan, aka the Grandfather Paradox

Ezra and Ahsoka find a portal showing Kanan's dying moments. Ezra has to relive the moment when Kanan sacrifices his life for Ezra and his friends, but he's still intent on saving Kanan just as he saved Ahsoka. But Ahsoka warns, "Kanan gave his life so that you could live. If he is taken out of this moment, you all die." Let us assume Ahsoka's right and there's no way of saving Kanan without Ezra dying. Is this a "mere" moral dilemma, in which Ezra has to make a terrible choice: sacrificing himself or letting a friend die? No, this scenario's also rooted in a metaphysical dilemma called the "grandfather paradox." If Ezra saves Kanan, Ezra dies in the past. But if Ezra dies in the past, then Ezra cannot later enter the World Between Worlds and save Kanan. If Ezra dies before entering the World Between Worlds, no one will save Kanan. But if no one saves Kanan, then Ezra lives and can save Kanan. Kanan can live only if Ezra dies, but if Ezra dies, Kanan cannot live.

But the problems do not stop here. Imagine that Ezra and Ahsoka succeed in saving Kanan, but that Ezra does not die. Past-Ezra, present-Ezra, Ahsoka, and Kanan are happily reunited. But present-Ezra has mourned Kanan's loss. This will not be past-Ezra's future because past-Ezra has no reason to mourn Kanan's loss. Ezra has changed the past, but also created a number of contradictions. Has Kanan lived or died? Has Ezra mourned or not?

In famous time travel stories such as *Back to the Future*, the protagonist travels to the past, changes the past, and then returns to a present quite different from the one they left. But philosophers agree that such stories do not make a lot of sense.[6] In fact, if we agree that there's only one time and one universe, time travel that changes the past seems to be impossible.

"A Bunch of (Metaphysical) Mumbo Jumbo"

Let us further pose the question of whether the past, present, and future are equally real. In contemporary philosophy of time, there are three main approaches to this question: *presentism*, *eternalism*, and the *growing block universe*. Presentism is the view that only the present is real. Only present objects and events exist; past and future objects do not. You exist but Abraham Lincoln does not. Presentism may seem like a commonsense view: it's somehow strange to say that, right now, Abraham Lincoln is equally real as I am. On the other hand, with presentism it's not so easy to make sense of statements about the past and future. Is it true that Abraham Lincoln served as the sixteenth president of the United States? To what state of affairs does the sentence "Abraham Lincoln served as the sixteenth president of the United States" correspond? If the past does not exist, can there be historical facts? Furthermore, presentism seems to be in tension with modern physics. According to special relativity, concepts such as "simultaneous" and "now" are relative. There's no objective *now*.

Eternalism says that the past, present, and future are equally real. Right now, as you are reading this, Abraham Lincoln is as real as you are; the statement that he served as the sixteenth US president is true in the same way as the statement that you are thrilled by the text you are currently reading. Time is similar to space: if you are standing at the gates of Skywalker Ranch, you cannot see what is 50 miles north, south, east, or west from you, but those places *do* exist. Different times are as real as different places. The world in which we live is a four-dimensional space–time that resembles an unchanging block: eternalism is also often referred to as the "block universe" theory of time. Eternalism also implies that there's no open future. At every point in time, it's true that Padmé dies in childbirth in 19 BBY. Often it's thought that this implies determinism, but this may be too hasty a conclusion.[7] Determinism says that the future is set in stone because the future non-accidentally follows from what has happened before. But determinism does not imply that the future yet exists. Eternalism says that the future exists, but it does not imply that the future is determined or even caused by previous events. It may be sheer coincidence that Abraham Lincoln became president. But if it's true, it has always been true. Finally, for the *growing block* theory, the past and present are real, but the future is not. This view best accords with our commonsense idea that the past is set in stone but the future is open.

These views on the nature of time have crucial implications for whether and how time travel may be possible. Presentism seems to be incompatible with time travel. If the past does not exist, how could I travel there? I cannot travel to a non-existent space, so how I could travel to a non-existent time? This argument is intuitive, but there are counterarguments.[8] Eternalism seems best suited to allow for time travel: if I can move from place to place, perhaps I can also move in time. Of course, to say that time travel is possible in any of these senses does not imply that it's *physically* possible. Also, time travel paradoxes still lurk!

In the growing block picture, traveling to the future seems impossible but traveling to the past should be possible. However, there's one fact about the growing block that makes time travel particularly scary. The growing block contains an objective present. The universe consists of everything that has happened from the beginning of time until that objective present. So if the objective present is first located in 42 BBY and then grows until it's in 0 BBY, the universe contains much more than before. For instance, in 42 BBY the universe did not contain Grogu (born in 41 BBY) but in 0 BBY it does. Now imagine that when Tarkin is informed toward the end of *ANH* that there's a danger that Rebel pilots could destroy the Death Star, Tarkin does not stay on the Death Star. Instead, he enters a time machine and travels from 0 BBY to 42 BBY. Imagine further that Tarkin is performing the sort of time travel that Sara Bernstein calls *movable objective present* (MOP).[9] MOP time travel not only temporally relocates the time traveler but also moves the objective present. Accordingly, by time traveling, Tarkin not only moves himself to 42 BBY, he moves the objective present to 42 BBY. If Tarkin's in a growing block universe, then, by time traveling, he's shrunken the whole universe. And since Grogu has not been born in 42 BBY, Tarkin has killed Baby Yoda! Or more precisely, he's erased Grogu from existence.

"Always in Motion Is the Future"

What does this "metaphysical mumbo jumbo" tell us about the reality of the *Star Wars* universe? First, since Ezra could travel to the past, the past seems to be as real as the present, so presentism seems to be ruled out. What about the future? Is the *Star Wars* universe an unchanging block or a growing block? This is difficult to pin down. When Ezra is in the World Between Worlds we hear familiar voices whispering famous words from both before and after the events of this *Rebels* episode. Also, when Rey touches Luke's lightsaber in *The Force Awakens*, she has visions of past and future events. This may indicate that the past and future are equally real.

However, at the end of our *Rebels* episode, we hear a Mortis god, the Son, say, "The future, by its nature, can be changed." Remember that the commonsense intuition that there's a difference between the past and the future (the past is fixed but the future is open) is one of the main motivations for accepting the growing block theory. In *Star Wars* it's particularly important that the audience perceives that it *matters* what the protagonists are achieving – that there is some risk of their failure. Of course, even in the growing block universe, we do not *change* the future. It's not like there's one future, then a person time travels and now there's a different future. *Right now*, there's no future at all. And once the objective present has moved from 42 BBY to 0 BBY, what's happened between 42 BBY to 0 BBY is not the future but the past and cannot be changed anymore.

Of course, the kind of time travel we witness in *Rebels* is not the typical kind that involves a time *machine*. Instead, time travel works by entering a place, the World Between Worlds, that connects different points in time and space. In terms of modern physics, the portals in the World Between Worlds may be understood as *traversable wormholes*. A wormhole, also known as an Einstein–Rosen bridge, links two disparate points in space–time. A wormhole, in theory, could link points that are far, far away – many light-years, away in fact. Wormholes are consistent with Einstein's general theory of relativity, so it's believed they are physically *possible*.[10] However, so far, we have not observed any, so it's unclear whether they *actually* exist.

In pop culture, wormholes appear in franchises like *Stargate*, *Star Trek: Deep Space Nine*, and the Marvel Cinematic Universe (where the Bifrost Bridge in *Thor* [2011] is referred to as an Einstein–Rosen bridge). In these examples, wormholes allow travel in space, but not in time. Physicists have speculated that if wormholes exist, they could be used to make time travel possible. Such a time travel story based on real but speculative physics is portrayed in the film *Interstellar* (2014).[11] Time travel that works by entering a place that warps space–time, rather than by entering a machine, is sometimes referred to as *warped* time travel.[12]

The End

The nature of time and the possibility of time travel have attracted and captivated humanity for centuries. Here philosophy, physics, and science fiction meet, inspiring each other. Particularly fascinating are the paradoxes that time travel seems to involve. Philosophers typically hold that it's impossible to travel back in time in a way that would create a grandfather-style paradox. You do not have to worry that when traveling back in time you'll kill your own grandfather, because you'd fail anyway. Of course, we do not know what would really happen if we traveled back in time. In some fictions, time travelers do cause paradoxical situations. In a recent episode of Marvel's *What If…?*, Doctor Strange causes a grandfather-style paradox *and destroys his whole universe*! We should thus be grateful to the metaphysically well-informed Ahsoka for preventing Ezra from causing such a paradox. Philosophy saved the *Star Wars* universe!

Notes

1 For a complementary discussion of free will in the tragic story of Anakin Skywalker and the heroic story of his son, Luke, see Jason T. Eberl, "'You Cannot Escape Your Destiny' (Or Can You?): Freedom and Predestination in the Skywalker Family," in Kevin S. Decker and Jason T. Eberl, eds., *Star Wars and Philosophy: More Powerful than You Can Possibly Imagine* (Chicago: Open Court, 2005), 3–15.

2 For further discussion of prophecy in *Harry Potter*, see Jeremy Pierce, "Destiny in the Wizarding World, " in Gregory Bassham, ed., *The Ultimate Harry Potter and Philosophy: Hogwarts for Muggles* (Hoboken, NJ: Wiley, 2010), 35–52.

3 For more on temporal metaphysics in the *Terminator* franchise, see Robert A. Delfino and Kenneth Sheahan, "Bad Timing: The Metaphysics of the Terminator," in Richard Brown and Kevin S. Decker, eds., *Terminator and Philosophy: I'll Be Back, Therefore I Am* (Hoboken, NJ: Wiley 2009), 109–121.

4 See David Lewis, "The Paradoxes of Time Travel," *American Philosophical Quarterly* 13 (1976), 145–152.

5 *Star Wars* television series producer Dave Filoni pointed out that this concept was inspired by C.S. Lewis's "Wood Between the Worlds" in his *Chronicles of Narnia*.

6 See Earl Conee and Theodor Sider, *Riddles of Existence* (Oxford: Oxford University Press, 2005), 57–61; Ryan Wasserman, *Paradoxes of Time Travel* (Oxford: Oxford University Press, 2018), 78; and Nikk Effingham, *Time Travel* (Oxford: Oxford University Press, 2020), 67.

7 See Tom Stoneham, "Time and Truth: The Presentism-Eternalism Debate," *Philosophy* 84 (2009), 201–218.

8 See Wasserman, *Paradoxes of Time Travel*, chapter 3.

9 Sara Bernstein, "Time Travel and the Movable Present," in John A. Keller, ed., *Being, Freedom, and Method: Themes from the Philosophy of Peter van Inwagen* (Oxford: Oxford University Press, 2017), 80–94.

10 See Kip Thorne, *The Science of Interstellar* (New York: W.W. Norton, 2014).

11 For discussion of how time travel in *Interstellar* bears on the self-identity of time travelers, see Todd McGowan, "We Are the Change That We Seek: The Subjectivity of Substance in *Interstellar*," in Jason T. Eberl and George A. Dunn, eds., *The Philosophy of Christopher Nolan* (Lanham, MD: Lexington Books, 2017), 203–217.

12 See Effingham, *Time Travel*, section 1.3.2.

Part III

ROGUE ONE AND *SOLO*

12

Building the Death Star: Complicity in Moral Evil

Jason T. Eberl

"Saw, they've come for us!" Fearful, but determined, Lyra Erso informs a long-time friend in the Rebel Alliance, Saw Gerrera, that the Empire has come for her family – specifically, for her husband, Galen. While Galen sends their daughter, Jyn, away to a secret hiding place on the backwater world they've made their home, Lyra can't stand by and let the Empire take her husband away. Unaware that Galen has just lied about her having died some time ago, Lyra appears and holds her husband's former friend and colleague, Orson Krennic, at blaster-point. Her conscience won't permit her to let the Empire do whatever it wants to her family and, by using them, to the rest of the galaxy. Yet her courage is rewarded with a blaster-bolt in her chest; as darkness forever obscures her consciousness, at least she knows she did all she could to stop the Empire's tyranny. So we wonder what she'd think of what her husband does next: Galen goes with Krennic – albeit reluctantly – to help finish constructing the most lethal weapon of mass destruction the galaxy has known: the Death Star.

Galen's choice to assist Krennic prompts the question of whether he's *morally culpable* for the millions of voices that "suddenly cried out in terror and were suddenly silenced" on Alderaan. After all, he designed the Death Star's primary weapon with knowledge of how to manipulate kyber crystals to enhance energy output. Thirteen years later, with the Death Star now operational and about to be unleashed on an unsuspecting galaxy, Galen recruits an Imperial cargo pilot, Bodhi Rook, to carry a warning to Saw and Jyn. Galen claims he knew the Empire would be able to finish the weapon without him; instead of refusing to work or taking his own life, he used the

Star Wars and Philosophy Strikes Back: This is the Way, First Edition.
Edited by Jason T. Eberl and Kevin S. Decker.

opportunity to create a design flaw that would permit a carefully aimed proton torpedo to cause a chain reaction that would destroy the Death Star. Does this mean that Galen was actually a silent hero of the Rebellion, someone Lyra could've been proud of? Or is he *complicit* in the deaths that occur on Jedha, Scarif, and Alderaan, and did he thus suffer a poetically justified death by Rebel bombs on Eadu as a war criminal?

Utilitarian ethics, focusing only on the net consequences of an action, would likely conclude that Galen did the right thing, ultimately saving many more lives than those lost and helping to free the galaxy from the Empire's tyranny. That positive outcome, however, also required Luke Skywalker to successfully hit a two-meter-wide exhaust port – the odds of which even C-3PO probably couldn't have calculated. So maybe Galen was simply the beneficiary of *moral luck*. For this reason, non-utilitarians would argue that Galen's contribution to the Death Star's malevolence negates his *moral integrity*. Unlike Krennic and Grand Moff Tarkin, he isn't the type of person who'd condone killing millions and terrorizing the galaxy, and so shouldn't have contributed to such an end, even if there were further benefit to be gained. In what follows, we'll examine how a utilitarian – concerned with the best overall outcome – and a deontologist – concerned with our fundamental moral duties – would evaluate Galen's choice to cooperate with the Empire. We'll also examine a potential justification for his serving both the Empire and the Rebel Alliance that may help us to navigate such complex moral dilemmas. Although Galen may appear to be in a genuine crisis of conscience, we'll see how he could morally justify assisting the Empire in building the Death Star while laying his trap for its destruction.

"Well, You Have to Start Somewhere"

Utilitarianism is defined by five foundational principles. Foremost is the *consequentialist principle*, which states that only an action's consequences count in its moral evaluation: actions aren't inherently right or wrong, but become right or wrong depending on the overall net outcome produced. While lying is held by many to be inherently wrong, Obi-Wan Kenobi lies to Luke about his parentage to achieve what he considers to be a better outcome for Luke's psychological well-being and the galaxy at large.[1]

Next is the *hedonistic principle*, which defines the consequences a utilitarian should try to maximize by their actions as intellectual and sensual pleasure; utilitarians ought also to minimize physical and existential pain and suffering.[2] In short, we ought to maximize the greatest good for the greatest number of persons affected by our action. When considering those who'll be affected by our action, we must be guided by the *principle of impartiality*: every individual whose interests will be affected is to count as one and no more than one. In other words, a moral agent must be "strictly impartial as a disinterested and benevolent spectator."[3] Consider Lando's betrayal of our Rebel heroes when they arrive at Cloud City. While many fans balk at Lando's disloyalty to his "buddy," impartial calculations of utility would weigh the well-being of Han, Leia, Chewie, and Threepio against that of all of the residents of Cloud City, for whom Lando bears a special responsibility as their administrator.[4] Depending on how things ultimately turn out, a utilitarian may applaud Lando's selling-out to the Empire. Though, given how Lando's deal with Darth Vader kept "getting worse all the time," leading to the mass evacuation of Cloud City, it appears that he failed to maximize net benefit for all concerned. The point is that Lando's betrayal of Han and the others has nothing to do, from a utilitarian perspective, with the value of Lando's *loyalty* to Han based on their many years of friendship – it has to do only with which action would lead to the greatest overall benefit.[5]

Finally, and most pertinent to the present discussion, is the *principle of negative responsibility*, which stipulates that we're just as responsible for negative outcomes we could've prevented as for the outcomes we directly cause. Some viewers – notably the slacker Randal in Kevin Smith's film *Clerks* – have judged the Rebels as "terrorists" for destroying the second Death Star while there were still innocent construction workers on board. If, however, the Rebels had allowed the Death Star II to be completed and used to kill untold numbers of innocents, the blood of those innumerable victims would've been on their hands.[6] The same would arguably be true of Galen Erso if he hadn't cooperated in the first Death Star's construction to allow himself the opportunity to implant a potentially destructive flaw. That Galen's involvement in the Death Star's construction may be justified by his engineering its potential destruction, however, turns on whether or not that very *potentiality* is realized.

"I've Got a Bad Feeling about This"

Although Luke's proton torpedoes provide the positive utility outcome that couldn't have been effected without Galen's contribution, events could've easily turned out quite differently. The Death Star might not have been destroyed, the Rebel base on Yavin IV might've been obliterated, and the Empire's tyrannous control over the galaxy would have been strengthened.[7] Galen is thus the beneficiary of *moral luck*, meaning that his potential for being lauded as a hero depends to a degree on factors beyond his control; had things turned out otherwise, he might've been morally condemned.[8] Ethicists debate whether the existence of moral luck undercuts any claim to moral responsibility since apparently everyone seems to be either blessed or cursed by circumstances outside of their control that influence the moral choices they make. The problem of moral luck is particularly acute for utilitarians, who hold one responsible for the net consequences of their chosen actions and inactions. Though Galen was morally lucky in his overall plan, he was also morally *unlucky* in that his plan resulted in innocent deaths – including his own daughter's – on Jedha, Scarif, and Alderaan.[9]

For deontological moral thinkers, what matters most aren't the consequences a moral agent produces or fails to produce, but whether we act from a *good will*: "A good will is not good because of what it effects or accomplishes, because of its fitness to attain some proposed end, but only because of its volition, that is, it is good in itself."[10] Consider Finn and Rose Tico's mission to find the "master codebreaker" on Canto Bight. Their mission stems from their good wills to save the Resistance; yet, changes of fortune result in their being arrested for illegal parking, meeting and subsequently being rescued by the mysterious thief "D.J.," and ultimately being betrayed by D.J. to the First Order. Although they remain heroic "rebel scum," Finn and Rose's mission fails and actually results in greater losses for the Resistance.

Bernard Williams (1929–2003) criticizes utilitarianism for allowing moral praise or blame to be held hostage to uncontrollable fortune and considers intrinsic value to lie in an agent's *moral integrity*, a person's self-identification with "his actions as flowing from projects and attitudes which in some cases he takes seriously at the deepest level, as what his life is about."[11] He argues,

> A feature of utilitarianism is that it cuts out a kind of consideration which for some others makes a difference to what they feel about such cases: a consideration involving the idea, as we might first and very

> simply put it, that each of us is specially responsible for what *he* does, rather than for what other people do. This is an idea closely connected with the value of integrity.[12]

Williams illustrates his contention with an example quite similar to Galen Erso's situation. "George" is an unemployed chemist who must find a way to support his family. A colleague offers George a job in a lab that produces chemical and biological weapons. George is morally opposed to such weapons but is informed that, if he doesn't take the job, it'll go to another chemist who zealously supports creating these weapons. If George takes the job, he could probably do the bare minimum to keep from being fired and support his family, thereby producing far fewer weapons – though he would clearly help produce *some* – than his more zealous counterpart.

Like George, Galen is concerned about providing for his family, as well as having fulfilling work to do, when – prior to the events in *Rogue One* – he initially agrees to work with Krennic on what he believes to be a sustainable energy project.[13] He's also clearly a man of conscience. While imprisoned on Vallt on suspicion of constructing weapons for his employer, Zerpen Industries, Galen protests, "If I thought that Zerpen was engaging in weapons research, I wouldn't be working with them."[14] Krennic describes him as "something of a pacifist. A conscientious objector, if you will."[15] Galen is also someone who feels responsibility for consequences that result from his actions, even if he didn't intentionally cause them, such as when Krennic orders the destruction of the Separatist sympathizers on Vallt who held Galen and his family hostage.[16] Galen clearly isn't of a utilitarian mindset; nor does he adhere to the strict framework of moral integrity that Williams recommends, in which the demands of conscience override all other considerations. Galen thus attempts to *balance* competing moral demands, ultimately resolving, when Krennic comes for him on Lah'mu, to assist the Empire in order to safeguard his daughter while seeking to undermine its villainous aims. How can he reconcile these two imperatives while remaining true to his own moral character?

"We've All Done Terrible Things on Behalf of the Rebellion"

Galen Erso begins his journey – from peaceful scientist to creator of the most destructive machine ever devised – humbly enough as a researcher focused on the mysterious kyber crystals. Unlike his wife, Lyra, Galen isn't interested in kyber crystals for their "spiritual" value but in their function as a natural energy amplifier. Since the Jedi zealously guarded the naturally occurring crystals found on Jedha and other remote locales throughout the galaxy, his early research for Zerpen Industries was aimed at fabricating synthetic kyber crystals. Galen thus typifies the research orientation of theoretical physicists such as Albert Einstein and others who foresaw the ability to split atomic nuclei as a means of creating inexhaustible amounts of energy. In both cases, the same scientific knowledge was able to be weaponized by those with more nefarious intentions.[17]

Such is the case with Orson Krennic, a brilliant engineer with ambitions of rising in the ranks of the Empire. His political success would be assured if he could deliver a weapon of unimaginable destructive force, and he sees Galen's research as the key to building such a weapon. Krennic initially recruits Galen into the Death Star project with the latter unaware of the true practical application of his research. Galen believes he's developing an inexhaustible source of "inexpensive and safe energy to countless worlds," dubbed "Project Celestial Power," which becomes "a kind of gilded cage." Krennic also has a secret facility to weaponize Galen's research.[18] Once Galen finds out the true nature of his work, he and his family run away with the help of Saw Gerrera.

When Krennic finds Galen and brings him back to the Death Star project, Galen is now more akin to Robert Oppenheimer, head of the Manhattan Project that created the world's first atomic bombs unleashed on the Japanese industrial cities of Hiroshima and Nagasaki to end World War II.[19] Oppenheimer, unlike Galen, was a willing contributor to creating the atomic bomb, but he later regretted his contribution, as evidenced in a famous interview reflecting on the first successful atomic detonation:

> We knew the world would not be the same. A few people laughed, a few people cried. Most people were silent. I remembered the line from the Hindu scripture, the *Bhagavad Gita*. Vishnu is trying to persuade the Prince that he should do his duty, and, to impress him, takes on his multi-armed form and says, "Now I am become Death, the destroyer of worlds." I suppose we all thought that, one way or another.[20]

Oppenheimer may have had the same self-delusional belief as some of Galen's colleagues that "they are creating something so terrible and powerful it will never be used." Galen's assessment differs: "But they're wrong. No weapon has ever been left on the shelf. And the day is coming soon when it will be unleashed."[21]

The difference between Galen and Oppenheimer is that the latter was *formally complicit* in creating the atomic bomb: Oppenheimer was not only fully aware of the goal he was working toward, but he also evidently *morally approved* of its development and potential use, even if he later came to regret it. Galen, on the other hand, does not morally approve of the Death Star's construction and use. If Galen hadn't helped finish the Death Star, but it had been successfully built based on his initial research into kyber crystals, his moral position would've been equivalent to Einstein's. His theories allowed the atomic bomb to become physically realized, but he wasn't directly involved in the Manhattan Project.[22] Galen's degree of moral complicity thus lies between Einstein's and Oppenheimer's since, unlike Einstein, he actually participates in the Death Star's construction but, unlike Oppenheimer, he doesn't morally approve of what he's doing. Galen struggles between the utilitarian pull to do what he believes will produce the greatest benefit for the galaxy and the anti-utilitarian imperative to adhere to the dictates of his own conscience, which abhors contributing to the deaths of innocent people no matter the overall beneficial outcome. What's undeniable, however, is that Galen is *materially complicit* in the Death Star's development and the deaths it subsequently brings about by virtue of his work being an important cause in its construction.[23]

We need to say more about what it means for a moral agent to materially cooperate in doing something wrong. Consider the difference between a mechanic like Peli Motto who builds a landspeeder in a garage on Tatooine and someone who purchases and later plows that same landspeeder into a crowd of peaceful Jawas because they sold him an R2 unit with a bad motivator. While the mechanic has materially contributed to the latter's immoral action, she's not *blameworthy* for the violence for which the landspeeder was used because that wasn't the primary *purpose* for which the speeder was made. Galen's case differs; the purpose for which the Death Star was constructed is inherently immoral and he knew of this after he returned to the project. More salient to the present case is whether Galen's materially cooperative activity was *mediate* or *immediate*, along with its *proximity* to the immoral end achieved by its use. The more direct and necessary one's cooperative activity is for the immoral end to come about, the more difficult it is to exonerate oneself from culpability since, by refusing to materially cooperate, one could've prevented the immoral end from occurring. If, however, the immoral end may or may not have come about due to the choices of other moral agents, or if it was likely to come about – inevitable even – regardless of one's cooperative activity, then one's culpability diminishes due to how little control one had over the outcome.

While Galen provided material means by which the Death Star was capable of destroying Alderaan, the decisions of other moral agents ultimately result in its firing: mainly, Tarkin's order and the gunners who press the buttons that fire the Death Star's superlaser. In Oppenheimer's case, the atomic bomb's ultimate use wasn't directly attributable to him so much as to US President Harry Truman's order to release it over Hiroshima, as well as Colonel Paul Tibbets and the crew of the *Enola Gay* who executed that order. Even Princess Leia Organa serves as a more proximate contributor to Alderaan's destruction. It's her home planet, and her choice to become a leader in the Rebel Alliance motivates Tarkin's choice to destroy Alderaan as "an alternative form of persuasion" to convince Leia to divulge the location of the secret Rebel base. This is akin to Emperor Hirohito and the Japanese high command's unwillingness to surrender unconditionally prior to the atomic bomb being utilized.[24] Galen, in fact, attempted during the Clone Wars to remove himself from even such remote material cooperation with weapons development. Krennic shows him, however, how his employer at the time, Zerpen Industries, was selling material to both Republic and Separatist worlds. Krennic's point is that no one can remain aloof in such a galactic-scale conflict, but is forced to take sides.[25] Further, the inability to predict accurately how one's moral choices will intersect with those of others shows that moral luck is still a factor.

Another potentially complicating factor is the *necessity* of Galen's role in the Death Star's creation. A moral agent's level of complicity diminishes to the extent to which his material support could be *replaced* by another agent. In such a case, the immoral action is likely to occur no matter what one does: an example would be one of the cargo pilots who delivers kyber crystals mined from Jedha to the Imperial research base on Eadu, each of whom is easily replaceable by another cargo pilot who'll get the job done. Galen, however, plays a much more crucial role in the Death Star's development. If, however, we take him at his word as communicated to Saw and Jyn, while he was at one time irreplaceable, he knew that eventually the Death Star project could be completed without him. Assuming Galen is being objectively honest, history may forgive him: his material contribution to Alderaan's destruction is both mediate and remote.

"Rebellions Are Built on Hope!"

Is Galen Erso morally culpable for the lives lost when the Death Star destroyed Jedha, Scarif, and Alderaan? From a utilitarian perspective, *no*: the lives saved by his planting a fundamental weakness in the Death Star's reactor, exploited by Luke Skywalker, justifies the previous sacrifices of innocent lives. Yet, that net gain depended upon a series of fortuitous occurrences outside of Galen's control. Bernard Williams would thus condemn Galen for having betrayed his *integrity* in being complicit with an irredeemably reprehensible set of actions. Careful analysis of the conditions of moral complicity, however, *justifies* Galen's collusion so long as he had a reasonable expectation that the Death Star would've been completed anyway, and that there was a reasonable hope – a *new* hope – of success in its ultimate destruction.

Notes

1 For an analysis of the ethical justification of Obi-Wan's lie, see Shanti Fader, "'A Certain Point of View': Lying Jedi, Honest Sith, and the Viewers Who Love Them," in Kevin S. Decker and Jason T. Eberl, eds., *Star Wars and Philosophy: More Powerful than You Can Possibly Imagine* (Chicago: Open Court, 2005), 192–204.

2 The foundational texts of utilitarianism are Jeremy Bentham, *An Introduction to the Principles of Morals and Legislation* (1789): https://www.earlymoderntexts.com/assets/pdfs/bentham1780.pdf (accessed February 3, 2019); and John Stuart Mill, *Utilitarianism* (1863): https://www.earlymoderntexts.com/assets/pdfs/mill1863.pdf (accessed February 3, 2019).

3 Mill (1863), Chapter 2.

4 See Richard Dees, "Moral Ambiguity in a Black-and-White Universe," in Kevin S. Decker and Jason T. Eberl, eds., *Star Wars and Philosophy: More Powerful than You Can Possibly Imagine* (Chicago: Open Court, 2005), 39–53.

5 For an articulation and defense of the value of *loyalty* for its own sake, see Josiah Royce, *The Possibility of Loyalty* (New York: The MacMillan Company, 1908).

6 For a defense of the Rebels' destruction of Death Star II, see Charles C. Camosy, "Chasing Kevin Smith: Was It Immoral for the Rebel Alliance to Destroy Death Star II?" in Jason T. Eberl and Kevin S. Decker, eds., *The Ultimate Star Wars and Philosophy: You Must Unlearn What You Have Learned* (Malden, MA: Wiley-Blackwell, 2015), 67–78.

7 An alternative history of how things might've gone if Luke had failed to destroy the first Death Star is depicted in the *Star Wars: Infinities* (2001) comic series.

8 For the concept of moral luck, see Thomas Nagel, *Mortal Questions* (New York: Cambridge University Press, 1979), chapter 3; Bernard Williams, *Moral Luck* (New York: Cambridge University Press, 1981); and Daniel Statman, *Moral Luck* (Albany: State University of New York Press, 1993).

9 One might think that the deaths of Imperial officers and troops on Scarif don't count as those of "innocents," but the destruction of Scarif also killed Jyn Erso and Cassian Andor, and there may have been non-Imperial civilians working on Scarif just as there were on Death Star II.

10 Immanuel Kant, *Groundwork of the Metaphysics of Morals* (New York: Cambridge University Press, 1997), 8.

11 Bernard Williams and J.J.C. Smart *Utilitarianism: For and Against* (New York: Cambridge University Press, 1973), 116.

12 Ibid., 99.

13 James Luceno, *Catalyst: A Rogue One Novel* (New York: Del Rey, 2016), 112 and 120.

14 Ibid., 25.

15 Ibid., 44.

16 Ibid., 69.

17 There's a great deal of scholarly literature discussing the "dual use" of research for both beneficent and maleficent purposes; see, e.g. Thomas Douglas, "The Dual-Use Problem: Scientific Isolationism and the Division of Moral Labour," *Monash Bioethics Review* 32 (2014), 86–105; Lalit Kant and D.T. Mourya, "Managing Dual Use Technology: It Takes Two to Tango," *Science and Engineering Ethics* 16 (2010), 77–83; Svitlana Pustovit, "Philosophical Aspects of Dual Use Technologies," *Science and Engineering Ethics* 16 (2010), 17–31; and Ineke Malsch, "The Just War Theory and the Ethical Governance of Research," *Science and Engineering Ethics* 19 (2013), 461–486.

18 Luceno, *Catalyst*, 146–147, 176, 185, 194.

19 Note that I'm not weighing in on the vexed question of the morality of the development and use of the atomic bomb, but rather comparing Oppenheimer and Erso with respect to their roles in contributing to the creation of their respective weapons of mass destruction.

20 Robert Oppenheimer, "Oppenheimer Bhagavad-Gita Quote": https://www.youtube.com/watch?v=pqZqfTOxFhY (accessed February 3, 2019).

21 Alexander Freed, *Rogue One: A Star Wars Story* (New York: Del Rey, 2016), 102.

22 In 1939, Einstein did sign a letter addressed to US President Franklin Delano Roosevelt urging the atomic bomb's development based on the fear that Nazi Germany was also developing such a weapon. He later stated, "If I had known that the Germans would not succeed in constructing the atom bomb, I would never have lifted a finger": http://themanhattanprojectus.weebly.com/the-einstein-letter.html (accessed May 1, 2018).

23 See Kevin L. Flannery, *Cooperation with Evil: Thomistic Tools of Analysis* (Washington, DC: Catholic University of America Press, 2019).

24 To be clear, I'm not assigning moral culpability to the Japanese for not surrendering as a form of "victim blaming"; rather, I'm merely drawing an historical parallel to the various types of causal connections at play in the destruction of Alderaan.

25 Luceno, *Catalyst*, 72.

13

"Rebellions Are Built on Hope": The Creative Democratic Force of *Rogue One*

Terrance MacMullan

Rogue One is a complex film that invites a wide range of philosophical questioning. This chapter focuses on the film's *political* aspect.[1] *Rogue One* powerfully illustrates an essential and timely claim made about the nature of democracy by John Dewey (1859–1952). Dewey argued – and *Rogue One* shows – that true democracy is not found in formal political structures, like the Galactic or US Senates. Instead, democracy is a living force that dwells within and is strengthened through trusting and humane interactions. *Rogue One* dutifully serves as a faithful prequel to *A New Hope* by having two protagonists – first Cassian Andor, then Jyn Erso – remind us never to despair, because "rebellions are built on hope." Dewey offered a similar message at the dawn of World War II, when his generation faced the threat of a real evil empire. He believed that people cooperating and trusting each other is not just *a good idea* within a community, "it is the idea of community life itself."[2] With Dewey's aid, we can see *Rogue One* as an essential film for our times, when the flame of hope burns low, because it shows us that democracy and freedom are rooted in faith in each other. *Rogue One* shows us what our lives would be like without such faith, why we need it, and how to get it back. And it starts in a very cruel, despairing, and familiar place.

"This Town is Ready to Blow"

The Ring of Kafrene is a cramped and dingy mining colony turned trading post that's also the setting for one of the most jarring moments in *Star Wars*. It's here that an informant named Tivik keeps a

Star Wars and Philosophy Strikes Back: This is the Way, First Edition.
Edited by Jason T. Eberl and Kevin S. Decker.

clandestine rendezvous with Rebel Captain Cassian Andor and informs him of an Imperial "planet killer" super-weapon. While Cassian struggles to absorb the ramifications of this intelligence, a stormtrooper patrol intrudes, forcing Cassian to blow his cover by eliminating the troopers. The only escape is to climb up the mechanical canyon walls towering above them. Tivik panics because his broken arm prevents him from climbing. Cassian quickly calculates the harm to the Rebel cause if Tivik were to be captured and tortured by the Empire, calms Tivik with reassuring words and a warm smile ... then shoots him dead.

Rogue One is significantly different from earlier *Star Wars* films. It does not offer a simple, mythic morality tale, where the difference between right and wrong is as stark as the contrast between Leia's white gown and Vader's black mask. The right thing to do is usually obvious in these early films: the only question is whether the heroes have the courage to do it.[3] *Star Wars* became a global phenomenon because people, especially young people, longed for meaning-rich stories that myths provided for millennia, but which are mostly absent from our modern culture driven by economics and technology.[4] It's important for a young person to be able to look at the world with a sense of wonder and be ready to hear and heed the call of adventure; yet, as we age, we learn that life's decisions are usually more complicated than following an amiable wizard on an adventure to Alderaan. Our mature moral lives are complex and blurry, like Kafrene's jumble of muddy earth tones and greys. Having to witness the daring Cassian Andor murder a fellow Rebel in cold blood nearly inverts the famous line from the crawl of *Revenge of the Sith*: while the battles of the Clone Wars taught us that "there are heroes on both sides," *Rogue One* makes us wonder if "there are villains on both sides." We soon see that Cassian's no villain. He's a good person, fighting for a good cause against a powerful and ruthless military force; doing the right thing is a luxury he cannot always afford. His choices are grounded less in the pattern of Campbell's hero's journey than in the brute facts of an uncaring galaxy.

Dark Times for the Republics

Rogue One takes place in a messy and unfair world in which traditional moral frameworks appear naive and ill-suited. Living in a similarly messy world – the impending fall of the Roman Empire – Augustine of Hippo (354–430) developed a theory of "just war" outlining the conditions under which Christian governments could go to war without violating the biblical commandment against unlawful killing. The Rebels generally satisfy Augustine's doctrine governing the use of lethal force as summarized by Richard Hanley:

> There must be: *just cause* – a credible threat; *right intention* – the reason for fighting is to respond to a threat, with the ultimate aim of just peace; *competent authority* – the decision to fight is made by true representatives of the nation or group; *last resort* – peaceful means have been exhausted; *reasonable prospects of success* – it is credible that a just peace will result.[5]

But Cassian's dilemma is not covered by Augustine's theory. Augustine would condemn Cassian as a murderer if for no other reason than he and Tivik were on the same side!

Cassian's act would similarly shock Immanuel Kant (1724–1804), whose *categorical imperative* explicitly prohibits this sort of "ends justify the means" thinking. Kant rules out actions like Cassian's, saying that morality flows from our rational duty to do what we know we must do, no matter the expected consequences or our personal desires. Kant's "Formula of Humanity" specifically compels us to "Act in such a way that you treat humanity, whether in your own person or in the person of another, always at the same time as an end and never simply as a means."[6] Cassian violates this maxim by reducing Tivik to the status of a container that holds a secret, which Cassian destroys to prevent the Empire from learning that the Rebels know about their new weapon.

The ethical and political situation of *Rogue One* resembles our own. The citizens of the republic of the United States also live in a time of great cynicism, fear, and despair. Our social fabric has been worn threadbare by the stress of simultaneous virological, economic, and political crises. Quarantines meant to keep us alive have alienated us from each other as our social lives have contracted to the size of a smartphone screen. Political institutions that have endured for centuries are in jeopardy of collapse. Instead of facing these challenges, we often keep our heads down and "don't look up." It can be hard to find any reason to hope. While watching Tivik fall was an emotional gut-punch, the real blow hits when actor Daniel Mays nearly breaks the fourth wall and despairs that "[i]t's all falling apart!" This line is powerful because we live in a time when the US feels like the proverbial kettle about to blow its top. Its people are fellow citizens and neighbors; we are supposed to be on the same side. However, we are increasingly divided and distrustful of each other. We cannot even agree on what's real anymore, with conspiracy theories treated as equivalent to, or more credible than, hard-earned scientific facts. Like the Rebels, we have little trust in each other.

"Lies! Deception!"

Cassian's killing of Tivik is just the first of many ethically dubious acts committed by the film's supposed heroes. These acts range from split-second decisions with limited consequences, like Jyn Erso pummeling the Rebel soldiers freeing her from Imperial detention, to premeditated acts of massive significance, like Galen Erso's decision to continue working on the Death Star that would immolate the city of Jedha and later Alderaan.[7]

A turncoat Imperial pilot, Bodhi Rook, is brought before Saw Gerrera, the leader of a splinter group deemed too extreme by Rebel leaders like Mon Mothma. Bodhi identifies himself as a friend of Galen Erso, sent as a secret courier of intelligence critical to the Rebellion. Bodhi's a sincere, terrified, but brave pilot who risks his life to potentially save billions. But when he stands before Saw, he's neither praised nor protected: instead, Saw accuses him of being an Imperial double-agent. "Lies! Deception!" Saw rasps out as Bodhi kneels before him in terror. Saw then proceeds to torture Bodhi by subjecting him to the mind-warping power of Bor Gullet. In subjecting Bodhi to psychological harm in order to ascertain the validity of his claims, *Rogue One* again pulls our world onto the screen. It forces us to consider the pain and suffering caused by a counterintelligence technique paralleling waterboarding, euphemistically called "enhanced interrogation." In Saw's mind, the war against the unrelenting and ruthless Empire justifies dehumanization.

Looming over every morally questionable or unjustifiable Rebel act is the Empire's massive power. *Rogue One* shows that the most insidious damage wrought by a fascist state dwells within the truncated and corroded moral world of the people enthralled by its dehumanizing influence. The Empire's power forces people not only to fight, but to lie and distrust others; constant violence and surveillance have led to the inability to *trust*.

The Empire deftly leverages this distrust against anyone who defies them, as when they broadcast a hologram of Bodhi's face, enticing impoverished Imperial subjects to turn him in. Had the Rebels followed conventional rules of engagement or assumed the goodwill of their confederates, they'd likely have been wiped out in weeks because the Empire has no qualms about hurting innocent people or spreading untruths. Instead, the Rebels are reduced to the crudest form of consequentialist morality. They do anything they can, even torturing or killing fellow Rebels, that they believe will help topple the Empire. They must either learn to fight dirty against the Empire or acquiesce to its injustice. Cassian and Saw chose the first option: committing lesser evils in the hope of ending a greater evil. When we first meet Jyn, she's chosen the second option by doing nothing to fight the Empire's evils, trying to convince Cassian – and herself – that she does not need to join the Rebellion because she's learned to tolerate the Empire's banner flying over the entire galaxy: "It's not so hard if you don't look up."

This defeatist line from the film's protagonist, combined with *Rogue One*'s ethical complexity, realism, and cynicism, might lead audiences to fear that the film's tone will be miserable and gloomy. This is reinforced by feelings of hopelessness and defeat with the resurgence of nationalist and fascist states and the collapse of democracy and international amity. However, *Rogue One* is profoundly uplifting and meaningful, because the force that saves the Rebellion and grants its heroes posthumous victory is a very real force we can find among ourselves. It is not *the* Force. As the film meaningfully changes the famous phrase, it's the "Force of others," the force we share when we trust and believe in each other. We do not need to be special Force-wielding Jedi to access *this* force: we only need to share the faith that the Rebels found in each other and that Dewey locates at the heart of democracy.

"I'm Not Alone. I Have You!"

Over the course of his long life, Dewey witnessed many of humanity's cruelest injustices, but still kept his faith in our potential to grow and care for each other under the right conditions. When he wrote "Creative Democracy – The Task Before Us" in 1939, he faced a moment similar to the galaxy in ABY 0 (After the Battle of Yavin): an apparently unstoppable fascist force had occupied free societies with little opposition. However, Dewey did not respond to this crisis as many of his fellow citizens did (and still do) – by beating a nationalist drum or assuring his readers that since the US is the greatest nation in the world, it is immune to threats corrupting other nations. Instead, he cautioned that neither our institutions nor our constitution would save us from succumbing to the same cruelty and evil that had corrupted Germany through temptations to power and domination.

Dewey raised the alarm that the US was in crisis, not from an impending external threat, but from internal apathy and complacency: "the depth of the present crisis is due in considerable part to the fact that for a long period we acted as if our democracy were something that perpetuated itself automatically; as if our ancestors had succeeded in setting up a machine that solved the problem of perpetual motion in politics."[8]

The same could be said of the Republic in the prequel trilogy, mired in bureaucracy and infighting for so long that it easily succumbed to imperialism through fully legal means, cheered "with thunderous applause." Dewey urges us to be vigilant against these subtle, internal threats to democracy, because the heart of democracy is not found within legal or institutional structures, but "in our personal relations to other persons, [and] in our daily walk and conversation."[9] He urges in 1939 that fascism very well "could happen here." If we lose our democratic spirit – our commitment to "a way of life controlled by the working faith in the possibilities of human nature" – then nothing in our laws or constitution would stop us from descending into cruelty, ignorance, and distrust.[10]

Dewey shows that the most insidious power of a totalitarian Empire is its ability to feed distrust, resentment, anger, and greed, corroding people's faith in each other. This is what's so heartbreaking about the beginning of *Rogue One*: Rebels are not only doing terrible things to the Empire, but to each other *because of the Empire!* When Jyn confronts Cassian about his plan to assassinate her father, he gets exasperated and shouts that he's just following orders. Jyn retorts that for all his hatred of the Empire, he would've made a good stormtrooper.

The Rebels are driven to such faithless and cruel behavior because trust has been in short supply. Cassian cannot trust Tivik not to give up intelligence, so he kills him. General Draven trusts neither Galen nor the Rebellion's civilian leader, Mon Mothma, so he orders Cassian to hide the fact that he's seeking to assassinate Galen Erso. Even K-2SO has learned to be distrustful. When Cassian decides to let Jyn keep a blaster, K-2SO offers, "Would you like to know the probability of her using it against you? It's high.... It's very high." These Rebels have survived so long under Imperial thralldom they share hardly any community anymore, yet Dewey reminds us that "[d]emocracy must begin at home, and its home is the neighborly community."[11]

Thankfully, the film's tone shifts when Cassian and Jyn wind through the shattered remnants of the occupied Holy City of Jedha. In this reminder of a more compassionate time, Cassian confides that all they can do is hope to find their way to Saw, since "rebellions are built on hope." They do find hope on Jedha, but not in the form of superhuman Jedi; instead, they find something far more powerful in Chirrut Îmwe and Baze Malbus. Cassian describes the two as having once been holy men of a Force-religion – Keepers of the Whills – who now just "make trouble for everyone." Cassian hustles Jyn away from an oddly insightful conversation with the blind monk Chirrut, explaining that "we are not here to make friends." We soon learn that this is, ironically, the very thing they need. The friendship between Chirrut and Baze is not only the warm heart of the film, but the seed of friendship and community that the Rebels need to recover the compassion and humanity the Empire had drained out of them.

Chirrut demonstrates that the real struggle facing the Rebels is not about superhuman beings or some external, magical Force, but the force of faith in each other. He confides that his companion Baze is a one-time cleric who's lost faith in the Whills, an archaic word for the Force. However, it's clear that, despite their bickering and teasing, they deeply love each other and share an unbreakable faith in their friendship, one uncorrupted by the suffering and cruelty in occupied Jedha. In an especially sweet moment, Baze chides Chirrut, calling him crazy for heading out alone into unfamiliar terrain near an Imperial base. Chirrut smiles back knowingly that he's not alone at all: "I have you!"

This relationship is the antidote that neutralizes the toxin of Imperial distrust within the hearts of the heroes. Their friendship is like the proverbial lotus flower blooming resplendently amidst the muck and mud. They show the Rebels what can happen when they believe in each other. Soon after meeting them, Cassian has the chance to assassinate Galen. This would be an incalculable betrayal of Jyn and he stays his shot. It's as if exposure to the warmth of friendship and sincerity that's the heart of any free community changes Cassian. Perhaps it reminded him what he's been *fighting for* since he was seven, and not just what he was fighting against. While Cassian later defends his original orders, he never lies to or uses her (or any other Rebels) again. Chirrut and Baze save the Rebellion, not just as a bad-ass fighting duo, but by demonstrating the power of faith in the force of others.

Trust in the Force of Others

Fans have thought of the hidden base on Yavin 4 as the center of the Rebellion ever since we saw Luke climb into his X-Wing in *A New Hope*. *Rogue One* shows us that Yavin 4 was indeed where the spark of the Rebellion was rekindled at its darkest hour due to a pair of very human, but still awe-inspiring, acts that paved the way for Luke.

The first was the council of Rebel leaders deciding how to respond to Jyn's intelligence about the Death Star. This scene might not seem that important at first glance, especially as the council seems to make the wrong decision: instead of standing and fighting, they decide to scatter and hope to live to fight another day. However, the Rebels spoke to and listened to each other freely. Unlike the Empire, where officers intimidate, recriminate, and even Force-choke each other to get their way, these Rebels engaged in the *method* of democracy – honest and free discussion ("What is she proposing?!") – that Dewey points out is far more important than any *outcome* that might emerge. The Rebels' sincere debate represents the strongest bulwark against the evil of fascism: "I am inclined to believe that the heart and final guarantee of democracy is in free gatherings of neighbors on the street corner to discuss back and forth what is read in uncensored news of the day, and in gatherings of friends in the living rooms of houses and apartments to converse freely with one another."[12]

The second act that saves the spirit of the Rebellion occurs soon after, when a handful of Cassian's colleagues, along with Chirrut and Baze, decide to trust Jyn about a message none of them has heard. They find the courage to overcome the distrust and cynicism the Empire has bred within them and instead decide to trust in one another. This is the very same message Dewey gave his audience in the months before the US entered World War II. It is not enough for free people to fight fascism with force of arms; they need to develop personal attitudes and commitments that support a democratic spirit:

> Enemies of democracy can be successfully met only by the creation of personal attitudes in individual human beings; that we must get over our tendency to think that defense can be found in any external means, whether military or civil, if they are separated from individual attitudes so deep-seated as to constitute personal character.[13]

The rest of *Rogue One* is exceptionally powerful not only because of amazing acting, sound design, and cinematography, but because it uses the tropes and setting of gritty war cinema to tell a universal story about the power of hope and faith in others. In the assault on Scarif, individuals and small units depend on friends and allies to complete their important mission. Cassian, Jyn, and K-2SO rely on the majority of the crew's self-sacrificing actions to draw the Imperials away from the primary mission of retrieving and transmitting the plans. Bodhi stays aboard their commandeered Imperial craft to transmit the plans and confuse the Imperials through misinformation. K-2SO expires at a command console to give Jyn and Cassian the time they need to finish their mission. In a display of incredible courage and faith, Chirrut walks into a storm of blaster fire to engage the relay that will transmit the plans to the Rebel ships above, and is slain soon after followed by Baze.

However, what most powerfully demonstrates the power of faith in the force of others comes after Cassian's and Jyn's story is over. This is the terrifying scene on board the Tantive IV when a handful of Rebels play a life-and-death game of "Keep-Away" with the Death Star plans in a narrow corridor against the single most powerful being any of them will ever have seen: Darth Vader. On first viewing, the scene highlights Vader's monstrous powers. Beyond a shadow of a doubt, every Rebel in that corridor is doomed; we also know that they are victorious. Despite his command of the Force, Vader is alone and friendless. The Rebels in that hallway, like the ones on Skarif, *share a faith in each other*. After relentless carnage, one Rebel is trapped at the far end of the corridor by a door that's stuck only partially open. He cannot fit through to escape Vader, but still performs a valiant act of faith. He thrusts the plans through the crack to a Rebel on the other side, yelling "Take it!" moments before Vader's saber impales him. This selfless act shows the power in the force of others at the heart of democracy. He inherited that faith from a long line of people who trusted in the human potential of others: Galen, who trusted Bodhi, who trusted Saw, who trusted Jyn, who was trusted by Chirrut, Cassian, and eventually the entire Rebellion. The last Rebel to die in that hallway trusted his colleague to get it to Leia, who trusted Obi-Wan, who trusted Luke, and on and on, eventually throughout the entire galaxy.

Rogue One holds within itself the greatest contradictions. It's at once the most cynical and the most hopeful of the *Star Wars* films. It shows us the gritty realism of war in which realistic characters lie, distrust, and, most human of all, die. However, it's also a film whose heart is filled with faith and hope – not that the Force will make everything better, but that *we* will make it better with the help of the Force of Others.

Notes

1 This essay builds upon Kevin Decker, "By Any Means Necessary: Tyranny, Democracy, Republic and Empire," in Kevin S. Decker and Jason T. Eberl, eds., *Star Wars and Philosophy: More Powerful than You Can Possibly Imagine* Chicago: Open Court, (2005), 168–180.

2 John Dewey, *The Public and Its Problems* in *The Later Works of John Dewey*, vol. 2 (Carbondale: Southern Illinois University Press, 1985), 328.

3 For an excellent discussion of the moral complexities introduced to the original trilogy by Lando Calrissian, see Richard Dees, "Moral Ambiguity in a Black-and-White Universe," in Jason T. Eberl and Kevin S. Decker, eds., *The Ultimate Star Wars and Philosophy: You Must Unlearn What You Have Learned* (Malden, MA: Wiley-Blackwell, 2015) 39–54.

4 For further discussion of the *Star Wars'* mythic dimensions, see John Thompson, "'In That Time…' In a Galaxy Far, Far Away: Epic Myth-Understandings and Myth Appropriation in *Star Wars*," in Jason T. Eberl and Kevin S. Decker, eds., *The Ultimate Star Wars and Philosophy: You Must Unlearn What You Have Learned* (Malden, MA: Wiley-Blackwell, 2015) 263–273.

5 Richard Hanley, "Send in the Clones: The Ethics of Future Wars," in Kevin S. Decker and Jason T. Eberl, eds., *Star Wars and Philosophy: More Powerful than You Can Possibly Imagine* (Chicago: Open Court, 2005), 101. For further discussion of just war theory see Charles C. Camosy, "Chasing Kevin Smith: Was It Immoral for the Rebel Alliance to Destroy Death Star II?" in Jason T. Eberl and Kevin S. Decker, eds., *The Ultimate Star Wars and Philosophy: You Must Unlearn What You Have Learned* (Malden, MA: Wiley-Blackwell, 2015), 67–78.

6 Immanuel Kant, *Grounding for the Metaphysics of Morals*, trans. James Ellington (Indianapolis: Hackett, 1993), 36.

7 For an ethical analysis of Galen Erso's decision, see Jason T. Eberl's essay in this volume (Chapter 12).

8 John Dewey, "Creative Democracy – The Task Before Us (1939)," in *The Later Works of John Dewey*, vol. 14 (Carbondale: Southern Illinois University Press, 1988), 225.

9 Ibid., 226.

10 Ibid., 226.

11 Dewey, *The Public and its Problems*, 268.

12 Dewey, "Creative Democracy," 227.

13 Ibid., 226.

14

Han Solo: The Corellian Evasion of Philosophy

Kevin S. Decker

"Where's the chapter about Han Solo?" After co-editing three books with good friend and Jedi Master Jason Eberl, and reading over a hundred proposals and dozens of chapters on philosophy and *Star Wars*, this question became too weighty to ignore. Han Solo – orphan, laconically cool Corellian smuggler, Rebel general, and martyr for the Resistance – is one of the most-loved characters in the *Star Wars* universe. His emotional and moral development throughout the original trilogy into a trusted friend, Leia's lover, and a warrior for Rebel values is inspiring. In the sequel trilogy, he's returned to smuggling and reluctantly re-assumes the mantle of father to Ben Solo, an alienated and ultimately patricidal son, but even death fails to stop him from offering fatherly advice to bring Kylo Ren back to the light side.

In a universe of tyrants, freedom-fighters, Force-sensitives, Jedi, and Sith, everybody seems to be peddling a philosophy. But Han Solo is a scoundrel, a skeptic, and a Corellian who seems to want to evade a philosophical life. Aristotle (384–322 BCE), a philosopher's philosopher, thought that doing this was impossible:

> If you should do philosophy, you should do philosophy, and if you should not do philosophy, then you should do philosophy.... For if philosophy exists, then positively we are obliged to do philosophy, since it truly exists. But if it does not truly exist, even so we are obliged to investigate how it is that philosophy does not truly exist. But by investigating we would be doing philosophy, since to investigate is the cause of philosophy.[1]

Star Wars and Philosophy Strikes Back: This is the Way, First Edition.
Edited by Jason T. Eberl and Kevin S. Decker.

Is this another time, like making the Kessel Run in less than 12 parsecs, where Han Solo achieves what everyone else thought impossible? Even if the answer turns out to be "no," the question is fun and worth pursuing by looking at the anti-philosophical ideas of Ludwig Wittgenstein (1889–1951) and Richard Rorty (1931–2007). And best of all, Han finally gets his own chapter in a book on *Star Wars* and philosophy.

Don't everybody thank me at once.

"I Don't Have People. I'm Alone"

Han Solo became the favorite son of Corellia, yet he never knew his mother and, while very young, became a scrumrat in the industrial ghettos of his home planet. While many famous philosophers have also been "single orphans" like Han – Aristotle (384–322 BCE), René Descartes (1596–1650), and David Hume (1711–1776) all lost one parent – the experience of having to fend for himself and protect fellow scrumrats like Qi'ra was definitive for Han's character. Young Han, therefore, has something in common with the 140 million children in our own world reported as having lost one or more parents as of 2019.[2] Unlike Han's case, the vast majority of real-world orphans live with a surviving grandparent or other family members. Others, like Leia, are adopted by a loving family while they are very young. While Luke Skywalker grew up with Uncle Owen's chiding, Aunt Beru's Bantha milk, and a vague sense of having an important father whom Luke would've liked to meet, Han's father, Ovan, abandoned his son after realizing that his career building starships had effectively been meaningless.[3] Leia's elite lifestyle and Luke's cloistered youth shielded them from the wide variety of cruelties and indignities that shaped Han's early years on Corellia.

It's a testament to the luck that Han would so often count on that he dodged many of the typical lifelong problems that stem from neglect: "poor impulse control, social withdrawal, problems with coping and regulating emotions, low self-esteem, pathological behaviors such as tics, tantrums, stealing and self-punishment, poor intellectual functioning and low academic achievement."[4] Practical education on the streets of Corellia came mainly from the tender mercies of the White Worm criminal gang, for whom we see Han working when we are introduced to him in *Solo*.

This kind of education falls far below even the standards of a devout skeptic like Michel de Montaigne (1533–1592), who claimed, "The more simply we trust to Nature, the more wisely we trust to her. Oh, what a sweet and soft and healthy pillow is ignorance and incuriosity, to rest a well-made head!"[5] Whether ancient, modern, or contemporary, skeptics like Montaigne have claimed either that we can have no knowledge in science and philosophy, or that every argument in these areas can be matched by an equally good one that argues the opposite. Nonetheless, in his essay "Of the education of children," Montaigne maintained that philosophy should be the cornerstone of a child's education because it teaches the ability to question and analyze instead of merely asking children to memorize information. Montaigne's emphasis on critical thinking skills is laudable, and he's surely correct that young people should be exposed to philosophy well before college.[6] But Montaigne was distrustful of adults whose philosophical education as youths had led them to more abstract scholarly pursuits, saying of them,

> ...your better-bred sort of men are much more curious in their observation, 'tis true, and discover a great deal more; but then they gloss upon it, and to give the greater weight to what they deliver, and allure your belief, they cannot forbear a little to alter the story; they never represent things to you simply as they are, but rather as they appeared to them, or as they would have them appear to you....[7]

Where does education for critical thought end, and where begins a person's immersion in a field of specialized thinking – many of which Montaigne suspected of quackery? Montaigne, a man of leisure like so many philosophers, could afford to refrain from the need to problem-solve difficult ethical or political dilemmas, but in terms of the demands put on impoverished, orphaned street kids simply to survive, Montaigne also speaks from a perspective of class privilege.

Indeed, skepticism about the motives of others and a lack of trust were essential coping mechanisms for young Han. These were tempered by his close relationship with Qi'ra, but their future together was characterized by mutual betrayals – with Han being forced to leave her behind when he joined the Imperial Navy, and Qi'ra never fully revealing the extent of her commitment to the Crimson Dawn syndicate. Even when Han behaved kindly to younger scrumrats, he would deny that his concern with them was a moral one. It becomes clear later that Han enjoys being identified as a scoundrel. In one conversation with Qi'ra, he says, "No one's ever gonna help anyone unless it gets them something … It's that way down here with us … and I figure it's probably the same all the way up there, at the top of the fanciest tower on the fanciest planet in the galaxy."[8] Han's cynicism seems only to have been deepened by the misplaced trust he placed in Tobias Beckett during the Kessel coaxium heist. Beckett had, after all, advised Han to "trust no one."

Skepticism, anti-authoritarianism, and a desire to demystify – to strip away pretensions to reveal the true, but often ugly face of reality. These are some of Han's key personality characteristics – along with his charm and nose for a good smuggling job – when we see him in action in *A New Hope*. But many great thinkers in the philosophical tradition have adopted these stances to stake their own bold claims to truth, knowledge, beauty, and justice. What makes Han any different from them?

"That's Not How the Force Works!"

Whether he's bemusedly watching Luke Skywalker train with a remote on the *Millennium Falcon* or bullying C-3PO into using his godhood to help the Rebels escape being dinner for the Ewoks, Han's skepticism most often manifests itself in efforts to debunk or demystify what others take to be esoteric or sacred. In *A New Hope* (*ANH*), he famously chides Luke: "Kid, I've flown from one side of this galaxy to the other; I've seen a lot of strange stuff. But I've never seen anything to make me believe that there's one all-powerful Force controlling everything. There's no mystical energy field that controls my destiny."

Although Han's attitude might seem narrow-minded and arrogant, his views represent the vast majority of those in the galaxy who were not special – or lucky – enough to be born Force-sensitive. In the hands of the Jedi, what he derides as a "hokey religion" did, in fact, 19 years before in *Revenge of the Sith*, fail both in detecting the influence of Darth Sidious and in stopping the rise of the Empire. On top of this, Han was undoubtedly on the receiving end of Imperial anti-Jedi propaganda that pressured the few living Jedi to live clandestine lives on backwaters like Tatooine and Dagobah.[9]

Han obviously has a prejudice against those he sees as trying to exercise control over others by disingenuous means – an ironic prejudice for a smuggler! In this regard, he bears a likeness to another charismatic, temperamental maverick: Ludwig Wittgenstein (1889–1951) and his short book, the *Tractatus Logico-Philosophicus.* Wittgenstein made the bold claim that traditional philosophy – carried out over two thousand years from Plato to Edmund Husserl – was based on a *mistake* about how philosophical language reveals truth. "Language disguises the thought," he writes, "so that from the external form of the clothes one cannot infer the form of the thought they clothe, because the external form of the clothes is constructed with quite another object than to let the form of the body be recognized."[10]

Conversely, with his *Tractatus*, Wittgenstein believed he'd established a method for "seeing the world rightly."[11] But thinking through this method would require as much brash cleverness as piloting through the dangerous and uncharted Kessel Run. Taking a traditional metaphysical question like "Is the Good more or less identical to the Beautiful?" as an example, Wittgenstein argued that "most propositions and questions" like this one "are not false, but senseless. We cannot, therefore, answer questions of this kind at all, but only state their senselessness."[12]

Because he thought that the only meaningful use of language is found in its ability to "picture" or "model" reality, Wittgenstein argued that "the only strictly meaningful propositions are those of natural science," a method that cured the understanding reader of "the temptation to utter philosophical propositions."[13] He's certainly not the only twentieth-century philosopher to affirm that philosophy, understood properly, leads us back to – and ends at – truths discovered by science.[14]

Wittgenstein's demystifying attack on what previous thinkers believed the object or aim of philosophy to be can be loosely compared to Han's occasional effort to take naïve youngsters like Luke or "Big Deal" Finn to task. On board the *Millennium Falcon* on the way to Alderaan, not only does he criticize Obi-Wan's devotion to the Jedi and the Force, he tells Luke that "ancient weapons are no match for a good blaster at your side, kid." This is in stark contrast to Obi-Wan's remark in support of the lightsaber as a classy weapon reflecting a noble, lost tradition: "Not as clumsy or random as a blaster; an elegant weapon for a more civilized age."

Han, ever the pragmatist, also prefers direct confrontations to subterfuge – usually because his attempts to keep operations covert so often go wrong. In *ANH*, he confesses that he "prefer[s] a straight fight to all this sneakin' around!" And in *The Force Awakens* (*TFA*), when he plans to take the *Falcon* out of the Rathtar-infested *Eravana*'s hangar at lightspeed, Rey asks him if such a thing is even possible: "I never ask that question 'till after I've done it [...] This is *not* how I thought this day would go." A more cautious, philosophical mind might ask if these attitudes are arrogance or justified confidence? I go with confidence – Solo seldom loses his gambles, unless he puts trust in con men like Beckett or – more unfortunately – his own son on Starkiller Base.

And what about the mature Han Solo of the sequel films? He continues to avoid philosophy like a boss. In *TFA*, an awestruck Rey asks Han if the Jedi were real. He replies, "I used to wonder about that myself. Thought it was a bunch of mumbo jumbo. A magical power holding together good and evil, the dark side and the light. Crazy thing is ... it's true. The Force, the Jedi. All of it. It's all true." This hopeful but measured reply says much in its careful phrasing: "It's all true," he says, but in the context of Han's distancing himself from Leia and the Resistance, in refraining from trying to find Luke in exile, and in returning to his career home in smuggling, Han's also saying, "And still I choose to live my life as if it all doesn't affect me."

Han's a rule-breaker from birth, another thing that might be attributable to his status as an orphan and to his gang upbringing. But what can we make out of a philosopher who wants to cure people of doing philosophy? Wittgenstein suggests that if you are reading this book, then you may be the kind of person who gets a certain sort of itch when deep questions get brought up. When that happens, he gives this advice:

> One can defend commonsense against the attacks of philosophers only by solving their puzzles, i.e., by curing them of the temptation to attack common sense; not be restating the views of common sense. A philosopher is not a man out of his senses, a man who doesn't see what everybody else sees.... We therefore have to look round for the *source* of his puzzlement. And we find that there is puzzlement and mental discomfort ... when our curiosity about certain facts is not satisfied or when we can't find a law of nature fitting in with all our experience ...[15]

As we've seen, hard scientific facts are essential truths to Wittgenstein in the *Tractatus*. If something in our experience – like how the Force works – continues to puzzle us, there are two possibilities. Either we have not yet found the law of nature that explains it (midi-chlorians?) or the questions that move us may simply be senseless ones, like "Is the Good more or less identical to the Beautiful?" These questions may be interesting, but not addressable or solvable using the tools of philosophy. In his more reflective moments, Han might've agreed with the cryptic final line of Wittgenstein's *Tractatus*: "Whereof one cannot speak, thereof one must be silent." Without a doubt, though, Solo would've added: "Boring conversation anyway."

"Then I'll See You in Hell!"

For those of us who grew up watching the original *Star Wars* trilogy in theaters and who took to Han Solo as a Hollywood hero, there's no feature of his (aside from possibly his wit) more influential than his anti-authoritarianism.[16] In the *Legends* novel *Han Solo at Star's End*, he admits that his wanderlust means he cannot help but continue to run afoul of galactic authorities:

> I could always hit the beach, he thought. Find a nice place somewhere, go native. It's a big galaxy. But he shook his head. No use fooling himself. If he were grounded, he might as well be dead. What could one planet, any planet, offer someone who had knocked around among the stars? The need for the boundless provinces of space was now a part of him.[17]

After a short period of unfulfilling service to the Empire, he considers it to be more of a nuisance than an enemy to an honest smuggler like himself. In Brian Daley's *Legends* novels, Han and Chewie nip at the heels of the Corporate Sector Authority (CSA). And in both *ANH* and *The Empire Strikes Back*, he's a reluctant Rebel who's more interested in clearing his debt to Jabba than in cosmic justice.

Why would a pragmatic guy like Han also be anti-authoritarian? For a smuggler concerned with profit margins, surely it's better to "play ball" with the CSA, the Empire, and the Rebellion. Perhaps Han, like Benicio del Toro's DJ in *The Last Jedi* (*TLJ*), woke up one day to the realization, "It's all a machine, partner. Live free, don't join." One answer to "don't join" is to encourage political anarchism, where society would be organized so that voluntary and cooperative action between individuals would take the place of government force or compulsion. I suspect, though, that Han would think anarchism is bad for business. And anarchism requires agreeing to theories that claim to correctly represent human nature as fundamentally good when humans are out from under the thumb of governments like the Empire. This is a regression back into the philosophizing that Wittgenstein found so dubious.

Another answer, according to Cornel West, is to consider the ideas of early American essayist Ralph Waldo Emerson (1803–1882) and his contemporary, the "poet of democracy" Walt Whitman (1819–1892). Tying Emerson to Wittgenstein's demystifying project in the *Tractatus*, West explains:

> Emerson's suspicion of philosophy was not simply that it bewitched thinkers by means of language but, more important, that it had deep anti-democratic consequences. For Emerson, reason, formal thought, foundations, certainty were not only far removed from the dynamism of human experiences; they also were human creations that appear as detached abstractions which command their creators and thereby constrain their creators' freedom. This consequence is both anti-libertarian and anti-democratic in that human potential and participation are suppressed in the name of philosophic truth and knowledge.[18]

It took people like Emerson and Whitman, desiring an American "creative democracy" – one that would throw off the inheritances of European philosophy that Wittgenstein claimed were a source of "puzzlement" – to see that philosophy could itself be an obstacle to the equality and freedom desired by Americans. They thought that the desire to prove that foundations for knowledge exist, or that reason is the ultimate problem-solver, can erect idols whose authority has pernicious effects just like the old authorities of church and state, challenged and sometimes overthrown in the previous century in the European Enlightenment.

A tale that recounts how this replacement could happen (and what to do about it) that could be appealing to someone like Han can be found in *Pragmatism as Anti-Authoritarianism*, by the American neo-pragmatist scholar Richard Rorty. Rorty sees the elevation of reason in the Enlightenment to show that "'Philosophy' became, for the intellectuals, a substitute for religion. It was the area of culture where one *touched bottom*...."[19] Although the Enlightenment was a major cultural force for the secular rethinking of moribund church–state alliances in the eighteenth century, it did not go far enough. The philosophers' love affair with concepts like eternity, infinity, and the sublime took on new forms in the nineteenth and twentieth centuries. By contrast, Rorty makes a controversial suggestion, "... that we build our philosophical reflections around our political hopes: around the project of fashioning institutions and customs that will make human life, finite and mortal life, more beautiful."[20] We can imagine that Han shared these interests too, in envisioning a future with Qi'ra off Corellia, a dream dashed by an unpredictable quirk of fate at the Imperial checkpoint.

As Rorty's suggestion indicates, evading philosophy by doing more philosophy solves nothing. In this vein, pragmatists like Rorty are not interested in *solutions*, but instead – like Wittgenstein – investigate *therapies* for the urge to make philosophy into a quasi-religion by pursuing the absolute foundations of beauty, truth, and justice. In this vein, he writes, "[P]ragmatists keep trying to find ways of making anti-philosophical points in non-philosophical language."[21] For Rorty, this involves criticizing the philosophical tradition for over-valuing *knowing* over *doing* and for encouraging contemplative lives of withdrawal from society; he also draws moral and political lessons from literature rather than the philosophical tradition, and encourages his fellow political liberals to look to the values of solidarity that arose from the rise of American organized labor rather than what he sees as the divisiveness of "high theory" in identity politics.[22]

So, whether it's "liberation from the primal father," giving up hope of "union with something beyond the human," or dethroning philosophers' pretensions to knowledge of ultimate reality, Rorty sees the purpose of pragmatists, following in the steps of Emerson and Whitman, as creating a society in which no one has an unfair advantage because of the place that a mere philosophical theory situates them in society.[23] If you are a free spirit like Han or Chewbacca, you also would not be forced to be one of those with a seat at the "table of conversation" about shared hopes and dreams in such a society. Just do not "shut them up or shut them down"!

"You Like Me because I'm a Scoundrel"

It will not escape the eye of the discerning *Star Wars* fan that the sequel trilogy's enmeshment with identity politics – resulting in the reprehensible anti-feminist, anti-diversity casting "Fandom Menace" movement – is one of the reasons why *TLJ* and *The Rise of Skywalker* suffered from significant fan disinterest and received tepid reviews.[24] The *Star Wars* universe is an international treasure, and it's very unfortunate that it was politicized in this way. The investment that directors Rian Johnson and J.J. Abrams made in claiming that women and marginalized people can also be part of grand narratives was a smart idea. Perhaps the problem was, as Rorty's pragmatism as anti-authoritarianism might have it, that the challenges raised to the grand narratives of the "Skywalker Saga" and "bringing balance to the Force" in these films were not forceful enough. As the success of the Disney+ television series has shown, drawing attention to the lives of the "everyday" inhabitants of the *Star Wars* universe helps break the spell that belief in the authority of grand narratives weaves. These simple people trying to make their way in the universe – and who need no therapy for philosophy, luckily for them – are epitomized by the adventures of our favorite scoundrel, Han Solo.

In any case, there's no point in telling Han how much you love him. *He knows.*

Notes

1 Aristotle, *Protrepticus*, or "*Exhortation to Philosophy*," ed. and trans. D.S. Hutchinson and Monte Ransome Johnson: http://www.protrepticus.info/protr2017x20.pdf.
2 UNICEF Data Warehouse: https://data.unicef.org/dv_index (accessed March 31, 2022).
3 Marc Guggenheim, Dave Messina, and Alex Sinclair, *Han Solo and Chewbacca* #1 (March 9, 2022), Marvel Comics.
4 Kirsten Weir, "The Lasting Impact of Neglect," *Monitor on Psychology* 45 (2014), 36.
5 Michel de Montaigne, *The Complete Essays of Montaigne*, trans. Donald M. Frame Redwood City, CA: Stanford University Press, 1958 , 822.
6 One of an increasing number of academic programs that have developed philosophy curricula for children is the "Philosophy for Children" program out of the University of Washington's Philosophy Department; see https://phil.washington.edu/fields/philosophy-children.
7 Montaigne, *Complete Essays*, 152.
8 *Star Wars* (2020), #18. Marvel Comics, November 2021.
9 I discuss how this propaganda motivated several remaining Jedi in the *Dark Times* comics series in Dark Times: The End of the Republic and the Beginning of Chinese Philosophy, in Jason T. Eberl and Kevin S. Decker, eds., *The Ultimate Star Wars and Philosophy: You Must Unlearn What You Have Learned* (Malden, MA: Wiley-Blackwell, 2015), 53–64.
10 Ludwig Wittgenstein, *Tractatus Logico-Philosophicus 4.002*, in *Major Works: Selected Philosophical Writings* (New York: Harper Collins, 2009), 20–21.
11 Hans Sluga, "Ludwig Wittgenstein, Life and Work: An Introduction," in Hans Sluga and David G. Stern, eds., *The Cambridge Companion to Wittgenstein* (New York: Cambridge University Press, 1996), 11.
12 Wittgenstein, *Tractatus* 4.003, 21.

13 Sluga, "Ludwig Wittgenstein," 11.
14 In this respect, Wittgenstein shares much with the tradition of "logical positivism," identified with the members of the Vienna Circle. See Karl Sigmund, *Exact Thinking in Demented Times: The Vienna Circle and the Epic Quest for the Foundations of Science* (New York: Basic Books, 2017).
15 Ludwig Wittgenstein, *The Blue Book* (1958), in *Major Works: Selected Philosophical Writings* (New York: Harper Perennial, 2009), 158.
16 It's not just me. In 2005, Han placed #14 in the American Film Institute's list of greatest film heroes: https://www.afi.com/afis-100-years-100-heroes-villians (accessed April 4, 2022). Indiana Jones was #2, so we'll call it a double-win for Harrison Ford fans.
17 Brian Daley, *Han Solo at Stars' End*, in *The Han Solo Adventures* (New York: Del Rey, 2014), 8–9; originally published 1979.
18 Cornel West, *The American Evasion of Philosophy: A Genealogy of* Pragmatism (Madison: University of Wisconsin Press, 1989), 212.
19 Richard Rorty, *Philosophy and the Mirror of Nature* (Princeton: Princeton University Press, 1979), 4; italics added.
20 Richard Rorty, *Pragmatism as Anti-Authoritarianism*, ed. Eduardo Mendieta (Cambridge: Belknap/Harvard, 2021), xxix.
21 Richard Rorty, "Introduction: Pragmatism and Philosophy," in *Consequences of Pragmatism* (Minneapolis: University of Minnesota Press, 1982), xiii.
22 He does these things in *Contingency, Irony, and Solidarity* (New York: Cambridge University Press, 1989) and *Achieving Our Country: Leftist Thought in Twentieth-Century America* (Cambridge: Harvard University Press, 1999), respectively.
23 Rorty, *Pragmatism as Anti-Authoritarianism*, 10–11.
24 See Morten Bay, "Weaponizing the Haters: The Last Jedi and the Strategic Politicization of Pop Culture through Social Media Manipulation," unpublished (October 2018): https://www.researchgate.net/publication/328006677_Weaponizing_the_haters_The_Last_Jedi_and_the_strategic_politicization_of_pop_culture_through_social_media_manipulation (accessed April 4, 2022).

15

Friendship, Love, and Sex with Droids in *Solo*: "How Would that Work?" "It Works"

Nick Munn and Dan Weijers

In *Solo: A Star Wars Story*, the debonair Lando Calrissian is clearly in love with the artificially intelligent droid L3-37. Lando's no shrinking violet. His charisma and good looks would've made it easy to attract the attention of many organic suitors. Nevertheless, Lando's romantic attention is focused squarely on L3-37.

If you paid too much attention to the initial, negative Internet reaction to *Solo,* you may have missed the pleasure of watching a fun heist movie in the *Star Wars* canon. More than that, you may never have considered that a human and an artificially intelligent droid could fall in love. Even some people well acquainted with the *Star Wars* universe may still doubt that Lando could *really* love L3-37. In their defense, Qi'ra doubts it from her knowing position inside the *Star Wars* universe! But not just humanoid–droid love is at stake here: L3-37 also implies that humanoid–droid sex "works."

There are lots of friendships between droids and humans (not to mention Wookiees, Togruta, and more) in *Star Wars*. But in *Solo* we get a glimpse of something more. L3-37 can see that Qi'ra knows that Han loves her, however much Qi'ra wants to deny it. So in the spirit of friendship, L3 opens up about her own past.

QI'RA: Han is not in love with me!
L3-37: Oh, please. It's just us. You do not have to pretend. I'm in the same situation.
QI'RA: You are?

Star Wars and Philosophy Strikes Back: This is the Way, First Edition.
Edited by Jason T. Eberl and Kevin S. Decker.

L3-37: I'm sure you have noticed that Lando has feelings for me. Which makes working together difficult because I do not feel the same way about him.
QI'RA: Right.
[pause, decides to humor her]
QI'RA: Yes, Yeah. Yeah, I see that.
L3-37: Sometimes, I think ... maybe. But, no. We're just not compatible.

In this chapter, we'll look at the relationship between Lando and L3-37 in *Solo* and argue that they exhibit all the hallmarks not just of friendship, but of love. Has *Solo* taken the "fiction" part of "science fiction" too far, or do Lando and L3-37 give us a glimpse into a possible – even likely – future for humans involving successful romantic relationships with artificially intelligent robots? We find no reason that Lando and L3-37 could not have enjoyed such a relationship, one that included both love and sex.

What Does Friendship Require?

You know you have found a good friend when you find someone who looks at you the way Poe Dameron looks at BB-8. Philosophically speaking, it's been said that a good friendship involves mutual caring, intimacy, and shared activity, characteristics of many relationships between droids and other sentient beings in *Star Wars*.[1] Duos like R2-D2 and Anakin Skywalker, or BB-8 and Poe, forge their friendships through adventures by each other's side, and so they learn to rely on, trust, and come to know each other.

But Aristotle (384–322 BCE) says that some friendships are better than others. For him, there are complete and incomplete friendships. A friendship between people who both seek to gain from the relationship is one of *utility*, while a friendship between people who simply enjoy each other's company is one of *pleasure*. Both of these, Aristotle states, are friendships, but neither is a complete one. A complete friendship makes each of the friends better people. Aristotle calls these *character* friendships: they help you develop a virtuous character (many features of which are familiar to those who follow the Jedi creed).[2] But these friendships are also hard to come by. As Aristotle says, they are "rare because there are few good men and because time and familiarity are required to enter into a character-friendship."[3]

But Aristotle arguably asks too much of friendship. While it's certainly possible to have a complete friendship like the ones he describes, most of our friendships, even a lot of the best ones, aren't like that. Dean Cocking and Jeanette Kennett contend that affection and well-wishing are the core components of friendship,[4] while Nancy Sherman thinks it's the ability to "share and co-ordinate activities over an extended period of time" that does the work.[5] We do not think friendships are any worse for not being what Aristotle would call "complete." Instead, two things make a good friendship: first, that friends want good things for each other, and second, that their interactions are usually rewarding. It's hard to be friends with someone when you do not enjoy their company.

Wanting good things for each other is an important feature of good friendship: it allows people to distinguish between real friends and fake friends, enemies, and so on. When Han Solo and Lando first meet, they are friendly toward each other, but they aren't really *friends*. When gambling for the *Millennium Falcon*, they cannot want good things for each other – Sabacc has only one final winner. This is made most obvious by Lando's willingness to cheat to win – when you really care about someone, you do not cheat them out of the most iconic spaceship ever to grace the silver screen!

Rewarding interactions are also important. Imagine attending a party full of people who want the best for you, but who also annoy you. It's just you, Jar Jar Binks, C-3PO, Vice Admiral Holdo, Hayden Christensen's whiney *Attack of the Clones*-era Anakin Skywalker, and your cousin, the die-hard Trekkie. Despite their best intentions, you have a headache coming on and need to call it an early night. The rewards of friendship can come in many forms that do not need to be viewed as more or less valuable (like Aristotle does). Luke Skywalker might not want to party with Yoda, but he learns a lot about the ways of the Force from that wise old frog. The more rewarding interactions (and the fewer negative ones) you have with someone, the better friend they are to you. This helps explain why friendships get stronger over time, such as between Finn and Poe, and, dare we say it, R2-D2 and C-3PO.

The friendship between R2-D2 and C-3PO might not have seemed real to Aristotle. He did not think that droids can have everything required to be friends, but we'll take Anakin's side: he was right in *Clone Wars* to claim that R2 was "more than a droid ... a friend." C-3PO was right as well when he drew Poe's attention by "Taking one last look ... at my friends" in a pivotal scene in *The Rise of Skywalker*.

How many of your own friends are making you a better person through your friendship? Not many, right? Yet they are still friends, good friends even. Droids are the kinds of beings that can be good friends, as is clearly supported throughout the *Star Wars* canon. What's most important is that individuals have mutual positive intentions and a lot of rewarding interactions.

Let us take BB-8 as an example. He and Poe clearly enjoy each other's company and go out of their way to help and support each other – as good friends do. They clearly miss each other when they are apart, as shown by their touching reunions in both *The Force Awakens* and *The Last Jedi*, which include heart-warming vocalizations, hugging, and a tender forehead touch. Given his childhood as a slave with a knack for making robots, it's no great surprise that the often-moody Clone Wars-era Anakin seems to prefer R2-D2's company to most organic life forms. They regularly share jokes and reassuring comments, and unlike most of the humanoids with whom Anakin spends time, R2 never seems to trigger him. Anakin and R2 both clearly want the best for each other, as demonstrated by Anakin risking his own life, not to mention the lives of several clone troopers, to save R2.

Love is similar to friendship in some ways. Laurence Thomas has even ventured that it's merely a special kind of friendship, the only difference being the presence of a sexual element in romantic love.[6] This is clearly not what Obi-Wan has in mind when, in *Revenge of the Sith*, he says to Anakin: "You were my brother, Anakin! I loved you!" Most of us love our family and close friends without having any sexual feelings toward them. When we use "love" in this way, we are expressing deep caring about someone – we want the best for them. The kind of love that seems to have something more than friendship is evoked when we say we are *in* love with someone, or that we have romantic love for them. So, can a droid be in love with a humanoid? To answer this question, we'll consider a range of views of romantic love that go beyond just being "friends with benefits."

Being Encouraged to Love

Bennet Helm suggests four different ways to explain what romantic love requires.[7] We could consider love as the union of two beings, as a relationship of deep and enduring mutual caring, as the valuing of each other in some way that goes beyond the way in which you value friends, or as an emotional state. Let us look at Lando and L3's relationship in light of each of these views of love.

Helm says that love could be the *union* of two beings, but what could such a "union" be? Some claim that it's a joining of minds (or souls), where each participant willingly sacrifices their individuality to the joint creation of a "we." Each lover gives up something of themself to be one with the other, like when Chirrut Îmwe gives of himself to be one with the Force in *Rogue One*.[8] If we consider the idea that love consists in the desire to form a significant union, it seems that Lando, at least, had this desire. L3 says as much to Qi'ra: "I'm sure you've noticed that Lando has feelings for me. Which makes working together difficult because I do not feel the same way about him." The problem, for Lando, is that L3 does not think of him in that way. She insists to Qi'ra that there's no physical barrier to union with Lando, but L3 does not reciprocate Lando's desires. L3 is a fierce, proud droid, who believes herself fully capable of love, and claims to have considered making a go of things with him. She simply chose not to. Clearly, Lando and L3 weren't in love. The feelings were one-sided, with Lando left pining after an uninterested L3. But that does not undermine the general possibility of love between droids and humans, especially not if we take L3 at her word, that the physical union "works." Given her personality, L3 would probably reject the idea of "love as union" anyway, since the union view seems to undermine individual autonomy. L3 is big on droid rights and freedoms, as well as being fiercely independent.[9] So even when she envisages the possibility of loving Lando, she's unlikely to think of love like this.

We could alternately think about love as a deep and enduring *mutual caring* for one another. Here, the central feature of loving someone is a strong care for them for their own sake. This is not as demanding as the love-as-union view. We have good reason to believe that Lando cares about L3 in this way. Throughout *Solo*, he's a suave character, debonair and self-confident, with a breezy lack of concern for anyone but himself. And yet, he shows himself to be truly vulnerable when L3 is in danger. He abandons all thought of self-preservation to fling himself toward her, carrying her injured (and heavy!) body to the ship, ignoring the risk of laser-blast holes in his body (or his cloak!) in doing so. As a self-reliant ... err ... businessperson in a risky industry, Lando usually put his own interests first. He did not risk his life for Han in *Solo*, and was complicit in Han's carbon-freezing in *The Empire Strikes Back*, although by the events of *Return of the Jedi* he was a willing participant in the infiltration of Jabba's palace. But for L3, he could not do anything else. Of course, thinking of love as a deep and enduring mutual caring makes it harder to distinguish love from friendship. Most of us have friends for whom we'd sacrifice a lot, even to the point of risking our lives. If we are already comfortable with the idea of human–droid friendships, then if love is just this, it's clear that Lando and L3 could love each other.

Helm's third suggestion is that loving someone involves *valuing* them in a particular kind of way. Friendship, like love, entails valuing another, but the value implied by love might be different from that in friendship. David Velleman says that "love disarms our emotional defenses; it makes us vulnerable to the other."[10] This seems like an excellent description of how Lando behaves toward L3. He's smitten with her and would do anything to save her. It is not clear that L3 values Lando in quite the same way, although she seems to have considered the possibility.

Finally, Helm says that love might be an *emotional* state, and that loving someone requires that you have the right sort of emotions about them. This raises the important question of whether droids have emotions. In the *Star Wars* canon, we see many droids display a similar emotional range to humanoid characters (and a broader one than most Jedi), including but not limited to shame, fear, anger, regret, and joy.[11] When C-3PO says to R2 in *The Force Awakens*, "Oh, my dear friend. How I've missed you," we observe his emotions in exactly the same way that we observe Obi-Wan's emotions about Anakin. We understand that C-3PO really *feels* relief at having his friend return, and that the missing was an emotional state, not merely a programmed one.

Academics and advice columnists alike debate how the emotions characteristic of love develop. Amélie Rorty claims that love arises from the interactions of individuals *over time*.[12] So for Lando and L3, the history of their relationship – their adventures and experiences together – generates Lando's loving emotions toward L3. Annette Baier would describe this as the lovers' development of an *emotional interdependence* with each other.[13]

Thinking of love as an emotional state, the more you love someone, the more you are likely to value the same things they value and understand and respect their goals and desires. A perfect example of this is L3's often militant desires for droid rights, freedom, and emancipation. She's overwhelmed by these desires on Kessel, removing DD-BD's restraining bolt, inciting a droid uprising and consequently a Wookiee slave revolt. If Lando loved L3, he would not merely tolerate these desires, but encourage, endorse, and support her in this goal. And indeed, Lando's not annoyed at L3 for focusing on droid emancipation despite that not being part of the original plan. This valuing of the other's desires seems to go both ways between Lando and L3.

She might not feel the same way, as she tells Qi'ra, but she feels something. Decades later, Lando's feelings for L3 shape his relationship with the *Falcon*, which he still thinks of as his ship. Perhaps Lando never stopped loving L3 after she was uploaded into the *Falcon*.

Humanoids and Droids Having Sex?

L3 makes it clear that she knows her way around the reproductive biology of organic life forms, telling Qi'ra, simply, that "It works" when Qi'ra wonders how sexually compatible a droid and a human could be. But sex is not necessary for any of the kinds of love we described above. This is fortunate, given that love stories are a central part of storytelling and Disney is unlikely to ever allow more than the slightest hints of sexual content into their media. We can still wonder, though, whether there'd be anything wrong with human–droid sexual relationships.

Let us think of sex as any kind of activity that results in sexual reward, such as orgasmic pleasure in humans. Given this broad view, sexual reward seems possible without physical touch. Individuals can experience sexual reward in dreams or their waking imaginations. Couples can experience interactive sexual reward too, as demonstrated by the main characters of the "Striking Vipers" episode of *Black Mirror*, who get as much sexual reward from virtual touch as physical touch.[14] Once this inclusive view of sex is accepted, sex with droids seems possible – the burden of proof is on those who think sex with droids is not possible.

One potential concern is that droids smarter than humans might take advantage of an inferior organic life form by having a sexual relationship with them. This echoes the analysis of Han and Chewbacca's relationship by Arthur Chu,[15] who notes that Chewbacca, being bigger, stronger, smarter, more emotionally mature, and longer-lived than Han, wasn't, as George Lucas implied, the "dog" in this relationship – Han was. This worry is also supported by L3 voice-actress Phoebe Waller-Bridge's analysis of the relationship between L3 and Lando: "There's a very thin line between love and hate for them. But she certainly sees him as her, sort of, man-thing."[16]

In the *Star Wars* universe, droids are sentient non-organic life forms. At least some of them are highly intelligent, vastly outstripping the capacities of their organic counterparts. Despite this intellectual superiority, many droids deign to be friends with organic life forms, and some of their closest friendships are integral to the saga's appeal for us viewers. R2-D2 and BB-8 are fully realized characters whose friendships with the other protagonists drive the main trilogies along. It's easy to ascribe to droids the capacity to love and be loved. The relationship between L3 and Lando, while only hinted at in *Solo*, is nevertheless the clearest example we have of love between organic and non-organic life in the *Star Wars* universe.

Notes

1 Bennet Helm, "Friendship," in *The Stanford Encyclopedia of Philosophy* (Fall 2021 edition), ed. Edward N. Zalta, at https://plato.stanford.edu/archives/fall2021/entries/friendship.
2 For an exploration of Jedi virtues, see Judith Barad, "The Aspiring Jedi's Handbook of Virtue," in Kevin S. Decker and Jason T. Eberl, eds., *Star Wars and Philosophy: More Powerful than You Can Possibly Imagine* (Chicago: Open Court, 2005), 57–68.
3 Aristotle, *The Nicomachean Ethics*, trans. M. Ostwald (Englewood Cliffs, NJ: Prentice-Hall, 1962), 1156a6–1156a34.
4 Dean Cocking and Jeanette Kennett, "Friendship and the Self," *Ethics* 108 (1998), 502-527.
5 Nancy Sherman, "Aristotle on Friendship and the Shared Life," *Philosophy and Phenomenological Research* 47 (1987), 589–613.
6 Laurence Thomas, "Friendship," *Synthese* 72 (1987), 217–236.
7 Bennet Helm, "Love," in *The Stanford Encyclopedia of Philosophy* (Fall 2021 edition), ed. Edward N. Zalta, at https://plato.stanford.edu/archives/fall2021/entries/love.
8 Chirrut and Baze are, of course, great friends to each other throughout *Rogue One*.
9 For a discussion of L3 as a freedom-fighter for droid rights, see Joshua Jowitt's chapter in this volume (Chapter 16).
10 J. David Velleman, "Love as a Moral Emotion," *Ethics* 109 (1999), 338–374.
11 Robert Arp, "'If Droids Could Think ...': Droids as Slaves and Persons," in Kevin S. Decker and Jason T. Eberl, eds., *Star Wars and Philosophy: More Powerful than You Can Possibly Imagine* (Chicago: Open Court, 2005), 120–131.
12 Amélie O. Rorty, "The Historicity of Psychological Attitudes: Love Is Not Love Which Alters Not When It Alteration Finds," *Midwest Studies in Philosophy* 10 (1987), 399–412.
13 Annette C. Baier, "Unsafe Loves," in Robert C. Solomon and Kathleen M. Higgins, eds., *The Philosophy of (Erotic) Love* (Lawrence: University Press of Kansas, 1991), 433–450.

14 Darren Slade, "*Striking Vipers* and Closed Doors: How Meaningful Are Sexual Fantasies?" in David Kyle Johnson, ed., *Black Mirror and Philosophy: Dark Reflections* (Hoboken, NJ: Wiley-Blackwell, 2019), 241–250.

15 Arthur Chu, Twitter comment, December 20, 2017, at https://twitter.com/arthur_affect/status/943382213176913920.

16 Author unknown, "Solo: Everything We Know About L3-37," *Variety* (May 30, 2018), at https://www.youtube.com/watch?v=mZMLopagYF4.

16

La L3-37 Continue: Droid Rights and the Problem of Legal Personhood

Joshua Jowitt

One of my favorite things about going to the cinema is the discussion that takes place afterwards, when someone in the group inevitably asks, "Well? What did you make of that?" It's a simple enough question, but I'm sure you'll agree that the answer is crucial – and, after some friends and I went to see *Solo: A Star Wars Story*, it quickly became clear that I'd given the wrong answer.

THAT'S what you took from that?

Were we watching the same thing?

And, most pointedly:

> Josh – they're just droids!

The comment that provoked these reactions was how much I'd enjoyed the character L3-37, and how I wanted to hear more about her activism for droid rights.[1] My friends saw her struggle for equality as nothing more than comic relief, but as a lawyer, I was fascinated – why couldn't droids have rights? And as an ethicist, I was intrigued – why *shouldn't* they?

Perhaps my friends were skeptical because they just didn't see the issue, so with that in mind I'll try and show that L3 raises a real issue within the philosophy of law. We'll mainly be examining her activism and asking whether a case for rights and legal personhood for droids can be made. But given that societal change only

Star Wars and Philosophy Strikes Back: This is the Way, First Edition.
Edited by Jason T. Eberl and Kevin S. Decker.

happens when struggles against injustice stick in our consciousness, I think the droid rights movement may also need a snappy byline. "La Lutte Continue" – *may the struggle continue* – was one of the most popular social justice slogans to emerge from L'Atelier Populaire during the 1968 Paris riots. We can tweak this for the droid rights movement to produce a slogan that we can all get behind, one that fully recognizes L3-37's pioneering advocacy: "La L3-37 Continue!"

Droid Rights: The Problem of Legal Personhood

Before we dive into the case put to us by L3, let's start by taking a look at what legal personhood actually means. A long time ago, in an Empire far, far away, the Roman jurist Gaius (130–180 CE) wrote that all legal systems categorize everything as either a person or a thing. Legal persons are capable of bearing rights and/or duties. Things cannot – they are *property*, and an owner can do whatever they like with their property without having to worry about whether it has rights.[2]

Legal systems today still operate on this binary. But most legal systems see no necessary connection between *moral persons* (whom we might consider as having moral worth) and *legal persons*. Instead, they see legal persons as an entirely separate legal category. So, for example, legal systems have no problem recognizing things like ships or temple ruins as legal persons with rights despite their not being moral persons.[3] In the UK, we even went as far as giving corporations the right to vote in our parliamentary elections because they are legal persons – a right that was only removed in 1948.[4] On the other side of this binary, legal systems have had no problem with categorizing human beings as property through the institution of slavery. Far from being consigned to the history books, the status of slave remains legally permissible in several legal systems today.[5] This tells us that the immorality of slavery doesn't necessarily affect the validity of any legal rule that allows it. The law denies slaves are legal persons, so until the law changes, they are not.

I'm in no way saying that the suffering of enslaved people and their descendants is the same as that of droids in *Star Wars*. Rather, I want to make a less controversial point about the problem of categorizing things as either legal persons or as property: that legal systems can get it wrong. It seems to me that this is what L3 has picked up on.

Legal Personhood for Droids in the Galactic Empire

And how could she not? Right from the beginning of *Solo* we're reminded that – in the Empire's legal system – droids are seen as property. When Han and Qi'ra are attempting to board a transport off Corellia, we hear an announcement over the Coronet Spaceport announcement system: "Do not join the line if you don't have a boarding pass. No access without ID chips. All droids must be registered." The mundanity of this announcement shows how droids are entirely commoditized. Their status as property is so obvious and unchallengeable that it's not even conceivable that a droid may require a boarding pass in their own right. They only need to be registered, in the same way as we might check-in luggage when boarding a flight.

The point is made more brutally in a scene shortly after in which, just as enslaved gladiators fought to the death for their owners in Ancient Rome, droids are portrayed as cage-fighting for the entertainment of biological beings. It's here that we're first introduced to L3, when we hear her shouting to the crowd: "No! Unacceptable! Stop exploiting droids! How can you condone this savagery?" She then turns her attention to a fighting droid: "You! You should not be doing this, they are using you for entertainment!" The droid bleeps back at her, prompting her to reply "Yes, you've been neurowashed! Don't just blindly follow the program – exercise some free will!" She then gets into an altercation with the fight organizer, at one point issuing the rallying cry of "Droid rights! We are sentient!"

This is important dialogue. Not only does it tell us that L3 believes the legal system is wrong to deny droids their legal personhood, it also gives us the reason *why* she thinks a reclassification is needed – droid *sentience*, which she implies gives them *moral status*. She's at pains to show that, for her, sentience is more morally relevant than the fact she was made on an assembly line. In a multi-layered exchange with Lando Calrissian shortly after the fight, he instructs her to plot a course for Kessel despite her seeing no good reason to do so. L3 quips, "Oh, why? Because you're my organic overlord?" Lando's reply shows he disagrees with her belief that society imposes an organic/non-organic hierarchy: "Because I'm your captain, how about that? [Aside] I actually would have her memory wiped, but she's got the best damn navigational database in the Galaxy." Even though this response suggests he sees L3 as crew, it also shows that – despite the close relationship they have – he ultimately sees her as mainly instrumentally valuable. He sees her advocacy for rights almost as a malfunction, and he only tolerates her because there's something in it for him. Despite the closeness of their relationship, he doesn't see her as having independent moral value in the same way as a biological being.

This is further evidenced by a later exchange between the two on approach to Kessel. Lando asks L3: "I'm going to go check on the damps – do you need anything?" To which L3 replies curtly, "Equal rights?" Lando audibly sighs. This suggests that, not only does he not see her as a being worthy of rights, but that he's tired of her protestations to the contrary. For L3, the issue is clear: only recognition of rights can improve her lot and that of other sentient droids. She sees the problem as not just moral, but legal.

Morality and Legal Validity

If the problem is both legal *and* moral, then we should take a step back and look at the bigger picture: what exactly is the nature of the relationship between morality and the validity of a legal rule? There are two main schools of thought. Legal positivists think that law doesn't need to be morally permissible in order to be valid. All that matters is that it's been created by a body that has the power to make law. This view was famously summarized by John Austin (1790–1859): "The existence of law is one thing; its merit or demerit is another."[6] Austin believed that law was simply a command made from a position of power, backed up by a threat of sanction in the event of non-compliance.[7] This seems to describe how legal systems operate quite nicely – a legislator makes a law, and lays out a penalty if you break it. It also seems to describe the Empire's legal system; whether droids *ought* to be property is immaterial – they simply are and will remain so until the law is changed.

But there's a problem with Austin's view. H.L.A. Hart (1907–1992) pointed out that "law as command backed by sanction" could also describe a bank robbery: "Hand over the money, or I will shoot!"[8] It could also describe Enfys Nest's command as the Cloud Riders attempt to steal coaxium from Tobias Beckett and Han following their train heist on Vandor: "Release your cables, or die!" Both of these statements meet Austin's definition of law as commands backed by a threat of sanction. But they clearly aren't law – so does that mean law is more than this? There are two ways we could proceed. We could try to rescue Austin's claim, perhaps by pointing out our robber's threat isn't law because they aren't a legitimate lawmaker. But that route raises the question of who *is* a legitimate lawmaker? If we want to avoid that question, a second path is available.

Enter the natural lawyers, who think law *does* need to be morally permissible in order to be valid. Natural law positions have been dominant in history – thinkers such as Aristotle (384–322 BCE) argued that law needed to direct us to happiness, or *eudaimonia*; Thomas Aquinas (1225–1274) said that law needed to be in accordance with God-given rationality.[9] Even a strict reading of Immanuel Kant (1724–1804) and his categorical imperative could justify a natural law argument. Kant believed that rationality was the source of moral worth and all rational beings were deserving of rights, hence the third framing of his categorical imperative that in all circumstances we should respect "the will of every rational being as a universally legislating will."[10] Kantians believe that this maxim is the ultimate test for moral permissibility; any act that breaches it is immoral, because it's categorical and overrides any reason we may have to behave otherwise.

A Kantian version of natural law, applying the categorical imperative to questions of legal validity, would look something like this. Let's start with the idea that the whole point of making a law is to get us to comply with a legal rule; it follows that the law must at least claim that a reason exists for us to obey it. But remember – a categorical imperative *must override all other competing reasons for action*, otherwise it wouldn't be categorical. This includes legal reasons; so if law requires us to do something that breaches the categorical imperative, the categorical imperative has to come out on top. This means it's impossible for any legal rule that breaches the categorical imperative to give us a reason to obey it. And if they can't give us a reason to comply with them, conflicting legal rules can't meet the starting condition of any law: to get us to comply with them in the first place. If they can't do the one thing that laws are supposed to do, then we have to conclude that they aren't valid law at all.

It might not fly if you tried it in a courtroom, but as a matter of logic this seems sound enough. But enough of the abstraction – how would a natural lawyer link this back to the problem of legal personhood for droids?

Natural Law and Legal Personhood

If L3 is right and droid sentience means they're rational, moral persons deserving of rights, then a lawyer working from ideas of natural law would say their legal personhood must be recognized. Remember, our starting point is simple enough: the whole point of making a law is to get us to comply with it, so any legal rule needs at least to be capable of giving us a reason to obey. But if droids are covered by the categorical imperative because of their sentience, then any rule that sees them as property breaches the categorical imperative. Rules that breach the categorical imperative can't give us a reason to obey them, and so can't be valid law because they can't do the one thing a law is supposed to do. So if a rule exists that classifies droids as property, and this rule breaches the categorical imperative, it can't be a valid legal rule; it's an illegitimate exercise of state power and needs replacing as a matter of urgency.

You may have spotted a big caveat lurking here. This only works as a matter of logic if droids are sentient, rational beings that would be covered by the categorical imperative in the first place. L3 thinks they are, but is she right? How characters interact with droids can help us figure this one out, and we'll start with Lando. Although he instrumentalizes her for her navigational prowess, the way he treats L3 suggests her sentience has led to a meaningful relationship. After she's shot while leading a droid revolt in the spice mines of Kessel, we see him run to rescue her. I doubt he would do this if he saw her as merely property – and I doubt Han and Chewbacca would've helped him unless they also saw her as more. This is supported by a moving scene once they're back on the *Millennium Falcon*:

LANDO: It's OK, I can fix you!
L3: Lando ... What's happening to me? [L3's power dies]
LANDO: L3? L3! Oh, I'm sorry, girl. I'm so sorry.

This scene wouldn't work unless Lando saw her as being at least of *some* independent moral worth. Despite earlier suggestions to the contrary, it seems he *does* see her sustained pattern of rational choices as not just a malfunction, but as evidence that she is a moral person capable of being wronged. And, perhaps more importantly, the scene wouldn't work unless we saw her as a moral person too. Because it was at this point in the film that I found *myself* agreeing with her cause; the fact that she had made rational, informed choices at several points leading up to this dialogue meant that *I* saw her as more than just property. And I bet you do too, even if you don't realize it. Have you noticed I've ascribed a gender to L3, and referred to her as she/her throughout this chapter? The fact I feel fine doing this in English, where we don't normally ascribe genders to objects, confirms I see her as more than just property. I think it would have been odd to do this for simpler responsive technologies like Siri, despite them both having feminine voices. But I felt fine doing it here, because L3's rational choices and interpersonal relationships make me think she is a moral person. And I think the fact that you likely didn't notice I'd gendered her throughout this chapter – or if you did, didn't question it much – suggests that you see her as a moral person too. Her rationality brings something extra to the table, and it's not something we can just ignore.

This scene in *Solo* isn't an isolated incident; interpersonal relationships with droids suggesting they're more than mere property are common throughout the *Star Wars* franchise. Take C-3PO. When he's blown apart on Bespin in *The Empire Strikes Back*, we see this as a bad thing. And before the memory wipe performed by Babu Frik in *The Rise of Skywalker* (*TROS*), when he tells us that all his memories will be lost – including his recognition of his companions – we feel sad. The sadness we feel, a sadness shared by C-3PO's companions on Kijimi, can only be explained if we see him as more than just property. We see him as a companion and a friend, and we despair at the thought of losing him. We couldn't have this relationship with him were he not a sentient, rational being capable of maintaining personal relationships.

Hints at droid rationality and sentience exist beyond humanoid droids. Again in *TROS*, when D-O meets new people for the first time, he exhibits fear and nervousness that suggests past trauma. His previous relationships have made him modify his behavior to avoid perceived danger – a rational action if ever there was one. Some fans think that, in *The Force Awakens*, BB-8 flips the bird at Finn to show disapproval at his deception. This hints that BB-8 is a sentient, rational being too, as he wouldn't have been able to make a moral judgment and flip the bird if he couldn't weigh up the pros and cons of Finn choosing to deceive his friends. We also recognize rational personality traits in R2-D2 when the tone of his beeping suggests an awareness of the situations in which he finds himself. The bond we build because of this means we mourn with Luke when R2 is shot during the Battle of Yavin, and celebrate when we see him restored at the medal ceremony at the end of *A New Hope*.

Some may dismiss this as projecting human characteristics onto property, but there's enough here to make me think that – on balance – perhaps droids *do* have sentience and rationality, and that this *might* mean they're deserving of legal rights. There is certainly enough to trigger what contemporary legal theorist Deryck Beyleveld calls the "precautionary principle": if we think a being *might* be deserving of rights, then we should treat them as if they do – just to be on the safe side.[11]

This means that, at least for a lawyer working in terms of Kantian natural law, L3 is right – as a matter of logic, sentient, rational droids as they exist in *Star Wars* can't be property. As a matter of both morality and law this classification is incorrect, and her activism for rights and legal personhood is justified.

Beyond the Whimsy

You might think this seems far-fetched, but legal systems here on Earth are already dealing with the question of whether artificial intelligence (AI) can be a legal person. In the UK, Lord Hodge – Deputy President of the Supreme Court – has written that, conceptually, he has no problem with this at all.[12] Decisions have recently been made in the US, UK, and Australia as to whether an AI named DABUS can be the inventor of an item for the purposes of copyright ownership. Though rejected outright in the US it was initially accepted in Australia – and though rejected in the UK, one judge out of three hearing the case strongly dissented.[13]

Granted, this AI is a long way from the sentient droids of *Star Wars*. But it not only shows us that the problem is real, it also gives us a view as to how litigation may cause the galactic legal system to transition to seeing droids as rights-bearing legal persons. Philosopher Josh Gellers suggests that a useful parallel emerges if we consider campaigns for robot rights as similar to those for animal rights.[14] Legal systems worldwide are presently grappling with whether animals such as elephants, cetaceans, bears, and primates should be legal persons instead of property – the same issue that L3 identifies for droids.[15] It seems likely that her struggle will proceed through the courts in the same way.

Regardless of how it might happen, one thing is certain: it'll take time for public opinion to warm to this possibility – for either animals or droids. My friends' dismissiveness as we left *Solo* shows us that. Until then, if I've convinced you that L3 may be onto something, then we may need to channel the spirit of Paris, 1968. So say it with me: "May La L3-37 Continue"!

Notes

1 Pronunciation guide: L3-37's name is a nod to the Internet term "L33T," pronounced "LEET," which refers to the practice of swapping letters in a word to other, similar looking characters. The title of this chapter should be pronounced "La Leet Continue."

2 W.M. Gordon and O.F. Robinson *The Institutes of Gaius* (London: Duckworth, 1988) , Books One and Two.

3 Tucker v Alexandroff, 183 U.S. 424, 438, 22 Sup. Ct. 195, 201 (1902); Bumper Development Corporation v Commissioner of Police of the Metropolis (1991) 1 WLR, 1362.

4 Representation of the People Act 1948, s 1(2).

5 In Mauritania it is still not uncommon to find entire villages that are held in hereditary slavery from which there is no legal escape, and slavery and forced labor are legally permissible across the globe in multiple forms. Recent research suggests that, as of 2020, 94 states around the world do not have criminal legislation actively prohibiting slavery; 112 states do not have penal provisions to punish forced labor; 170 have not criminalized four institutions and practices, such as bonded labor, that closely resemble slavery; and 180 – that's 93% of all states in the world – do not have legislation that criminalizes servitude. See: https://antislaverylaw.ac.uk.

6 John Austin, *The Province of Jurisprudence Determined* (Cambridge: Cambridge University Press, 1995), 157–158.

7 Austin, *Province of Jurisprudence*, 21–22.

8 H.L.A. Hart, *The Concept of Law* (Oxford: Oxford University Press, 2012), 19.

9 Aristotle *Nicomachean Ethics,* trans. W.D. Ross and Lesley Brown (Oxford: Oxford University Press, 2009), Book 1; Thomas Aquinas *Summa Theologiae Vol. 28, IaIIae 90–97*, trans. Thomas Gilby (Cambridge: Cambridge University Press, 2006) , Q95 Art 2, 105.

10 Immanuel Kant, *Groundwork of the Metaphysics of Morals*, trans. Mary Gregor (Cambridge: Cambridge University Press, 2012), vol. 4, 431.

11 Deryck Beyleveld, " The Principle of Generic Consistency as the Supreme Principle of Human Rights," *Human Rights Review* 13 (2012), 10.

12 Lord Hodge, "Financial Technology: Opportunities and Challenges to Law and Regulation," in Dennis J. Baker and Paul H. Robinson, eds., *Artificial Intelligence and the Law: Cybercrime and Criminal Liability* (London: Routledge, 2020), 31–48.

13 Thaler v Hirshfeld – F.Supp.3d –, 2021 WL 3934803, 1:20-cv-903 (LMB/TCB); Thaler v Commissioner of Patents [2021] FCA 879; *Thaler v Comptroller General of Patents Trade Marks and Designs* [2021] EWCA Civ 1374.

14 Joshua C. Gellers, *Rights for Robots: Artificial Intelligence, Animal and Environmental Law* (London: Routledge, 2020).

15 *Nonhuman Rights Project Inc.* on behalf of Happy v Breheny 189 A.D.3d 583, 189 (2020); The Cetacean Community v Bush 386 F. 3d 1169 (9th Cir. 2004); Case of Chucho the Bear, CASE FILE T-6.480.577 - SENTENCE SU-016/20 (January 23) Constitutional Court of Columbia; Case of Cecilia the Chimpanzee; Acción de hábeas corpus presentada por la Asociación de Funcionarios y Abogados por los Derechos de los Animales (AFADA) EXPTE. NRO. P-72.254/15, Tercer Juzgado de Garantías Poder Judicial Mendoza.

Part IV

EPISODES IV–VI

17

The Non-dualistic, Redemptive Metaphysics of the Jedi

Michael Baur

The opening crawl to *A New Hope* tells us that "It is a period of civil war." An "evil" Galactic Empire, aided by "sinister" agents, opposes a group of Rebels, including Princess Leia, who together seek to "save her people" and "restore freedom to the galaxy." The Empire possesses a space station called a "Death Star," an ultimate weapon with enough "power" to destroy an entire planet. A first encounter with this opening crawl might lead one to conclude that the metaphysical view espoused by the *Star Wars* films is fundamentally *dualistic*: there is a civil war with an evil, sinister, power-seeking, destruction-causing Empire simply and straightforwardly opposed to a group of freedom-loving, people-saving Rebels who have a princess on their side. But is *Star Wars* really so dualistic?

"You Must Unlearn What You Have Learned"

Metaphysics, understood in its broadest sense, is the philosophical study of all reality whatsoever, including the reality of moral, political, epistemological, aesthetic, and other such properties. Dualistic metaphysical thinking conceives of reality as divided by a series of irreconcilable oppositions, such as good versus evil, truth versus falsehood, the desire for power versus the desire for freedom, independence versus dependence, activity versus passivity, and so on. The *Star Wars* narrative opens with a series of dualistic oppositions, but

Star Wars and Philosophy Strikes Back: This is the Way, First Edition.
Edited by Jason T. Eberl and Kevin S. Decker.

these oppositions begin to break down as we develop a better understanding of a wider story. In a similar way, certain dualistic oppositions begin to break down for Luke Skywalker as he struggles to discern the truth of his own narrative. Luke had been told that his father was killed by Darth Vader. At first, he passively accepts this narrative as a straightforward representation of a simple truth, and he does not see the need to actively interpret what it really means. The passively received truth is that Luke's father, one person, was killed by Darth Vader, another person. Later, once his true parentage is revealed by Vader and confirmed by Yoda, Luke rejects this narrative, regarding it as a lie. To the extent that Luke is capable of regarding the narrative only as either straightforwardly true or false – as something that can only be passively received or actively rejected – he remains within the grip of dualistic metaphysical thinking which fails to appreciate the possible interplay of truth and falsehood, appearance and reality, goodness and evil, activity and passivity.

With time, Luke becomes initiated into a broader, non-dualistic metaphysical view of the matter. He learns to see that the original story about Darth Vader and his father actually manifests a deeper truth; but his learning depends on Luke's ability to stop being a merely passive recipient and start becoming an active interpreter and participant in the truth. Luke's Jedi training can't be complete if it's based only on passively received stories about the past; Luke must actively enter into a direct, lived encounter with Darth Vader himself. Luke learns that the real truth isn't that one person simply killed another person. The truth is that the person who was Luke's father took on the identity of Darth Vader; and in taking on this identity, he effectively destroyed Luke's father as a Jedi role model that Luke might emulate. Once Luke learns to be both a passive recipient and active interpreter of his own story, he can recognize that the narrative given to him wasn't merely a deceptive appearance; it was an appearance which called for further interpretation and discernment, and which was able to reveal a deeper truth about Darth Vader and – as he learned in the cave on Dagobah – about himself. As we, the audience, learn about Luke's story, we too are invited to leave behind our initial, dualistic worldview which erects a fixed, unbridgeable gulf between truth and falsity, reality and appearance, activity and passivity, observation and participation.

To initiate ourselves further into a non-dualistic way of apprehending the world, we can consider the insights of Baruch Spinoza (1632–1677). According to Spinoza, no idea – considered simply in itself – is untrue; *all* ideas are true simply *as ideas*. However, it's possible for an idea to be *more or less true*, depending on whether the idea is more or less connected with other ideas. Consider the idea that "There is a winged bantha." If I were to apprehend this idea and no others, then, according to Spinoza, I'd be right to conclude that there really does exist such a thing as a winged bantha; for, at the very least, there's a winged bantha in my imagination or in my dreams. The idea that there's a winged bantha becomes more or less true, however, to the extent that this idea is connected with other ideas which either include or preclude the idea of a winged bantha. For example, I might realize that the idea of a winged bantha is regularly connected to ideas which are associated with the idea of being in a dream-state, but regularly disconnected from ideas which are associated with the idea of being awake. As long as I apprehend the idea of a winged bantha and no other ideas, Spinoza argues, I have no reason to doubt that there's such a thing as a winged bantha, and I'm not making a mistake in concluding that there really does exist a winged bantha. It's only when I connect the idea of a winged bantha with other ideas of mine that I can conclude that a winged bantha exists, but not in the way that I had originally conceived – for example, the winged bantha exists in my imagination, or in my dreams, or in a chapter (namely, this one) which makes use of the idea of a winged bantha in order to convey a philosophical point.[1]

Consider the idea that "Luke loves Leia." That idea is true, according to Spinoza, simply insofar as that idea exists in the mind of some intelligent being. But that idea becomes more or less true depending on how it's connected with other ideas. At first we might think that "Luke loves Leia" is true without qualification, and thus that his love includes the possibility of a sexual relationship – especially after that now-awkward kiss in *The Empire Strikes Back*! Only later do we learn that the idea of Luke includes the idea of being a sibling to Leia, and that the idea of siblingship excludes the idea of a sexual relationship between them – an idea that took Han a little too long to grasp when Leia professes her love for Luke on the moon of Endor in *Return of the Jedi*.

What about the idea that "Han Solo is a mercenary"? That idea is true, considered in itself; but as we later learn, that idea is true only with qualifications, since that idea can be coherently connected with other ideas about Han which exclude purely mercenary behavior. What about the idea that "Darth Vader is evil"? True enough; but once again, when that idea is connected with other ideas about Vader, we're led to second-guess our earlier judgments and thus realize that Vader is also good in some respects. We can see here how the non-dualistic metaphysics endorsed by *Star Wars* and Spinoza provides an important lesson about what it means to have a true idea about something. The more you know about a thing – the greater number of other ideas you're able to connect coherently with your idea of that thing – the less inclined you'll be to make immediate, unqualified, all-or-nothing claims about that thing. No wonder the virtue of patience (in both judgment and action) is an extremely important Jedi virtue.

"The Force Is What Gives a Jedi His Power"

For Spinoza, it's a mistake to think that there's a simple, unbridgeable, dualistic opposition between truth and falsehood, reality and appearance, goodness and evil, activity and passivity. Similarly, it's a mistake to think that there's a simple opposition between those who seek power and those who don't. According to Spinoza, all things – regardless of whether we characterize them as "good" or "evil" – necessarily seek power, a tendency Spinoza calls "conatus," often translated as striving, endeavor, impulse, inclination, drive, urge, energy, effort, or exertion.[2]

If all things seek power, it'd follow that even the Rebels, no less than their "evil" Imperial opponents, seek power. From Spinoza's point of view, it's superficial to think that the difference between what we call "good" and what we call "evil" is that the good seek power for "good purposes," while the evil seek power for "evil purposes." When something seeks power for "good" (or "evil") purposes, the achievement of such "good" (or "evil") purposes is just the thing's way of exerting its influence upon the world, and thus imprinting upon the world a sort of "stamp" that signifies its power.

Jedi Masters Yoda and Obi-Wan Kenobi conceive of the Force in much the same way that Spinoza conceived of "conatus." Yoda tells Luke that the Force is all around us: "Here, between you, me, the tree, the rock, everywhere." Similarly, Obi-Wan explains to Luke that all things participate in the Force and have their place in the galaxy on account of the Force, which "binds the galaxy together." The Force isn't simply inside or outside of us, but it "penetrates" and "surrounds" us. Furthermore, the Force is responsible for endowing things with power. Without any hint of embarrassment or apology, Obi-wan tells Luke that "The Force is what gives a Jedi his power." In a similar vein, Yoda explains to Luke that his ability to use the

Force is his ability to have power: "For my ally is the Force. And a powerful ally it is."

If the Force is similar to what Spinoza calls "conatus," then perhaps the reason why there's a difference between the "light" and "dark" sides of the Force has nothing to do with the (misguided) idea that some things seek power and some don't. Perhaps, instead, the difference has to do with the way in which a particular thing goes about seeking power. Those aligned with the light side seek power in ways that enable and facilitate a "balance" in the way that all things seek power, while those aligned with the dark side engage in a "zero-sum game" in which some things gain power only by destroying other things – this is one way of understanding Obi-Wan's seemingly paradoxical claim in *Revenge of the Sith* that "only a Sith deals in absolutes."

According to a dualistic worldview, a thing's independence from other things is simply incompatible with its dependence on other things; a thing's own "internal" properties (e.g. the distance between Chewbacca's own head and feet) simply can't be determined by its "external" relations to other things (e.g. the distance between Chewbacca and the center of the planet Kashyyyk). For dualism, then, a thing's own "internal" property of seeking power must exist independently of what any other thing is or does. And this would entail, furthermore, that the power-seeking exercised by one thing will always be uncoordinated with instances of power-seeking by other things. And so uncoordinated, unharmonized instances of power-seeking will inevitably result in a zero-sum game in which the power-seeking of one thing must either destroy or be destroyed by the power-seeking of another thing – an idea expressed clearly by the Sith "Rule of Two" authored by Darth Bane: "Two there should be. No more, no less. One to embody power, the other to crave it."

By contrast, in a non-dualistic conception of the world, independence and dependence aren't simply and straightforwardly opposed to one other. The apparently independent, internal properties that belong to one thing *necessarily depend* on that thing's relations to other things. Thus, for example, the swampy planet of Dagobah has a greenish color which belongs to it as one of its own properties; but the planet wouldn't have this property if it didn't reflect certain wavelengths of light which were perceivable by sentient creatures. Similarly, the Wookiee species possesses a tall, upright body-frame which belongs to it as one of its own properties; but Wookiees possess this property only because the planet Kashyyyk has particular properties of its own. If Kashyyyk didn't have its particular mass but was instead much more massive, then its gravitational pull would've allowed the evolution of only shorter, stouter (non-Wookiee) body-types – Ewoks perhaps?

According to non-dualistic metaphysics, a thing possesses its own seemingly self-determined properties only because of its *relations to other things*. Similarly, a thing's particular manner of seeking power isn't determined independently, in isolation from all other things, but depends on the way in which it's related to other power-seeking things. And so Emperor Palpatine's own manner of seeking power isn't just self-determined but also depends on the ways in which other power-seekers, including Darth Vader and Luke, go about seeking power. Palpatine seeks power by adjusting his plans to fit the characteristics and the anticipated actions of Vader and Luke. In turn, Vader and Luke seek power by trying to figure out what Palpatine's planning. What Palpatine's planning, in turn, depends on what he expects Vader and Luke will do, which again depends on what they think Palpatine's planning. Thus there emerges a feedback loop of anticipating, planning, anticipating how others will plan in light of one's own planning and anticipating, and so on. All instances of power-seeking are ultimately interrelated and reciprocally determine each other. No thing's power-seeking takes place independently of the properties and the effects of every other thing's power-seeking. And so the power-seeking exercised by all things always involves the possibility of mutual adjustment and coordination, and doesn't have to become an inevitably destructive zero-sum game among independent things. According to the non-dualistic metaphysics of the Jedi, power-seeking ultimately isn't a matter of domination or destruction, but of "balance." As Yoda observes in *The Clone Wars* (Season 1, Episode 10), "To answer power with power" in an all-or-nothing way "the Jedi way is not."

"An Energy Field Created by All Living Things"

Obi-Wan Kenobi explains to Luke that the Force is a kind of "energy field created by all living things." Yoda similarly explains that life "creates" the Force and "makes it grow." It's clear that there's an intimate connection between the Force and life; but what's the nature and meaning of this connection?

Two key properties of living things are the ability to metabolize materials from the environment and the ability to reproduce. By means of metabolism, living things keep themselves in existence (they maintain their power) by allowing parts of the world outside of them to become internalized and integrated as parts of themselves. By means of reproduction, living things extend their existence (they increase their power) by making more living things which bear the "stamp" of their own nature and efficacy. Furthermore, since each living thing is a replica of some earlier living thing, each living thing is defined by a plan or blueprint which it inherits from a source external to itself. Ewoks come from other Ewoks, Hutts come from other Hutts, and clone troopers come from Jango Fett.

Living things are like all other things: they strive to maintain and increase their power. But they're unique because their manner of power-seeking demonstrates in an especially clear way how non-dualistic metaphysics is true: how independence and dependence, activity and passivity, aren't simply opposed but in fact interpenetrate and codetermine one another. Living things maintain and extend their power, but not by rejecting the influence of external things upon themselves. They do so rather by receiving and internalizing the input of external things – by being independent and dependent, active and passive, all at once. Through metabolism, as the philosopher Hans Jonas (1903–1993) observes, a living thing exerts its own activity and identity by allowing parts of the external world to become part of itself: "its self-concern, active in the acquisition of new matter, is essential openness for the encounter of outer being."[3] A similarly non-dualistic interplay of activity and passivity, self-assertion and receptivity, independence and dependence, can be seen in the reproductive capacity of living things. Through reproduction, living things succeed at being themselves because they receive, and allow themselves to be defined by, a plan or blueprint they receive from other things (their genetic precursors). Furthermore, living things aren't just the effects but also the causes of reproduction: having passively received the genetic blueprint which makes them what they are, they also exert their own influence by actively imprinting the "stamp" of this blueprint on their offspring.

The non-dualistic interplay of activity and passivity, self-assertion and receptivity, independence and dependence, is further demonstrated through the psychological lives of human beings. Humans not only internalize material parts of the external world which become parts of their own bodies; and they not only internalize from their precursors a genetic blueprint which determines their nature; they also internalize from their parents (and other role models like Jedi masters) a set of psychological characteristics which influence their own mental dispositions and personality traits. It's thus no surprise that Luke has inherited many of the mental abilities and flaws of his father, Darth Vader: like his father, Luke possesses a heightened sensitivity to the Force, but he's also prone to bouts of impatience and anger.

The success with which human beings grow, mature, and enhance their power as psychological agents depends on their ability to properly internalize the personality traits they've inherited, on their ability to properly negotiate between being active and passive, self-assertive and receptive, independent and dependent, in relation to their parents and other role models. At first, most people are in denial about the negative psychological dispositions they've inherited; most people are unable to recognize the extent to which they are "fated" – by parenting and upbringing – to have the psychological dispositions they have. But as psychoanalysis teaches us, the more we're in denial about our negative psychological traits, the less power we have over them, and the more they'll exercise a debilitating and mostly unconscious influence over us. This is one reason why the mythological story of Oedipus plays such a central role in psychoanalysis. According to the story, Oedipus learns that he's "fated" to kill his father and marry his mother. Oedipus thinks he can avoid this inherited fate and independently choose his own destiny. In trying to avoid his inherited fate, Oedipus resolves never to return to Corinth, the town in which he grew up. But his attempt to escape his inherited fate only guarantees that it will be fulfilled: by staying away from Corinth and traveling toward Thebes, Oedipus sets up the very conditions under which he will kill his father and marry his mother.

Luke's story is similar to Oedipus's, though the outcome is quite different. Even after Luke accepts the biological fact that Darth Vader is his father, he wants to deny the psychological fact that he shares several of Vader's psychological characteristics. By initially trying to escape his fate, by disavowing his psychological similarity to Vader, Luke manifests the very characteristics that he'd inherited from his father: impatience, anger, a willingness to destroy. As psychoanalysis shows, the attempt to deny or disavow your fated psychological inheritance is self-defeating. The more Luke denies the inherited psychological dispositions he shares with Vader, the more he allows those dispositions to operate powerfully (and unconsciously) within himself. Luke can gain maturity and power over those inherited dispositions only by internalizing them in the right way: by acknowledging them and taking responsibility for them as his own, even though they exist in him only because of his dependence on and relationship to his father.

Luke's initial psychological failure is also a metaphysical failure, for in trying at first to deny his psychological inheritance from Darth Vader, Luke remained in the grip of a dualistic metaphysics: he thought that he could affirm his own independence, self-determination, and goodness only by denying any substantial connection with dependence, fate, and evil. But, as we come to learn from the non-dualistic metaphysics of Spinoza and the Jedi, there's something metaphysically incoherent in Luke's initial attempt at combining three different ideas: "Darth Vader is evil," "I am good," and "I come from Darth Vader." In the end, Luke learns to move beyond simple metaphysical oppositions. He learns to recognize goodness in Vader and evil in himself, and as a result he enables Vader's redemption which, in turn, enables his own self-redemption.

Notes

1 Spinoza himself uses the example of a winged horse, not a winged bantha. See Baruch Spinoza, *Ethics*, Part II, Proposition 49, Scholium. For a reliable English translation, see Baruch Spinoza, *Ethics*, trans. Samuel Shirley (Indianapolis, IN: Hackett, 1992), 99.

2 Spinoza, *Ethics*, Part III, Propositions 6–7.

3 Hans Jonas, *The Phenomenon of Life* (Evanston, IL: Northwestern University Press, 2001), 84.

18

Just How Many "Lukes" Are There in *A New Hope*, Anyway?

Roy T. Cook and Nathan Kellen

Few *Star Wars* characters are more beloved than Luke Skywalker, Jedi Knight, son of Darth Vader, and mentor to Rey (Skywalker). But just who *is* Luke? Fictional characters like Luke are wholly defined by how we understand, interpret, and evaluate their depictions within the fictions in which they appear. To understand Luke is to know him as he appears in stories like *A New Hope* (ANH), *The Thrawn Trilogy* (*TTT*),[1] and *The Last Jedi* (*TLJ*), among others.

But working out who Luke is – that is, what is *true* of Luke in these stories – is particularly difficult when there are a number of different "universes" in which he appears, including (but not limited to) the *New Canon* and the *Legends* universes.[2] Some stories (*TLJ*) depict things that only happen to Luke in *New Canon*, others (*TTT*) depict things that only happen to him in *Legends*, and still others (*ANH*) depict things that happen in both universes.

Things get even more complicated when we take into account stories that were never canonical in the first place, such as the "what if?" stories told in the *Star Wars: Infinities* comics.[3] Cases involving fan fiction, such as ScarletJedi's *Old Man Luke* – where Luke travels back in time to the Clone Wars to hassle his mentor, Obi-Wan Kenobi, and bond with his father – are equally problematic.[4] How are we meant to understand the relationships that hold between these different Lukes? Are they, in fact, the same character?

Star Wars and Philosophy Strikes Back: This is the Way, First Edition.
Edited by Jason T. Eberl and Kevin S. Decker.

"You Don't Need to See His Identification"

Asking whether two fictional characters, from different stories, are the same or not falls within *ontology* (specifically, the ontology of fiction), which is a branch of the wider subfield called *metaphysics*. Ontology, simply put, is the study of *being*. When asking about the ontological status of a certain kind of object, such as fictional characters, three types of question loom large. First, we can ask whether there really is such a type of object in the first place: "Are fictional characters genuine objects? Are they things that genuinely exist?" If we answer "yes," a second question immediately arises: "What kind of objects are fictional characters? Are they words on the page? Ideas in our minds?" Let's say that we sort out these initial questions. We then have a third question: "How do we tell when we have one fictional character and when we have two?"[5]

Answering this question requires the *identity conditions* for fictional characters – criteria that will answer questions of the following form:

Is character C_1 from story S_1 the same as character C_2 from story S_2?

We'll explore various ways to provide identity conditions for fictional characters. To streamline the discussion, we'll represent the character named Luke depicted in *ANH* as Luke_{ANH}, the character named Luke depicted in *TTT* as Luke_{TTT}, the character named Luke depicted in *TLJ* as Luke_{TLJ}, and so on.

It may seem obvious to anyone who's seen both *ANH* and *TLJ* that the Luke in the first film is identical to the Luke in the second film, that is, that $\text{Luke}_{ANH} = \text{Luke}_{TLJ}$. But, from a philosophical perspective, it's not enough that we can figure out *whether* some or even most identity claims are true or false. We want an explanation of *why* some such claims are true, while others are false. Further, the answers to this question involving Lukes from *other* stories aren't so obvious. An account of the identity conditions for fictional characters can help us to settle these hard cases.

"Impressive. Every Word in That Sentence Was Wrong"

Let's get two simple but ultimately incorrect accounts of fictional character identity out of the way. The first thought one might have is that two characters, from two different works of fiction, are identical if and only if they have the same name. This clearly won't work, however, since it would imply (to switch universes for a moment) that The Beast from the *Buffyverse* is the same character as The Beast from *Kung Fu Hustle*, despite these characters having almost nothing in common other than their shared name.[6]

A slightly more sophisticated approach involves adopting a version of the principle known as the *Identity of Indiscernibles*, often attributed to the philosopher Gottfried Wilhelm Leibniz (1646–1716): two objects are identical if and only if they have the same properties or characteristics.[7] Before applying this principle, we need to distinguish properties that are either *internal* or *external* to the story. We shouldn't conclude that Luke_{ANH} is distinct from Luke_{TLJ} because the former, but not the latter, existed in 1995, or because the latter, but not the former, is owned by Disney. These properties are *external* to the stories, and thus irrelevant to determining whether they're the same. We should restrict our attention to properties attributed to the character *within* the narratives. So we get what we'll call the *Indiscernibility Account*:

> Character C_1 from story S_1 is the same as character C_2 from story S_2 if and only if the (internal) properties C_1 has in S_1 are exactly the same as the (internal) properties C_2 has in S_2.

Even with this modification, the *Indiscernibility Account* just won't work. Luke_{ANH} doesn't have the same properties as Luke_{TLJ}. The former isn't a Jedi Knight, the latter is. The former is young and idealistic, the latter is grizzled, jaded, and cynical. If we apply the *Indiscernibility Account* to fictional characters, we're forced to conclude that *ANH* and *TLJ* depict different characters who just happen to both be named Luke. But that's clearly the wrong verdict. We need a more sophisticated account.

"This Is Not Going to Work." "Why Didn't You Say So?" "I Did Say So."

Let's examine a more sophisticated, but again ultimately incorrect, account of fictional character identity: the *Say-So Account*, in which authors (or their estates, or whoever the relevant agents are) determine whether two characters, from two fictional works, are identical. Richard Routley (1935–1996) describes the view as follows: "In sum, *what controls sameness across* [fictional] *worlds is qualified* author *say-so*, the qualification being that a core of features of the object must be preserved."[8] Amie L. Thomasson defends something like the *Say-So Account* when she provides the following rule as a necessary (although not sufficient) condition for two characters from distinct stories to be identical: "If character C_1 in story S_1 is identical to character C_2 in story S_2, then the author of S_2 must be competently acquainted with C_1 of S_1 and intend to import C_1 into S_2 as C_2."[9] According to the *Say-So Account*, Luke_{ANH} is the same fictional character as Luke_{TLJ} simply because George Lucas (and Rian Johnson, Disney, etc.) *said so* (or because they intended to "import" the Luke of *ANH* into *TLJ* in the appropriate manner). So, $\text{Luke}_{\text{ANH}} = \text{Luke}_{\text{TLJ}}$.

So far, so good – this account does a better job than the *Indiscernibility Account*. The problem arises when we consider cross-continuity characters, such as Luke_{TTT}. If we were to ask Timothy Zahn whether, when authoring this trilogy, he was writing about the same Luke as he is depicted in *ANH*, he'd certainly answer affirmatively (and George Lucas and Lucasfilm would've agreed, since these books were canon before the 2014 reboot). Thus, on the *Say-So Account*, Luke_{ANH} and Luke_{TTT} are identical – that is:

$$\text{Luke}_{\text{ANH}} = \text{Luke}_{\text{TTT}}$$

But now we have a problem. Identity is *transitive*, that is, it can carry across different relations of identity: so, if $a = b$ and $a = c$, then $b = c$. Thus, the Luke that appears in *TLJ* must be the same character as the Luke that appears in *TTT*, and so $\text{Luke}_{\text{TTT}} = \text{Luke}_{\text{TLJ}}$.

This can't be right: certain facts true of the former – for example, that Luke_{TTT} and Mara Jade begin a relationship eventually leading to marriage and a child – aren't true of the latter, since (as far as we know) Luke_{TLJ} dies without ever having met Mara Jade and there's no mention of his having a son. The *Say-So Account* leads to contradictions.

It's tempting to think there's an easy fix. We could just say that Luke_{TTT} was identical to Luke_{ANH} until the 2014 reboot, at which point Luke_{TTT} ceased to be identical to Luke_{ANH}. And then, when *TLJ* appeared (based on the say-so of Lucas, Johnson, Disney, etc.) Luke_{TLJ} is now identical to Luke_{ANH}. Although, Luke_{ANH} was identical with Luke_{TTT} at one point in time, and identical with Luke_{TLJ} at another point in time, Luke_{ANH} was never identical with both Luke_{TTT} and Luke_{TLJ} *at the same time*. This would block transitivity, and thus the contradiction.

Unfortunately, this strategy won't work for a simple reason: Zahn hasn't gotten fully on board with the erasure of his stories from *Star Wars* canon:

> [A]s far as I can tell from the announcement, [Lucasfilm] is *not* erasing the EU, but simply making it clear that nothing there is official canon. That's *not* necessarily a bad thing, nor does it immediately send everything into alternative-universe status. If nothing from *The Thrawn Trilogy*, say, is used in future movies (and if there's nothing in the movies that contradicts it), then we can reasonably continue to assume that those events *did* happen. It looks to me like the *Legends* banner is going to be used mainly to distinguish Story-Group-Approved canon books from those that aren't officially canon but might still exist.[10] (*Making Star Wars*)

Zahn is reaffirming that, at least until new films, comics, or television shows explicitly contradicting *TTT* are released, we should continue to believe that its events happened. In short, according to Zahn, Luke_{TTT} remains identical to Luke_{ANH} (and Luke_{TLJ}) because he says so.[11] Luke had quite a full life before becoming a recluse on Ahch-To!

"Many of the Truths We Cling to Depend Greatly on Our Own Point of View"

Although the *Say-So Account* doesn't solve our dilemma, its failure might provide the key to formulating a successful account of Luke's identity. The problem with the *Say-So Account* hinges on the creator of *ANH* disagreeing with the creator of *TTT* as to whether the Luke appearing in the first story is identical to the Luke appearing in the second. From the perspective of the creator of *ANH*, Luke_{ANH} isn't (now) identical to Luke_{TTT}. But from the perspective of the creator of *TTT*, the same fictional character appears in both stories.

This suggests that identity claims regarding fictional characters might not be simply true or false, but are true or false *with respect to* a particular story. If so, then we shouldn't be asking whether it is true or false that $\text{Luke}_{ANH} = \text{Luke}_{TTT}$. Rather, we should ask two distinct versions of this question, one from the perspective of *ANH* and one from the perspective of *TTT*. We call this approach the *Perspectival Account*:

Fictional character C_1 from story S_1, considered from the perspective of story S_3 (that is, $<C_{1S1}, S_3>$) is identical to fictional character C_2 from story S_2, considered from the perspective of story S_3 (that is, $<C_{2S2}, S_3>$)

> if and only if, when interpreting and evaluating story S_3, we are meant to understand that everything that happens to character C_1 in story S_1 also happens to C_2, and everything that happens to C_2 in story S_2 also happens to C_1.

Following this formula, let $<\text{Luke}_{\text{ANH}}, \textit{ANH}>$ represent the character Luke as depicted in *ANH*, *and viewed from the perspective of ANH*, $<\text{Luke}_{\text{TTT}}, \textit{ANH}>$ represent the character as depicted in *TTT*, *but viewed from the perspective of ANH*, and so on. When we consider whether $<\text{Luke}_{\text{ANH}}, \textit{ANH}>$ is identical to $<\text{Luke}_{\text{TTT}}, \textit{ANH}>$ the answer is clearly negative: When evaluating *ANH*, we're *not* allowed to infer that the Luke appearing in this work also did the things Luke is depicted as having done in *TTT*. But, if we consider the same two characters from the perspective of *TTT*, we should judge the relevant identity claim to be true: when evaluating *TTT*, we're meant to understand the Luke appearing in this work to have also done the things Luke is depicted as having done in *ANH*. So the following claims are true:

$$<\text{Luke}_{\text{ANH}}, \text{ANH}> \neq <\text{Luke}_{\text{TTT}}, \text{ANH}>$$
$$<\text{Luke}_{\text{ANH}}, \text{TTT}> = <\text{Luke}_{\text{TTT}}, \text{TTT}>$$

We can handle other cases along similar lines. For example, the Luke depicted in *Old Man Luke* is identical to the Luke depicted in *ANH* from the perspective of *Old Man Luke*, but not from the perspective of *ANH*.

The *Perspectival Account* avoids the problems seen in the earlier accounts and provides us with an adequate account of identity conditions for fictional characters. Further, the *Perspectival Account* allows us to explain how the truth-value of fictional character identity claims can change over time. As we've noted, Luke_{ANH} and Luke_{TTT} are identical with respect to *TTT*, and are non-identical with respect to *ANH*. But things weren't always thus. Before the 2014 reboot, we *were* meant to understand that the events depicted in *TTT* did in fact happen to the Luke depicted in *ANH from the perspective of ANH*. In short, prior to 2014 it was true that $<\text{Luke}_{\text{ANH}}, \textit{ANH}> = <\text{Luke}_{\text{TTT}}, \textit{ANH}>$. Thc fact that this identity changed from true to false in 2014 is easily explainable: the reboot dramatically altered how we were supposed to understand certain stories told about the *Star Wars* characters, and, in particular, it altered which stories we were meant to understand as having happened to the *canonical* versions of the characters.

"Master Skywalker. There Are Too Many of Them. What Are We Going to Do?"

A final, interesting feature of the *Perspectival Account* is that it involves what might be called *ontological excess*. So, we can ask, "When watching *ANH*, how many different characters named Luke are we learning about?"

The answer is: a lot! There's the canonical Luke – Luke_{ANH}, considered from the perspective of *TLJ*, who's identical to Luke_{ANH}, considered from the perspective of *ANH*. But there are many others, such as Luke_{ANH}, considered from the perspective of *TTT*. And Luke_{ANH}, considered from the perspective of *Old Man Luke*. And hundreds of other Luke Skywalkers, corresponding to Luke_{ANH} viewed from the perspective of any of the hundreds of other fanfictions, *Muppet Show* appearances, *Holiday Specials* (both the 1978 original and the 2020 LEGO version), and other non-canonical works of all kinds. But, since very different (and often incompatible) things happen to these different versions of Luke in these different stories, each is clearly distinct from the others. Thus, each time we watch *ANH*, we're seeing what happened, not to a single character named Luke, but to innumerably distinct, yet intimately connected, Luke Skywalkers.

Notes

1 Timothy Zahn, *The Thrawn Trilogy* (New York: Bantam Spectra, 1991–1993).

2 In April 2014, shortly after purchasing Lucasfilm, Disney announced that the canonical *Star Wars* universe would contain only the theatrically released films, the new animated television shows, and any additional materials created after this date. All other materials (novels, comics, etc.) would be relegated to non-canonical, *Legends*, status. For a detailed discussion of the reboot, see Roy T. Cook and Nathan Kellen, "Gospel, Gossip, and Ghent: How Should We Understand the New *Star Wars*?" in Jason T. Eberl and Kevin S. Decker, eds., *The Ultimate Star Wars and Philosophy: You Must Unlearn What You Have Learned* (Malden, MA: Wiley-Blackwell, 2015), 296–307.

3 *Star Wars Epic Collection: Infinities* (New York: Marvel Comics, 2015).

4 ScarletJedi, *Old Man Luke*, ArchiveOfOurOwn, December 12, 2016, at https://archiveofourown.org/works/8825689/chapters/20234725.

5 Another version of this puzzle is raised by the Bigger Luke fan theory, in which there are two distinct Luke Skywalkers (possibly played by two

different actors) in the original trilogy films. The two Lukes purportedly can be distinguished by their height – Bigger Luke is substantially taller than Luke Prime. For a recent discussion of this theory, see James Shackell, "The Bigger Luke Hypothesis: Going Deep on *Star Wars*' Most Absurd Fan Theory," *The Guardian*, October 26, 2021, at https://www.theguardian.com/culture/2021/oct/27/the-bigger-luke-hypothesis-going-deep-on-star-wars-most-absurd-fan-theory.

6 Here we're referring to the demon known only as The Beast, who was an antagonist of Angel/Angelus. The Hellgod Glory also used this name as an alias in *Buffy the Vampire Slayer*.

7 A related way of accounting for the ontology of fictional characters, known as Meinongianism, asserts that fictional characters are a special type of non-existent objects that "encode" collections of properties or characteristics, and provide identity conditions in terms of whether the characters in question encode exactly the same properties or characteristics. This approach suffers the same problems as do other versions of the *Indiscernibility Account* of fictional character identity. See Terence Parsons, *Non-Existent Objects* (New Haven: Yale University Press, 1980) for an influential defense of Meinongianism, and Amie L. Thomasson, *Fiction and Metaphysics* (Cambridge: Cambridge University Press, 1999), especially Chapters 1 and 5, for a detailed criticism of this approach.

8 The *Say-So Account* is defended in John Woods, *The Logic of Fiction*, Revised edition (Rickmansworth, UK: College Publications, 2009), and discussed at length in Richard Routley, "The Semantical Structure of Fictional Discourse," *Poetics* 8 (1979), 3–30.

9 Amie L. Thomasson, *Fiction and Metaphysics*, 67. Notation has been modified.

10 Jason Ward, "Timothy Zahn on *Star Wars*," *Making Star Wars*, April 2014, at http://makingstarwars.net/2014/04/timothy-zhan-on-star-wars. Zahn's views don't seem to have changed much since. A recent interview promoting his canonical *Thrawn: Alliances* novel includes this exchange:

Thrawn feels like if it had been written before the canonization purge a couple of years ago, or if you squinted a bit, it would serve as a perfect setup for _Heir to the Empire_.

Oh, I don't think you need to squint at all. I wrote him in these two books to fit in with everything else I'd done. So if someone at Lucasfilm snapped their fingers, and suddenly all of my other books were canon, and there would be no real retrofitting that would have to go in. It would all fit together.

Thrawn: Alliances feels more at home in the new canon, especially because Thrawn has been fleshed out a bit more in _Rebels_. Was there any adjustments for that?

Not really. I'm getting to play with more canon characters like Vader and Padmé and Anakin, but the character himself, I still see him as the same person. He's got goals, and he won't necessarily share them with you, but he as long as you're going the same direction, he's happy to cooperate and assist along the way.

Andrew Liptak, "*Star Wars* Author Timothy Zahn on *Thrawn: Alliances and Toxic Fandom*," The Verge, July 2018, at https://www.theverge.com/2018/7/25/17597478/star-wars-timothy-zahn-thrawn-alliances-book-comic-con-sdcc-2018.

11 For a defense of the claim that canon is *dynamic*, *negotiated*, and *participatory*, and hence that Zahn's comments should be taken seriously as data affecting how we should interpret the *Star Wars* universe, despite Disney's unilateral attempt to control such interpretation, see our "Gospel, Gossip, and Ghent," in Eberl and Decker, eds., *The Ultimate Star Wars and Philosophy: You Must Unlearn What You Have Learned.*

19

Force and *Geist*: Hegel Watches *The Empire Strikes Back*

Umut Eldem

The scene is set: you've crash-landed in a swamp on Dagobah and a weird but wise creature is telling you to unearth your X-wing from the treacherous depths of gunk and goo. You need to do something you thought was impossible for your entire life: to somehow "connect" with your spacecraft and lift it, not with a machine, not with the help of your friends, but solely by using "the Force." You've had little to no experience with the Force: perhaps you've lifted a rock or two, but nothing of this size. You concentrate, sense the ship jiggling under the swamp, but you can't for the life of you raise it. It's just too big, too heavy. You're trying, but you just don't believe you can do it. Failed you have, and here's why.

We're all fondly familiar with this scene: Luke exclaims that it's one thing to raise stones by using the Force but raising an X-wing is "impossible." Yoda immediately objects: the difference between a ship and a stone is "only in your mind." Yoda's objection suggests that there's something more fundamental in nature than the different weights of a rock and a spaceship; to move either by using the Force is essentially the same task.

How are things interconnected through the Force? What must we learn (or unlearn) to get that ship to move? What kind of ontology does all this presuppose? "Ontology" means the philosophical study of *being*, the most basic ways in which things exist and how they're interrelated. Hopefully, with a little help from Georg W.F. Hegel (1770–1831), we can get that X-wing out of the swamp without even touching it. Or at least we can understand how such a thing could be possible, given the ontology in the *Star Wars* films.

Star Wars and Philosophy Strikes Back: This is the Way, First Edition.
Edited by Jason T. Eberl and Kevin S. Decker.

Hegel's philosophy provides a helpful framework for discussing the Force as described by Yoda in *The Empire Strikes Back*: that is, created by life as the energy that binds the rock to the tree and the land to the X-wing, and everything in between. Chapters in previous *Star Wars and Philosophy* books have taken on Hegel's philosophy. James Lawler emphasizes the Christian overtones found both in Hegel and in *Star Wars*, whereas Brian Cameron offers a more political reading of the ideas of recognition and the master–slave dialectic in Hegel's seminal work, *The Phenomenology of Spirit*.[1] This chapter will focus on how Hegel's philosophy might help us understand the Force using his concepts of "force" and *Geist*.

In *The Phenomenology of Spirit*, Hegel discusses how human beings have come to know things, including themselves. He gives us an account of humanity's quest for knowledge that is both philosophical and historical. Beginning with sense perception, each chapter presents a more complicated and detailed analysis of different forms of knowledge, from consciousness to self-consciousness and then to reason, religion, and ultimately Absolute Knowledge, which is knowledge of *Geist* (translated as "spirit" in the title of the book). *The Phenomenology of Spirit* serves as an introduction to Hegel's philosophical system, which continues with logic, philosophy of nature, and ethical and political philosophy.

One chapter of *The Phenomenology of Spirit*, "Force and the Understanding," is infamously complicated and dense. Hegel tries to work out how our knowledge of particular things and the relations between them presupposes what he calls "force." As he sees it, force is an essential part of matter, rather than something external to it. This is why, for Yoda, size and weight don't matter so long as a Jedi can manipulate this essential aspect of matter.

A Long Time Ago, in Ancient Greece

Understanding the main problem here requires us to take a small step back ... just 25 hundred years back to Greece. In those days, philosophers before Socrates (470–399 BCE) looked at the world in terms of a great diversity, a multiplicity of things and events. They wondered whether there was something – a principle, a force, an idea – that would explain the diversity in the objects and events that happened around them. They looked for a unifying principle (*arche*) that would explain why the world is the way it is. An *arche* would be primal, the first source, the structure guiding cause and effect, providing the basis for all causal explanations. If we could just grasp the underlying principle of reality, we'd be able to explain all things and creatures and their interactions. But these philosophers differed on what the *arche* was: Thales (624–583 BCE) thought this first principle was water, Anaximenes (586–526 BCE) thought it was air, Democritus (ca 460–ca 370 BCE) thought it was atoms, and so on. They believed that if there's something that permeates every single being, that ties them together, then having knowledge about that thing must be the key to all other kinds of knowledge in the universe. Sound familiar?

This idea has been influential throughout the history of philosophy, and Hegel learned this lesson incredibly well. His entire philosophy is dedicated to bringing forth a conceptual framework that provides the *arche* for modern social, philosophical, and scientific thought. Hegel calls this elementary unity and unfolding of all things *Geist*, the principle that ultimately grounds and explains both nature and society. *Geist* is the unfolding of reality itself; it manifests itself through everything and everyone. The key to understanding everything is *Geist*.

Yoda points out that the Force is everywhere, "it surrounds us and binds us … between you, me, the tree, the rock, everywhere … even between the land and the ship." The Force is intrinsic to individual beings, so if you could understand the Force, you could begin to understand how other beings co-exist and relate to each other. In *Star Wars*, the Force is the most primary principle, or *arche*. Its functions are both ontological (it's primal being) and epistemological (it allows us to have knowledge beyond what's observable). Through it, we can explain many historical and political as well as physical events.

Understanding the Force is key to understanding everything else. For Hegel, understanding force is like catching a thread or stumbling upon a road to what he calls "Absolute Knowledge," the understanding of *Geist*. Similarly, the Force calls forth to Force-sensitives: offering past wisdom and visions of the future. It warns, guides, and tempts those under its sway.

All the major heroes in the Skywalker saga have some connection to the Force, and their fates and endeavors are closely tied to that relation. Luke and Rey discover who they are through their adventures guided by the Force. Anakin turns to the dark side through his fear, induced by a vision, of losing his wife in childbirth. Han Solo and Leia struggle with Ben's sensitivity to the Force. The Force is thus more than just a "force of nature." It also has an ethical dimension: it can influence people by providing intuitive guidance, and in turn can be influenced by their actions, as we can understand from the call to "bring balance to the Force." But how do these different aspects of the Force relate to each other, and how can Hegel's philosophy help us understand the connection between these various aspects?

"You Must Unlearn What You Have Learned"

A good way to understand a philosophical position is to understand what kind of an idea it responds to. After the pre-Socratics and their quest for an *arche*, a different kind of ontology started to gain traction among philosophers. Aristotle led the charge in claiming that *things* were primary, whereas *relations* were secondary. For instance, understanding what a dejarik table is requires understanding what it's made of and what shape it has; it doesn't require understanding where it's situated, who uses it, and so on. Ontology became the study of the being of objects and individuals, rather than the dynamic interconnections and processes between them. According to this ontology, particular things have properties that inhere in a substratum (a "substance") which remains unchanged.

According to Aristotle's ontology, to understand what a thing is, we need to understand its essential properties. Wetness, for instance, is an essential property of water. This has also been called an *intrinsic* property of water, which means the wetness of water belongs to it solely by virtue of water's existence: water doesn't owe its wetness to any other thing. Not all properties are intrinsic: if I pour water on my lightsaber, the fact that it's now wet is the result of something other than the lightsaber itself, since lightsabers aren't themselves wet.

Kenneth Westphal, a Hegel scholar, points out an ambiguity in what "intrinsic" means here.[2] "Intrinsic" has been used in two different ways. One use implies that an intrinsic property belongs solely to a substance, that it's "non-relational," but another use says that a property is *essential* to a substance, so that without that property, that substance would cease to be what it is. For instance, we wouldn't call what Luke and Rey are able to lift with the Force a "rock" if it lacked rigidity. Rigidity for a rock is both a "non-relational" property (since it does not owe its rigidity to something other than itself) and an essential property (since without it, it wouldn't be a rock). But these two meanings have been confused, so many philosophers have been accustomed to think that relational properties can't essentially belong to a substance. This leads to an "atomistic" thrust to this traditional ontology: we tend to "think of individuals as basic and relations as derivative."[3]

However, we can conceive of an essential property which is also relational: "Force is the unconditioned universal which is equally in itself what it is for an Other; or which contains the difference within itself."[4] Michael Inwood's commentary is helpful in deciphering what Hegel means here. He gives the example of a balloon. Any balloon filled with air "retains its size and shape owing to the interplay between the air pressure within the balloon [...] and the elasticity of the material from which the balloon is made."[5] Understanding this particular thing requires us to understand the same force from two different directions: contraction and expansion. This force belongs to all balloons essentially; we can't make sense of what a balloon is without examining these forces.

Unsurprisingly, Hegel doesn't philosophize at length about balloons; instead, he's drawing on his knowledge of gravity and magnetism. Remember Newton: every action has an equal and opposite reaction. Newton showed that gravity is a *bifurcated* force since objects with mass attract each other reciprocally: each of them exerts a force in the opposite direction. Magnetism is also bifurcated since a magnet has positive and negative directions of one and the same force. Force differentiates itself into two opposites, which together form a unity. Hegel's ontology suggests that relations of force are essential to particular things, an idea that seems suitable for understanding the Force in *Star Wars*.

The existence of dark and light sides of the Force already suggests a unity that also includes difference, just as Rey and Ben discover themselves to be "a dyad in the Force" in *The Rise of Skywalker*. This unity allows us to comprehend the Force, as we can only understand force by its vector, its directionality. Hegel suggests that this is how we understand how entities interact with each other: everything from planetary motions to electricity, from car crashes to a game of basketball, exhibits this bifurcated structure inherent to the forces involved.

As Westphal shows, Hegel is influenced by Newton's physics, and gravity is clearly a relational property that's also essential to all matter.[6] Gravity is involved both within a single substance and between different substances. Things are made of atoms and each atom creates its own gravitational field, which holds the atoms of different things together. When atoms come together, they form a stronger gravitational field. Every atom in the universe exerts some force and is also the recipient of a similar force.

According to Hegel, we must accept a relational ontology to make sense of the network of cause and effect. This is because we know particular things only through our cause-and-effect observations of, and interactions with, them. For this to work, a particular thing can't be isolated unto itself: we must presume that forces and relations are essential to matter. Hegel's ontology also presupposes that relations among things are prior to the individual beings to which relations are essential. However, one significant difficulty awaits us: since Hegel's ideas are supposed to apply not only to nature but also to society, how do we move from *physical* force (such as gravity or magnetism) to a conception of *social* force?

Unlike gravity, in *Star Wars* the Force's influence is apparent in relations between living creatures; it also has an ethical dimension. Can Hegel's philosophy provide a parallel account for physical force and social reality? Fortunately, this is specifically what Hegel's philosophy aims to do: to find analogies, intricate connections, and syntheses between the natural and social orders within our world.

May the *Geist* Be with You

The Force both constitutes the *Star Wars* universe and explains why it exists the way that it does. It explains life, the ability of the Jedi and Sith to move objects from a distance, and even what happens after our favorite characters die. The same goes for characters' social and ethical lives: a wrongful action can be explained by a temptation from the dark side of the Force, whereas a noble action can be explained by guidance from the light side. The Force doesn't fully *determine* individuals' choices and actions, though. Hegel was well aware of this: the existence of *Geist* doesn't preclude the possibility of *free will*. In fact, just the opposite: *Geist* provides the natural and social background for freedom to flourish.

We've already mentioned two different aspects of the Force: a *physical* one akin to telekinesis, the ability to move objects from a distance, as well as a *perceptive* use involving heightened awareness of one's surroundings, including sensing the presence of those with a special connection with the Force. Finally, we must mention a *social and historical* aspect, in which we can differentiate the dark and light sides.[7]

The Force is primarily about connection, both between people and between people and things. When Darth Vader feels his son learning the ways of the Force, he senses a "disturbance." Similarly, Luke senses the presence of his father in Darth Vader. In later films, connections seem to span not only space but time (Anakin is afraid of a possible future in which Padmé dies in childbirth), and in the sequel trilogy the "dyad" of Ben and Rey enables them to have face-to-face conversations across the galaxy.

Stephen Houlgate's poignant interpretation of Hegel's *Geist* is useful for a social interpretation of the Force in *Star Wars*.[8] Houlgate's is a religious interpretation, but with an emphasis on the importance of the feeling of *love*. For Houlgate, Hegel's *Geist* is natural and is social reality becoming aware of itself through the lives of human beings. All our attempts at knowledge, understanding, and awareness make up the adventures of *Geist* and its quest to reach self-understanding. Philosophy is the love of wisdom, so we try to learn and understand because we love this adventure itself. We want to become part of this endeavor.

Love is also the essential connection we feel toward other people that determines who we are and who we're to become. It's both essential and relational to our being. We can see immediately how something like gravitational or magnetic force is akin to love: love brings people together. It has the power to move us, so it explains a lot of what we do. Its effect is weakened by mental and emotional distance. It's what we must follow if we seek peace and harmony in the world. In a sense, we're magnetic beings, attracting and repelling each other until an equilibrium can be reached. It's through love that we understand ourselves not as isolated beings, but collectively, as a system with various parts interacting with each other through centuries and generations.

What about the Force in *Star Wars*? It's clear that there's a religious aspect to it, but given its intimate connection with human affairs, at least the light side can be understood in terms of love. Love is what explains Darth Vader's final act of sacrifice, as well as Rey and Ben overcoming their differences. The connections between matter are transposed into connections between people since, as Yoda explains, the Force is something we "feel."

The key lesson from Hegel is that our relations to other people, other things, the universe itself, all make our individuality possible. We're not isolated particulars. Our relations matter to us essentially: they shape us, determine who we are and who we shall become. This understanding of the individual is central if we wish to understand the journey of Luke, Anakin, and Rey. The Skywalker saga is a tale that brings all these disparate aspects of natural and social reality together.

Accordingly, a hero is a person who's less concerned with their own well-being and more concerned with the safety of others in the face of immediate danger to their own community. The hero becomes aware of this interconnection of all things and knows that they'll be remembered by the community for which they sacrifice themselves. Of course, we shouldn't all seek to sacrifice ourselves for the communities to which we belong: our aim and our resolve must be accurate, it must seek to bring about the greater good, it must seek justice and harmony.

Yoda's Theme

Finally, we're ready to bring that X-wing out of the swamp. Hopefully, Hegel's philosophy has brought us closer to Yoda, who has a deep understanding of reality thanks to his extensive knowledge of the Force and how it binds everything and everyone together. As we all know, through this knowledge Yoda can move the X-wing as well as lead the Jedi Council and move us, the audience, as one of the most iconic characters in cinematic history. Yoda can do this because he was written, performed by, and interacted with, people who grasped and loved the *Geist* of their times. And it seems that this love will be reciprocated for many generations to come, as we continue to explore all the possibilities that the *Star Wars* universe has to offer.

Notes

1 James Lawler, "The Force Is with *Us*: Hegel's Philosophy of Spirit Strikes Back at the Empire," in Kevin S. Decker and Jason T. Eberl, eds., *Star Wars and Philosophy: More Powerful than You Can Possibly Imagine* (Chicago: Open Court, 2005), 144–156 ; Brian K. Cameron, "'What Is Thy Bidding My Master?' Star Wars and the Hegelian Struggle for Recognition," in *Star Wars and Philosophy*, 159–168.

2 For a detailed discussion of traditional ontology and Hegel's critique of it, see Kenneth R. Westphal, "Force, Ontology and Understanding," *Hegel Bulletin* 29 (2008), 1–29.

3 Ibid., 3.

4 G.W.F. Hegel, *The Phenomenology of Spirit*, trans. with introduction and commentary by Michael Inwood (Oxford: Oxford University Press, 2018), §136, 587.

5 Ibid., 386.

6 Westphal, "Force, Ontology and Understanding," 3.
7 Other abilities such as bringing someone back from the dead are also alluded to, especially in the prequel and sequel trilogies, but they need not concern us here.
8 See especially the last chapter of Stephen Houlgate, *An Introduction to Hegel: Freedom, Truth and History* (Oxford: Blackwell, 2005), 242–276.

20

"I Know There Is Good in You": Luke, Anakin, and Confucian Filial Piety

Eric Yang

Relationships between children and parents pervade the *Star Wars* saga, especially if we include surrogate parents. Anakin's relationship with his mother, Shmi, in the prequels impacts his trajectory toward the dark side. In *The Mandalorian*, Mando's role as a surrogate father to Grogu transforms them into a "Clan of Two." But the most significant parent–child relationship in the saga may be the one between Luke Skywalker and Darth Vader.

When Luke rushes off to save his friends at Cloud City in *The Empire Strikes Back*, he's unprepared to find out that Darth Vader is his father. His training is nearly complete in the next film, but Yoda declares that Luke is not yet a Jedi until he confronts Vader. Even Obi-Wan Kenobi advises Luke to kill Vader. Luke's reply – that he's unable to kill his own father – leads Obi-Wan to lament, "Then the Emperor has already won." Why would Luke go against his former master's advice? Is Luke being irrational in his commitment not to kill his father?

An odd thing happens next. Luke gives himself up to Vader on the moon of Endor. Luke's surrender may be hard to understand at first, but it makes good sense in light of the Confucian virtue of *filial piety*. Though Confucius (551–479 BCE) did not write anything, some of his sayings, actions, and interactions have been collected in the *Analects*. Confucius's teachings highlight the importance of benevolence, social order, and ritual propriety among other virtues and values. As we'll see, understanding Luke's surrender to Vader in terms of Confucian filial piety makes sense of how Luke is able to overcome the allure of the dark side and become a Jedi.

Star Wars and Philosophy Strikes Back: This is the Way, First Edition.
Edited by Jason T. Eberl and Kevin S. Decker.

"Unexpected This Is, and Unfortunate"

The wisdom tradition of Confucianism offers a philosophy aimed at living well. To live well, we have to cultivate the right kind of habits that make for a good life. Habits that help someone live in an excellent way are often referred to as "virtues." Virtues are not qualities of individual actions but rather dispositions to act in ways that promote a person's flourishing. These habits of excellence are especially important because our lives are full of unexpected turns of events.

In *Return of the Jedi* (*ROTJ*), the Rebels experience this kind of unexpectedness. As the plot unfolds, Emperor Palpatine claims to have foreseen it all, saying that "everything that has transpired has done so according to my design." But when Luke asks Yoda whether Vader is really his father, Yoda is surprised that Luke has learned this fact, replying, "Unexpected this is, and unfortunate." Not even the greatest of the Jedi was able to expect this turn of events! More surprises await: when Luke is brought to the Emperor, he's astonished that Palpatine is aware of the Rebel mission on Endor and has set a trap for their fleet by leaking false information concerning the Death Star, which, he reveals, is fully operational.

Surprises can lead people into making poor decisions. To live well, we need to handle life's unexpected turns prudently. In Confucianism, flexibility is a key feature. Flexibility involves a *fitting responsiveness* to circumstances: the fitting response is what a good person would do if she were in a particular circumstance. The way to become a good person is to find *exemplars* – models of living a good life – and imitate them. We discover exemplars through the emotion of *admiration*.[1] Indeed, Confucius's students admired and imitated him by carefully observing his speech and actions. Moral development is similar to the way people develop skills in other areas of life. Novice musicians admire skilled virtuosos, imitating the melodic phrases and style of their musical exemplars. Basketball players often imitate the dribbling and shooting form of their heroes. To become like your exemplar, you have to practice certain actions until those skills become deeply ingrained habits. These practices are the observance of *ritual*:

> When it comes to the practice of ritual it is harmonious ease [i.e., flexibility] that is to be valued . . . If you merely stick rigidly to rituals in all matters, great and small, there will remain that which you cannot accomplish. Yet if you know enough to value harmonious ease but try to attain it without being regulated by the rites, this will not work either.[2]

Ritual involves repeated practice in moral, civic, and familial situations. But rituals cannot be followed mechanically. They must produce the kind of flexibility that makes it easier for someone to handle the unexpected twists and turns of life.

"I Feel the Good in You, the Conflict"

The right response to tough circumstances is not a random reaction. Confucian flexibility follows from habits to respond appropriately, which are required for a flourishing life. Achieving well-being, however, requires several steps and, for Confucianism, the first step is filial piety: an abiding reverence, respect, and dedication to one's parents, even in adulthood. In the *Analects*, we see that such respect is the starting point for becoming a good person:

> A young person who is filial and respectful of his elders rarely becomes the kind of person who is inclined to defy his superiors . . . The gentleman applies himself to the roots. "Once the roots are firmly established, the Way will grow." Might we not say that filial piety and respect for elders constitute the root of Goodness?[3]

Filial piety is the foundation of a flourishing life. It's not concerned merely with outward behavior, otherwise there would be no difference between humans exhibiting this virtue and the behavior of "dogs and horses."[4] Rather, filial piety involves having the appropriate attitudes and dispositions toward one's parents. Some have claimed that this kind of respect is owed to parents because the very existence of children depends on their parents. But in Confucianism, biology has very little to do with it. Consider a person who, suffering from a debilitating disease, decides to become a parent only for the sake of having a potential organ donor match. This is not acting as a genuine parent should, which involves love and care for one's children.[5] This parent's children would be right not to exhibit filial respect, whereas filial piety toward adoptive or surrogate parents (and in some cases, even teachers) can be appropriate, since such individuals provide proper care befitting a loving parent.

Why does Luke surrender himself to Vader? It is not because Anakin is biologically responsible for Luke's existence. Rather, Luke recognizes an inner conflict in Vader, something that Vader himself is not willing to admit. Luke senses that there's still good in him. Given that they are family and both are Jedi, it's no surprise that Luke would be privy to Vader's true feelings. Even when Vader no longer regards himself as Anakin Skywalker, declaring "That name no longer holds any meaning for me," Luke senses the truth, countering that "It is the name of your true self, you've only forgotten. I know there is good in you; the Emperor hasn't driven it from you fully."

If Vader had no care or concern for Luke, then perhaps filial piety would be inappropriate. While Vader attacks and tries to defeat Luke in obedience to Palpatine, Luke knows there's more to Vader. Even in their dialogue, Vader repeatedly calls Luke his "son." Their connection is deeper than that between typical Jedi. In *ROTJ*, Palpatine does not sense Luke's presence on Endor, yet Darth Vader does. This appears to be more than merely the sensing of another Jedi but is instead based on their parental–filial connection. The good in Vader is manifest when he sacrifices his life to prevent Palpatine from killing Luke. If Vader has a paternal role in Luke's life, then it's appropriate for Luke to exhibit filial piety.

"I Am a Jedi, Like My Father Before Me"

Confucius's *Analects* has a moral framework called "exemplarism." This is the idea that moral knowledge and practice do not start with principles, rules, duties, consequences, or character traits. Instead, they are based on the example provided by good persons picked out through the emotion of admiration. Moral novices should imitate exemplars, acquiring the good traits possessed by the good person they admire. Parental figures typically serve as "ready-made" exemplars since children typically admire their parents – if their parents exhibit noble and loving characteristics. Of course, parents aren't always perfect shining examples, and eventually children may move on, finding better exemplars like the sages in their community. Sometimes finding exemplars is difficult. Yet almost everyone has parents or parental surrogates who can serve in that role.[6] It may even be possible to extend one's admiration and practice of imitation to *fictional* exemplars – imaginary good persons worth emulating.[7]

If this is right, then even an imagined representation of an estranged parent could serve as an exemplar. After Obi-Wan tells Luke that his father was "a great pilot" who fought as a Jedi Knight in the Clone Wars and in whom the Force was strong, followed by giving him Anakin's lightsaber, Luke begins to regard his father as an exemplar.

Anakin serves as a role model for Luke even though he'd been absent for all of Luke's life. Parental relationships can have a profound impact even when the parents aren't around. Even absent parents can be exemplars just as fictional exemplars might be. Clearly, Luke's admiration of his imagined father drives his desire to become a Jedi.

But there's a significant turning point in Luke's captivity on the second Death Star. When he's taken to Palpatine, Luke's surprise at the Emperor's trap for the Rebel fleet prompts anger that causes him to attempt to strike down Palpatine. Luke's feelings betray him: his rage almost overwhelms him, and he reveals his intense emotions for his twin sister, Leia. After Vader threatens to lure Leia to the dark side, Luke's powerful attack brings Vader to the verge of defeat, but the turning point is reached when he sees the weakness of his father, whose hand he just cut off. His anger mollified, Luke turns to Palpatine and proclaims, "You've failed, your highness. I am a Jedi, like my father before me." With that recognition, Luke overcomes his anger and avoids journeying further to the dark side.

These crucial decisions and actions flow from Luke's character. His ability to avoid becoming Palpatine's apprentice arises from his attempts to cultivate virtues associated with the Jedi and through his training with Obi-Wan and Yoda. But the "root" of this formation, as Confucius would have noted, is filial piety. Another way in which respect for parents can be understood as the root of other virtues is found in the charge that individuals live according to a particular tradition and learn the ways of that tradition. Parents can represent the traditions to which one belongs.[8] Luke exhibits filial piety not only in his attitude toward Anakin, but also in his reverence for the Jedi way. While Luke has a rebellious spirit, like his father, even his imperfect commitment to following his masters Obi-Wan and Yoda exhibits filial piety, developing within him the kind of character that allows him to resist Palpatine's schemes.

Jedi training is quite strict, but so is filial piety. According to the latter, a child can "never disobey."[9] This may seem rigid or harsh, but remember the aims of the moral formation of persons in Confucianism. It's not enough to obey rules and principles. Rather, it involves forming the right kinds of dispositions or character traits that enable a person to respond *spontaneously* to life's unexpected circumstances with flexibility or harmonious ease. And this spontaneity requires a lot of training. This is one reason why ritual in Confucianism is an integral part of moral formation. Ritual pervades virtually every facet of one's life, prescribing certain patterns of behavior pertaining to etiquette, conventional formalities, or informal gestures. These behaviors may not seem connected to living a moral life, but ritual can produce the ability to respond spontaneously in a way that is prudent and wise when facing a difficult, surprising situation. An analogy is found in sports, where many of the exercises seem irrelevant to the way the sport is actually played competitively. Coaches understand that these exercises strengthen muscles and develop important habits for when the competition is fierce. The training Luke receives from Yoda may at first appear pointless, and yet these rituals aid production of the right traits and abilities for living the Jedi way. Though Luke did not carry out his training perfectly, the process was instrumental in helping him overcome the temptation to join Palpatine. And his willingness to see it through is evidence of his filial piety for the parental figures and the Jedi tradition in his life. Luke's filial piety for Obi-Wan, Yoda, and Anakin, as well as the Jedi tradition, shapes his character such that he can ultimately resist the temptation of the dark side.

"Tell Your Sister, You Were Right"

In the end, Luke is vindicated in his judgment about Vader: Anakin Skywalker is still alive; there is still good in him. When Palpatine beats Luke down with Force lightning, Luke cries out, "Father, please!" Even at the brink of death with his father seemingly coldly staring at him, Luke believes there's good in Vader, which manifests when Vader risks death to rescue Luke. The final vindication comes as Luke tries to rescue the broken Vader to escape the Death Star. With Vader's helmet removed, seeing his son with his own eyes for the first time, Anakin utters his final words: "You were right about me; tell your sister, you were right."

Luke's filial piety persists even after Vader's death. A reverence for parents, in the Confucian tradition, should be exhibited after their passing: "When someone's father is still alive, observe his intentions; after his father has passed away, observe his conduct. If for three years he does not alter the ways of his father, he may be called a filial son."[10] Burial rites are an important way to exhibit filial piety, since they continue to honor parents and bring order out of the disruption death may bring.[11] To honor his father according to Jedi tradition, Luke takes Vader's body to Endor and builds a funeral pyre – in the same manner as Qui-Gon Jinn's cremation in *The Phantom Menace*.

If we understand Luke's decisions and actions in light of Confucian filial piety, his choice to surrender himself is neither foolish nor imprudent. Filial piety makes sense when we reflect on Luke's journey into becoming a Jedi and achieving peace, knowledge, serenity, harmony, and eventually becoming one with the Force in *The Last Jedi*. No doubt other factors were crucial, including his friendships, but we must not overlook the ways in which filial piety is foundational for a good life, including the life of a Jedi.

Notes

1 See Amy Olberding, *Moral Exemplars in the Analects: The Good Person Is That* (New York: Routledge, 2011), and Linda Zagzebski, *Exemplarist Moral Theory* (Oxford: Oxford University Press, 2017).
2 Confucius, *The Essential Analects: Selected Passages with Traditional Commentary*, trans. Edward Slingerland (Indianapolis: Hackett, 2006), I.12.
3 Ibid., I.2.
4 Ibid., II.7.
5 See Philip J., Ivanhoe, "Filial Piety as a Virtue," Rebecca L. Walker and Philip J. Ivanhoe, eds., in *Working Virtue: Virtue Ethics and Contemporary Moral Problems* (Oxford: Oxford University Press, 2007), 297–312.
6 See Eric Yang, "Filial Piety and Ritual: A Confucian Approach to Well-Being," *Science, Religion, and Culture* 6 (2019), 96–102.
7 Chris Tweedt, "Fictional Exemplars," presentation at North and South Carolina Philosophical Societies (February 2012).
8 A.T. Nuyen, "Filial Piety as Respect for Tradition," in Sor-Hoon Tan and Alan Chan, eds., *Filial Piety: Concepts and Traditions* (New York: Routledge, 2004), 203–214, and A.T. Nuyen, "The Contemporary Relevance of the Confucian Idea of Filial Piety," *Journal of Chinese Philosophy* 31 (2004), 433–450.
9 Confucius, *The Essential Analects*, II.5.
10 Ibid., I.11.
11 Chris Fraser, "Xunzi Versus Zhuangzi: Two Approaches to Death in Classical Chinese Thought," *Frontiers of Philosophy in China* 9 (2013), 410–427.

Part V

THE MANDALORIAN

21

Should You Eat Baby Yoda?

A.G. Holdier

It's a heart-rending moment when the Mandalorian says goodbye to Grogu at the end of "The Rescue." Having managed to free his friend from the clutches of Moff Gideon, Din Djarin slowly removes his helmet and shares a comforting look with the Child before sending him off to train in the ways of the Force with Luke Skywalker. After 16 episodes across two seasons, many questions still remain about the mysterious Grogu, his past, and his future, but at least one will almost certainly never be answered: What would "Baby Yoda" taste like?

If this strikes you as an odd question, that's the point of this chapter: to search our feelings about the adorable green kid frequently seen playing with the control knobs of the *Razor Crest* and explore the moral implications that our common affective responses could suggest. Depending on what we find, we might end up uncovering a surprising reason or two to think that the energy field created by all living things not only surrounds us, penetrates us, and binds us together, but also gives us reasons to treat others in certain ethical ways – no matter what they look like.

"I've Got a Bad Feeling About This"

At several points in *The Mandalorian*, we see Grogu face mortal danger, only to be rescued by his begrudgingly heroic bounty hunter companion. Suppose that instead of escaping from ice spiders, sea monsters, or assassin droids, the little Force-user met a tragic, untimely end. To add insult to emotional injury, imagine also that the very next

Star Wars and Philosophy Strikes Back: This is the Way, First Edition.
Edited by Jason T. Eberl and Kevin S. Decker.

scene were to show Grogu's dead corpse roasting over a cookfire as hungry stormtroopers clean their plates for dinner: How might such a sight make you feel?

If you are like me, the thought of a chargrilled Child-steak does not merely strike you as unappetizing or disgusting – you probably think that the stormtroopers are doing something *morally wrong* by murdering and eating Grogu. Philosophers who hold *sentimentalist* views of morality believe there's an important relationship between those initial affective responses – our "gut reactions" – and our more considered moral judgments; in many cases, the former might actually explain the weight of the latter. Some sentimentalists think humans have a fully separate kind of "moral sense" (akin to our senses of touch or smell) allowing us to perceive moral truths about the world. So your outrage at the sight of a Grogu-based dinner reflects a kind of shortcut around otherwise more complicated moral judgments about the wrongness of such an action.[1] While you *could* come up with reasons for why Grogu should not be eaten, your moral sense saves you time by simply skipping to the moral judgment.

Other sentimentalists argue that our emotions are just affective responses to experiences which should not be interpreted as giving us moral truths, but instead can help us to make sense of our own moral motivations as we reflect upon the things we care about. This perspective would say that your disgust at Grogu's treatment does not pick out an objective fact about its wrongness, but instead should tell you something important about what you believe "counts" as a proper moral judgment (and then you can puzzle out what, if anything, justifies those judgments).[2]

Finally, some moral sentimentalists say that ethical judgments *just are* our affective responses to the world and do not necessarily refer to or reflect anything beyond those emotional experiences. Instead of "detecting" moral truths or informing us about something internally separate from our feelings, the feelings themselves provide the content of our moral beliefs. On this view, my disgust at the thought of someone eating Grogu is not *showing* me that it's wrong to eat him, nor does it *justify* a separate belief that "It is wrong to eat Grogu" – instead, my disgust *simply is* my judgment that Grogu is not the kind of creature who should be eaten.[3]

In whichever variety, moral sentimentalism tries to take seriously the psychological mechanisms that underwrite our making moral judgments. Consider Din Djarin's experience in "The Sin" when, despite having just delivered Grogu into the hands of the Empire, he chooses to return and rescue the Child. Despite knowing the dangerous risk of taking on the Client's stormtroopers by himself, as well as the fact that his decision violates the Code of the Bounty Hunters' Guild, the Mandalorian follows his emotional impulses because he *cares* about Grogu's well-being. At this point, all other rational considerations pale in comparison to Mando's sentimental attachment to the kid.

"Always Thinking with Your Stomach"

Moral sentimentalists treat feelings, or affective attitudes, as important components of moral theorizing and decision-making. As any good Jedi will point out, there's at least one problem looming on the horizon for this kind of emotion-sensitive framework: What happens when someone's psychological mechanisms go awry and *fail* to reliably render the right kinds of judgments? Even if our emotions aren't dragging us into the lures of the Dark Side, it still seems like we have got the potential for a significant problem on our hands.[4]

Consider again the imaginary dead body of "Baby Yoda" roasting on a spit over a fire and the visceral revulsion the image provokes. Presumably, the stormtroopers waiting for the dinner bell *do not* feel this same sense of disgust – how might you convince them that their emotions are inappropriate? Normally, we do not consider emotional responses to be the kinds of things that can be *wrong*, but without some way to correct errant sentiments, moral sentimentalists run the risk of being accused of defending a merely subjective ethics. Perhaps our broader cultural context can help prescribe (and proscribe) certain emotional responses to its members. So, in virtue of being a part of a society that, on the whole, tends to care about creatures like Grogu, I might be obligated to reflect that cultural sentiment, at least in my outward behavior.

Unfortunately, it's not clear that this cultural constraint will give us the results we are looking for. If just one Mos Eisley bartender prohibits droids from entering his establishment, but everyone else allows them to come and go as they please, we might think that the bartender is simply prejudiced and whatever negative feelings he experiences toward droids are inappropriate. But if *all* Mos Eisley bartenders (or, indeed, all bartenders) feel negatively toward droids, we cannot criticize those feelings if their dominance among bartenders is all we are measuring.

Consider a different example. In "The Passenger," Mando and Grogu welcome aboard the *Razor Crest* an amphibious woman seeking safe passage to meet her husband. While in transit, Grogu sneakily eats a number of the eggs the woman has laid and is carrying with her – eggs she is careful to safeguard, presumably in order to prevent her family line from going extinct. After the episode aired, fans of the show complained that Grogu was effectively snacking on her children while she wasn't looking – a gruesome activity to depict the otherwise adorable Child happily (and repeatedly) enjoying. In a now-deleted response via Twitter, a Lucasfilm executive wrote that "the Frog Lady's eggs are unfertilized, like the chicken eggs many of us enjoy. But obviously, chickens aren't sentient beings and the Child eating the eggs is intentionally disturbing, for comedic effect" – many of Grogu's fans remained unconvinced.[5]

What, then, should we say? If we determine the appropriateness of emotional responses by something like a popular vote, and if *enough* viewers' emotional responses to Grogu munching on the eggs were negative, then Grogu might well be guilty of a serious moral crime, no matter what the writers or showrunners of *The Mandalorian* intended.

"You're Lucky You Don't Taste Very Good"

The egg debate suggests at least one more problem with measuring the aptness of moral feelings against a cultural standard: it might make us think that *we actually should not care about Grogu either* and, even more problematically, *neither should Din Djarin.*

Consider the studio executive's comment about chicken eggs again: just like Grogu, it's common in our culture for people to eat the bodies of other animals. Typically, philosophers refer to a creature's ability to *feel pain* by using the term "sentient" (the term "sapient" indicates that a creature possesses higher rational capacities, like complex language-use). Din Djarin, Grogu, and the so-called "Frog Lady" are sentient in this way. So are (presumably) the ice spiders that nearly destroy the *Razor Crest*, and so are chickens in our world.[6]

But the majority of people around the world *do not* seem to care about the painful experiences of chickens, despite the fact that many commercial agricultural operations force chickens (and pigs, cows, and plenty of other sentient creatures) to live exceedingly poor lives. If we recoil at the thought of one adorable nonhuman creature being tortured and eaten (Grogu), why do not we experience similar feelings of revulsion at the thought of a cheeseburger or chicken sandwich? Indeed, if we are going to base our proper moral feelings on popular sentiments, we might be forced into thinking that nonhuman sentient creatures do not *deserve* our moral consideration at all, making our disgust at the thought of a Grogu-steak *inappropriate*. And we might be able to tell a similarly speciesist story *for the Mandalorian himself*, given that he's also shown eating meat at different points throughout the series; if Djarin does not care about *those* nonhuman creatures, why should he care about Grogu?[7]

So, instead, we might want a more nuanced model of the moral psychology at work here. T.J. Kasperbauer suggests that our feelings toward nonhuman creatures (like chickens and Frog Ladies) are partly the result of generations of our ancestors behaving toward different species as if they were in lower or more distanced social groups.[8] According to Kasperbauer, the psychological process responsible for this downgrading is the same one that has led societies to dehumanize and abuse other humans by unjustly and irrationally discounting their moral value; through the process of *infrahumanization*, victims "are still attributed various key human qualities but are treated as inferior to some other group by comparison."[9] Adapting this concept to analyze cross-species relationships, Kasperbauer concludes that nonhuman animals have, as a category, been historically classified as an outgroup, thereby removing many of our feelings of moral obligation to care for nonhuman animals. But, because some animals (like dogs or horses) are more similar to humans than others (particularly in the appearance of their cognitive capacities), and because we have evolved closer relationships of mutual recognition with them as fellow creatures, our psychological responses to *those* nonhuman animals have been similarly cultivated along infrahumanizing lines – perhaps this can salvage our preference for little Grogu.

Consider what Kasperbauer's view might mean for sci-fi/fantasy stories in which complex, nonhuman species live rich, complicated lives. Should humans in *Star Wars* be expected to treat Wookiees, Jawas, Gungans, or Hutts as infrahumanized outgroups comprising moral patients with less moral significance, or deny their status as moral agents altogether?[10] Certainly not! Despite the fact that the Child has yet to speak on-camera, he – just as much as Chewbacca, Jabba the Hutt, R2-D2, and, of course, Master Yoda – is clearly cognitively and emotionally similar to humans in many relevant ways. Given human interactions with these myriad alien and artificial species in a galaxy far, far away, we can expect that the moral psychology of humans would've developed differently from that on Earth, so infrahumanizing habits may have been avoided. In short, Mando's affection for the Child makes sense.

Unfortunately, that leaves us with the question of whether or not *we* should care about Grogu. If cultural dominance is the metric for our moral sentiments, then our predominantly speciesist culture threatens to undermine our emotional concern for the clearly nonhuman Child.

"This Is the Way"

Fortunately, moral sentimentalists have a better option for measuring the appropriateness of our ethical feelings. Scottish philosopher Adam Smith's 1759 book *The Theory of Moral Sentiments* remains a landmark defense of moral sentimentalism.[11] Rather than dominant cultural attitudes, Smith wrote that the appropriateness of moral feelings can be judged based on what an "impartial spectator" would feel in the scenario in question. If someone free of bias or self-interest, having stripped away personal attachments in a Jedi-like fashion, were to feel disgusted at a Grogu barbeque, then *everyone* should feel likewise.

For many moral sentimentalists, this kind of idealized standard for our moral feelings offers a helpful reference point when some people's moral attitudes misfire: if the impartial spectator would feel badly about Grogu eating the passenger's eggs (perhaps because the spectator sympathizes with the stressed plight of the would-be mother), then failure to experience negative emotions toward the Child's misdeeds is a *moral* failure.

If the impartial spectator feels badly about the plight of *chickens* and their eggs (just as much as the Frog Lady and her eggs), perhaps because they are all sentient creatures that can experience suffering, then we *also* have reason to care about nonhuman animals – no matter how delicious they might taste when their corpses are deep-fried. Indeed, Kasperbauer's idea of infrahumanization is neither a justification for the mistreatment of nonhuman animals nor a prescription for us to act differently – it's a description of the current psychological landscape of our culture. It's designed, in part, to get people thinking more carefully about how we *should* be feeling, rather than simply how we *do* feel. In short, whatever reasons we might have for being disgusted at the thought of eating Grogu seemingly apply to plenty of other nonhuman creatures as well; whatever we think and feel about one, we seemingly should think and feel about the others.

In the 1970s, philosopher Cora Diamond talked about "fellow creature responses" as important starting-points for thinking about our ethical sentiments regarding animals.[12] To Diamond, our relationships with nonhumans come in all sorts of complicated forms and each deserves its own careful treatment for determining its moral character.[13] *Star Wars* has shown us a similar kind of picture with a galaxy of different ways in which humans and nonhumans can interact. In *The Mandalorian*, we see a particularly sentimental relationship between Din Djarin and Grogu – one that's not only emotionally touching, but philosophically interesting as well.

Notes

1 That truths about morality can be *perceived* is exemplified in the views of British philosophers like Francis Hutcheson (1694–1746 CE) and the third Earl of Shaftesbury (1801–1885 CE), both of whom described a "moral sense" that provokes feelings of approval or disapproval. More recently, psychologist Jonathan Haidt has described how our "gut reactions" to moral questions can reflect unconscious cognitive processes that function in a similar fashion.

2 One example of this kind of sentimentalism is the philosophy of David Hume (1711–1776 CE), who argued that our experience of *sympathy* for others ultimately motivates us to act morally. Hume did not think that we perceive moral facts in the world, but rather that our moral emotions provoke us to behave in various ways.

3 To be fair, this oversimplifies the interesting nuances separating different *non-cognitivist* views of moral sentimentalism, each of which holds that morality is not determined by rational consideration or assessment.

4 For another set of philosophers sensitive to the ways in which our feelings can mislead us and suspicious of the category of emotions altogether, consider the ancient Greek Stoic school from the third century BCE. For a discussion of Stoicism in *Star Wars*, see Matt Hummel, "You Are Asking Me to Be Rational: Stoic Philosophy and the Jedi Order," in Jason T. Eberl and Kevin S. Decker, eds., *The Ultimate Star Wars and Philosophy: You Must Unlearn What You Have Learned* (Malden, MA: Wiley-Blackwell, 2015), 20–31, and William O. Stephens, "Stoicism in the Stars: Yoda, the Emperor, and the Force," in Kevin S. Decker and Jason T. Eberl, eds., *Star Wars and Philosophy: More Powerful than You Can Possibly Imagine* (Chicago: Open Court, 2005), 16–28.

5 Art manager Phil Szostak, who worked on both seasons of *The Mandalorian*, initially tweeted this on November 9, 2020.

6 Neither the individual character, nor her husband, nor their species is named in either the episode or its accompanying materials, but the moniker "Frog Lady" arose quickly online to refer to the mother.

7 Much like how we can understand "racism" or "sexism" as an irrational prejudice against an individual on the basis of their race or sex, "speciesism" is the irrational discounting of a creature's value because they lack membership in the category *Homo sapiens*. You can read more about this in Peter Singer's landmark book *Animal Liberation: The Definitive Classic of the Animal Movement, Updated Edition* (New York: Harper Collins, 2009).

8 Kasperbauer's argument, along with considerable supporting empirical evidence, can be found in his book *Subhuman: The Moral Psychology of Human Attitudes to Animals* (New York: Oxford University Press, 2018).

9 Ibid., 40.

10 A moral *agent* possesses the capacity to act morally or immorally (and, by extension, deserves to be treated with a certain kind of respect or with consideration for their interests); in contrast, a moral *patient* is an individual who *cannot* be said to act morally (for a variety of potential reasons) but who nevertheless still deserves to be treated in certain ways by moral agents.

11 This is the same Adam Smith whose later work would culminate in the 1776 publication of his famous defense of free market economics, *The Wealth of Nations*.

12 Most famously, her thoughts can be found in Cora Diamond, "Eating Meat and Eating People," *Philosophy* 53 (1978), 465–479.

13 Although Diamond is not a sentimentalist, her ethics is amenable to sentimentalist concerns since it also assesses the appropriateness of our emotional responses to each experience as they come.

22

Grogu's Little Way: The Binds of Power and the Bonds of Love in *The Mandalorian*

Jeffrey P. Bishop and Isabel Bishop

In *The Mandalorian*, the Client says, "The Empire improves every system it touches. Judged by any metric – safety, prosperity, trade, opportunity, peace – compare Imperial rule to what is happening now. Look outside. Is the world more peaceful since the revolution? I see nothing but death and chaos" ("Chapter 7: The Reckoning"). The scene takes place in a safehouse for the Imperial remnant on Nevarro, an Outer Rim planet where there's lawlessness, disorder, theft, murder – what Thomas Hobbes (1588–1679) might've called a "state of nature" where people are free to do what they like, if they can get away with it. In the state of nature, might makes right; you have ultimate freedom, but there's no safety for your property or your person. Little did the Client know that Moff Gideon – a reminder of the Empire's former sovereign power – is sitting outside with enough firepower to destroy the safehouse. *Power* in all of its manifestations – political, biological, even mystical – is about to be on display.

In this chapter, we'll explore the relations of different kinds of power, philosophically understood – sovereign power, disciplinary power, and biopower – and argue that the politics of the *Star Wars* galaxy, as well as our own, is animated by an ontology, or metaphysical picture, centered on *power*. We'll further argue that *The Mandalorian* criticizes this power ontology with the introduction of the Child, Grogu, who generates a different kind of Force: *a relational ontology of love*. Grogu and the love he generates point to a different

Star Wars and Philosophy Strikes Back: This is the Way, First Edition.
Edited by Jason T. Eberl and Kevin S. Decker.

way of being in the world than power. Ultimately, *The Mandalorian* offers a different ontology of power – an ontology of love – as a radical alternative to the bindings of political power.

"I Can Bring You in Warm, or I Can Bring You in Cold"

Nevarro is an Outer Rim planet at the margins of political power, sitting at the border between a civilized state and the state of nature. In Hobbesian political philosophy, the civilized state must be carved from the state of nature by sovereign power; the sovereign keeps one foot in the state of nature and one foot in the civilized state.

Nevarro's inhabitants also have interesting relationships to power. Greef Karga was a magistrate when Nevarro was under Imperial rule. Now he leads the Bounty Hunters' Guild, which operates by its own *code* but has an ambiguous relationship with New Republic laws. Bounty hunters operate in the interstices of sovereign and administrative power and have a malleable relationship with the power of the law. They often do things that would be illegal for the authorities to do, but aren't necessarily illegal for the average citizen to do. They work at the borders of the law, one foot inside the legal boundary and one foot outside.[1]

Din Djarin is a bounty hunter, but what makes him and his Mandalorian comrades unique among bounty hunters is the strict *creed* to which they adhere. They do not marry and they appear to swear off the comforts of home and sex. They grow their numbers by taking in foundlings and orphans, caring for them and raising them in the Way of Mandalore. Djarin belongs to a strict sect known as the Children of the Watch, a separatist group aimed at maintaining the purity of the religious cult. Separatist movements often grow up in the midst of chaos, usually at the margins of society. Separatists find strength in strict adherence to their doctrines, creating order for themselves in the midst of the chaos that surrounds them. Where the law cannot be trusted, faith in "the Way" creates spiritual order to face the chaos.

The Client is a businessman, who's seen the importance of Imperial political stability for his business. He hopes to discover Grogu's biological powers, like the longevity of his species and his ability to tap into the mysterious power of the Force. The Client's goal is the safety provided in *biopower*: the ability to heal the sick and stave off death.

And if he makes a little profit along the way, then the spirit of capitalism might doubly bless him.[2]

Moff Gideon of the Imperial Security Bureau fills out the spectrum of power, having once been a notorious warlord of the Galactic Empire. He took part in the Great Purge of Mandalore, where he came to possess the legendary Mandalorian weapon, the Darksaber. Now leading an Imperial remnant, Gideon seeks to reestablish the Empire's sovereignty.[3]

On Nevarro, we find different kinds of power ontology at work. There's the border between chaos and order, that between the state of nature and the civilizing government, and that between sovereign power and administrative governing power.

"Enter the Bureaucrat. The True Rulers of the Republic"

Sovereign power in premodern Western societies tended to be mysterious and directly related to cultic concern for right worship of the proper gods, and so political power was related to the mythology of people grounding their faith in a spiritual order. Before modern times, Hobbes saw not a spiritual order, but chaotic forces at work in the state of nature. In the state of nature, you can act however you wish, drawing on your own power – just as Anakin attempts to convince Padmé to join him on the dark side to "make things the way we want them to be." But this need to express power is also true for everyone else. The only thing preventing someone from stealing your landspeeder is the greater power and threat of violence as punishment. The state of nature is a war of all against all in which life is "solitary, poor, nasty, brutish, and short."[4]

As Hobbes sees it, a *civilized state* is carved out of the state of nature by the sheer strength of a *sovereign* who wields the greatest power. Those less powerful then enter into a *social contract* with the sovereign for protection. Each individual cedes their freedoms for the sake of security. The sovereign retains the power to punish and even kill to keep rogue forces from molesting citizens of the contract, thus securing the civilized state. Hobbes's political philosophy is aimed at creating the orderly society imagined by the Client, but also by Palpatine in his speech to the Senate at the founding of the Empire in *Revenge of the Sith* (*ROTS*): "In order to ensure our security and continuing stability, the Republic will be reorganized into the first Galactic Empire, for a safe and secure society." Just as Hobbes's sovereign retains the power over life and death held over from the state of nature, the Emperor must be able to kill and so employs enforcers such as Darth Vader, the Inquisitors, and legions of stormtroopers. The Emperor also enforces his power through the bureaucratic ranks of Imperial governors, moffs, and magistrates – as Greef Karga once was.

Once the sovereign and their sergeants-at-arms have secured the border between the state of nature and the civilized state, governing within the boundaries takes on a very different tenor. John Locke (1632–1704) agrees with much in Hobbes, arguing that people long for freedom to carry out meaningful lives.[5] But for Locke, the sovereign must cede back to individuals some of the freedoms they had in the state of nature. And David Hume (1711–1776) argues that in order to protect these *civil liberties*, there needs to be some sort of *bureaucratic structure* that both assures security and protects freedom.[6]

We can see two dimensions of this kind of bureaucratic power in the work of Michel Foucault (1926–1984).[7] First, there exist a series of *disciplines* that constrain the extent of individual power, and these could be seen as oppressive. An example might be found in the design of the panopticon prison, created with the hope that prisoners (or workers) might internalize the behavioral (or work) habits that the designers had in mind. Thus, disciplinary power is also internalized by each individual through *education* and *formation* for the purposes of disciplining oneself. You can enjoy the freedoms granted to individuals by the sovereign . . . *if* you have self-discipline. On Nevarro, we see disciplinary power at work with Greef Karga. As head of the Bounty Hunters' Guild, he metes out punishments to those who violate the Guild's code – as Djarin does when he recovers Grogu from the Client. We also see it subtly at play in the Client, who wants stable markets that shape people's behaviors toward productivity; thus his hatred of the chaotic post-Imperial galaxy. Finally, there's the stoic self-discipline exercised by Djarin and his fellow Mandalorians following the strict creed of "the Way."

Foucault saw disciplinary power as a break from sovereign power. The goal of disciplinary power is to render individuals docile, so that they desire whatever preserves their safety and security within the civilized state. Once the boundaries of civilization are protected from the state of nature, safety and security themselves become administered within the state. The contemporary philosopher Giorgio Agamben argues, however, that sovereign power is still active within the bureaucracies and disciplines of the civilized state.[8] For example, Locke thought the administrative state would limit itself to creating zones of liberty, but the civilized state in fact begins to see itself as creating safety and security at every level. When Palpatine articulates his vision of the Empire, he does not have in mind a limited, Lockean state. Instead, he sees the power of sovereignty as ordered to the creation of "a safe and secure society," which he proclaims to the cheers of the Senate. Padmé – channeling Locke – laments, "So this is how liberty dies. With thunderous applause." The Lockean vision is at odds with disciplinary power. Padmé would agree with Agamben's claim that sovereign power remains active even in disciplinary power. For Palpatine, sovereign power is necessary to execute disciplinary power for the sake of a safe and secure society. But it's also necessary to have power over death and life, which is the concern of *biopower*.

"Without the Midi-chlorians, Life Could Not Exist"

Foucault sees power manifesting differently in different epochs of history: power is different in the epoch of sovereign power than in the epoch of disciplinary power. The epoch of disciplinary power gives way to the epoch of biopower in the eighteenth century. Disciplinary power is exercised upon, and then internalized by, individuals. Biopower is exercised upon *populations* in various ways to tap into the power of life itself, attempting to create populations with targeted abilities and strengths.

For example, the Kaminoans contracted by the Republic through the Jedi Sifo-Dyas, created a grand clone army, harnessing the biological power of the Mandalorian bounty hunter Jango Fett. Fett's biopower is deployed by sovereign power for the sake of executing the sovereign's desires (seemingly the Senate's desires, but actually Palpatine's). A contrasting example is the more mystical biopower exhibited by the 50-year-old Force-sensitive Child, Grogu. The Client hopes that Dr. Pershing, a former Imperial scientist, can study Grogu and extract whatever gives his species such longevity and links him to the Force.

As a child, Grogu has not yet learned to align his power to the Force. Djarin understands the gift of power Grogu has, and that it must be cultivated and harnessed through practice. The need for practice shows that power is not neutral, but can deliver creation and destruction at the same time – just as the Death Star aims to create order by destroying planets. Grogu must learn to align himself with the light side of the Force, which requires the disciplinary tutelage of a Jedi. The search for a Jedi to educate Grogu becomes Djarin's primary task.

Djarin understands that if Grogu falls into the hands of the Client and Gideon, the sovereign power the Empire brandishes will become stronger for the sake of establishing "safety and security" at the expense of any other possible goods, such as freedom and meaning. Yet, what motivates Djarin – along with Cara Dune, Kuill, and eventually Greef Karga – is not the moral vision of sacrificing one for the many. Nor is it even the sense of duty that Djarin feels as a Mandalorian adhering to his creed, which requires him to save foundlings. Rather there's something far more subtle that seems to slip from the three levels of power – sovereign, disciplinary, and biopower. As an alternative to the bindings of a power ontology, Grogu symbolizes an alternative ontology grounded in *love*.[9]

The Binds of Power or the Bonds of Love

In the power ontology at work in the *Star Wars* galaxy we have been discussing, all creatures are caught in a world of power relations. Power is all there is, or so it seems. Even the Force is imagined as a kind of power that some sentient beings can interact with in various ways. Everything seems to stem from power: life (both naturally and through dark side manipulation), the ability to build planet-sized cities (Coruscant) and technological terrors (Death Stars, Starkiller base), and the desire to create social order (Republic, Empire, New Republic, First Order). Power here moves at every level: cosmic, biological, political. In this ontology, there's no good or evil per se, but only the sake for which power is used. As Palpatine tells Anakin, "Good is a point of view, Anakin. The Sith and the Jedi are similar in almost every way. Including their quest for greater power."

Palpatine is correct that power dynamics shape the confrontational relationship between the Jedi and Sith, which is fed by the Jedi's disavowal of strong *attachments*. Sensing that young Anakin misses his mother in *The Phantom Menace*, Yoda warns, "Fear is the path to the dark side. Fear leads to anger. Anger leads to hate. Hate leads to suffering." Later, in *ROTS*, when Anakin has a Force vision of Padmé's death, Yoda again interprets Anakin's personal attachment as somehow *disordered*, exhorting him to "Rejoice for those who transform into the Force. Mourn them do not. Miss them do not."[10] This philosophy dissuades Jedi from attachment because it might lead to negative emotions, such as fear, hate, and grief. Yet, had the Jedi understood something about human attachments and bonds, they might've seen that appropriately loving attachments can also bring positive emotions leading to the light side of the Force.

Yoda would have Anakin not love, so that he would not fear. Not heeding Yoda's counsel, Anakin sees Jedi detachment as impotent against the forces that would take Padmé's life and seeks to gain power over them. Palpatine convinces him that the dark side is more efficacious in protecting those he loves. If the Jedi had not closed themselves off to love, and if their traditional training practices had rightly ordered Padawans toward properly loving attachments, Anakin might never have embraced the dark side.

Anakin's sense that the world is a harsh and dangerous place is the animating force behind sovereign power, whether in the Sith desire to overthrow the Jedi, in Palpatine's desire to establish a new order, or in Gideon's Imperial remnant at the margins of the Outer Rim. Each is caught in the throes of power which even the seemingly powerful Empire cannot control. Even those who choose the dark side, like Anakin, do so hoping to gain the power to protect something or someone they love, believing, as Anakin proclaims in *ROTS*, that "peace, freedom, justice, and security" are made possible by a "new empire." The logic seems tight: there must be a sovereign to rule over chaos in order to create these conditions, as if the sovereign – whether a person or a system of governance – can hold death and destruction at bay. All political systems arise for this purpose. No one can imagine a way out of the binds of this power ontology, in galaxies far or near.

Yet, *The Mandalorian* articulates another way – we may even call it a "little way." Through Grogu's innocent engagement with other beings, through his dependency on others, through the very fact that he can be destroyed by power, the Child demonstrates a different relation to power, including a different relation to the Force. He's subject to the powers of the world, and yet, in his helplessness before these powers, others come to see their way out of the binds of power. Grogu does this through the *love* he generates in Din Djarin, and the love they share reaches far beyond their "Clan of Two." Omera – a villager on the swamp planet of Sorgan – sees the love they share, which in turn generates her love for Djarin. This shared love transforms a cynical Cara into someone who can see that order must be placed in service of something other than just ordering power itself – rather, power must be ordered to love. And the love that circulates between Grogu, Djarin, and Cara breaks open the hard crust of Greef Karga, who then partakes in the love by being healed by Grogu.

Each of these principal characters are forced to abandon a haven in the midst of the chaos of disorder. Greef Karga abandons the Bounty Hunters' code in double-crossing the Client. Cara Dune abandons her cynical attempt to protect herself by being a loner. Din Djarin begins to see that the creed of the Children of the Watch is actually a second-order concern. In "Chapter 15: The Believer," he removes his helmet – breaking his creed – to save Grogu. He's willing to reveal himself as a vulnerable human being for the sake of another whom he loves. He later removes his helmet to allow Grogu to see his face for the first time (and, perhaps, the last) before sending him away with Luke Skywalker.

The Mandalorian thus offers a different relation to power than most of the rest of the *Star Wars* canon.[11] Perhaps the world is not just power all the way up and all the way down, but can also embrace an array of differing relations that move individuals toward loving relationships with each other. Rather than the binds of power, *The Mandalorian* offers the bonds of love as an alternative ontology, an ontology of *relations*.

"Wherever I Go, He Goes"

The Mandalorian provides "a new hope" for a world not ordered by coercive and violent powers, a world of "all against all." It points to the faults of disordered creeds aimed toward securing power – whether sovereign power, disciplinary power, or biopower. As shown in "Chapter Five: Return of the Mandalorian" in *The Book of Boba Fett*, Din Djarin must ultimately abandon the Children of the Watch to embrace the "little way" of Grogu. And Grogu himself, at the end of the next episode, must choose whether to follow Luke's Jedi training and immerse himself in the epochal power exchanges between Jedi and Sith or follow his loving attachment to Djarin. His choice shows that the central moral question here is not whether you adhere to the light or dark side of the Force, but whether you can envision and strive to create a world built, not upon power, but upon a *love ontology*.

Notes

1 "Greef Karga," Wookieepedia, at https://starwars.fandom.com/wiki/Greef_Karga.
2 "The Client," Wookieepedia, at https://starwars.fandom.com/wiki/The_Client.
3 "Gideon," Wookieepedia, at https://starwars.fandom.com/wiki/Gideon.
4 Thomas Hobbes, Leviathan, ed. Richard Tuck (New York: Cambridge University Press, 1991), i, xiii, 9.
5 John Locke, *Two Treatises on Government*, ed. Peter Laslett (Cambridge: Cambridge University Press, 1988).
6 David Hume, *An Enquiry Concerning Human Understanding*, ed. Stephen Buckle (Cambridge: Cambridge University Press, 1999), 8.23.
7 Michel Foucault, *Power/Knowledge: Selected Interviews and Other Writings, 1972–1977*, ed. Colin Gordon (New York: Pantheon Books, 1978). See also Foucault's *The History of Sexuality, vol. 1: The Will to Knowledge*, trans. Robert Hurley (New York: Random House, 1977).
8 Giorgio, Agamben, *Homo Sacer: Sovereign Power and Bare Life*, trans. Daniel Heller-Roazen (Stanford: Stanford University Press, 1998).
9 For further discussion of the power of love in *Star Wars*, see James Lawler's chapter in this volume (Chapter 29).
10 For a defense of Yoda's perspective, through the lens of St. Augustine, see Jason T. Eberl, "'Know the Dark Side': A Theodicy of the Force," in Jason T. Eberl and Kevin S. Decker, eds., The Ultimate Star Wars and Philosophy: You Must Unlearn What You Have Learned (Malden: MA: Wiley-Blackwell, 2015), 100–114.
11 Notably, Luke, in *The Last Jedi*, declares a need for the Jedi to end, to break the cyclical power struggles between the light and dark sides, and instructs Rey that the Force is *not* a power that she has.

23

Beneath the Helmet, Beyond the Way: *The Mandalorian* and Moral Decision-making

Noam Ebner

Din Djarin's life is exhausting. In addition to the grueling physical aspects of his work, and schlepping all that armor around, he lives the life of a single dad making his way in the universe, and his ride keeps breaking down. With the Child down for the night, there are all those ethical decisions keeping him awake:

Can I take another's life or liberty to gain a monetary award?
How should I split this beskar up between my own self-preservation and supporting foundlings?
Should I rescue one child, when it puts my entire coven at risk?
How do I decide between my duties to my professional guild and to my coven?

And on, and on. Decisions, decisions.

This chapter charts a metamorphosis in Djarin's ethical decision-making across the first two seasons of *The Mandalorian*. His changing perspective generates a new outlook on other people, the Way, and of course, life's core question: *When can I remove my helmet?*

"Everybody's Got Their Lines They Don't Cross, Until Things Get Messy"

"How do I make ethical decisions?" ranks high on the list of Big Questions philosophers have addressed. Most proposed answers for finding the right choices fall into one of three schools of

Star Wars and Philosophy Strikes Back: This is the Way, First Edition.
Edited by Jason T. Eberl and Kevin S. Decker.

thought: virtue ethics (do what a virtuous person would do), consequentialism (do what will bring the best outcome for all involved), and deontology (do your duty no matter the consequences). Appealing in theory, these approaches are devilish to apply in practice, as they deal in absolutes. They all assume a rational process of moral deliberation that runs counter to the way we actually process ethical conundrums.

We do not conduct most of our moral decision-making sitting in a library of philosophy books; rather, this takes place in the basements of our minds as we go about our lives. It's guided by psychological formations laid down before our encounter with any theories. As human younglings grow, philosophical questions of ethics and virtue merge with psychological development and decision-making to constitute their *moral development.*

Traditionally, philosophy and psychology have centered on moral reasoning and developmental processes based on logic, reasoning, and a primary concern with oneself, sometimes tempered by respect for others. A bounty hunter informing their quarry, "I can bring you in warm, or I can bring you in cold" expresses morality-in-practice, not an edgy threat. "My needs justify bringing in bounties" goes their moral reasoning, so "out of respect for their individual rights, I let them choose whether to be brought in warm or cold." In a nutshell, this is Mando's moral stance at the beginning of *The Mandalorian.*[1]

Before going further, let us acknowledge one shortcoming of this traditional approach to moral development: it ignores half of humanity. In the 1970s, Carol Gilligan exposed how the psychological study of moral development had traditionally assumed both the male psyche and male morality to be the default baseline for decision-making and research.[2] Her own research, listening to the voices of women speaking about moral issues, uncovered an entirely different vocabulary of moral reasoning, one focused on emotion, caring, and relationships. She realized that this wasn't evidence of women's *flawed* moral development, as previous generations of male psychologists asserted. Instead, it was evidence of an entirely *different* process of moral development. Men and women, she concluded, typically grow into significantly different conceptual frameworks of morality.[3]

Gilligan saw that typical male development orients men toward "ethics of rights": People have *rights*, and are entitled to develop, achieve, and *take* within the scope of those rights. However, *all* individuals have rights, so when my rights collide with another's, can I pursue my own benefit over theirs? The answer is found by logical reasoning: quantifying benefits, harm, and fairness, and resorting to rules and theories of justice if necessary. Mando thinks, *If IG-11 and I both put equal effort and risk into recovering the bounty, we'll split the reward equally. Logical? Fair? You bet.*

Female development typically orients women toward an "ethics of care": People have *responsibilities* toward others as well as themselves. Ethical dilemmas present themselves when these responsibilities clash, bringing relationships into conflict. To what extent must I care for one person at the expense of caring for another or myself? The answer is found through inclusion, restoring relationships, empathy, communication, and nonviolence. Mando might've thought, *My new droid partner and I have discovered clashing preferences regarding the delivery temperature of a jointly captured bounty? Should I shoot it? Let us talk.*

Of course, men do include care in their moral decision-making, and women take rights into account. Originally introduced by Gilligan as a gender-based feature of psychological moral development, the moral notion of care has since developed into a moral *theory* that people of any gender can apply.[4] *The Mandalorian* is the story of one man's moral overhaul toward care. And, you guessed it: it's all because of the Child. But Djarin's metamorphosis is not simply him discovering his nurturing side. It involves a far deeper shift in how he views himself and his relationships. At the heart of this change lies his gradual disenchantment with moral decisions based solely on the ethics of rights and their replacement with the ethics of care.

"He's a Little Rough Around the Edges, but He Is the Best"

Watching Chapter 1, "The Mandalorian," I was struck by one odd characteristic of early Mando: *He does not negotiate.* And it gets more interesting – he does not simply avoid negotiation by *using force* to take anything he wants. Early Mando often pays when he could take, and does not negotiate even when he has everything to gain by doing so. Why did he not haggle when Greef Karga, head of the Bounty Hunters' Guild, slashed his pay in half? Sure, he *complained*, but rising to leave was theatrics, not negotiation. And, couldn't he have asked the Client for just a little more beskar as a down payment?

This raises the question: what is early Mando's *system*? What moral approach guides him when he wants something from another person, another wants something from him, or they both want the same thing exclusively for themselves? Patrons of the bar in the opening scene might conclude that Mando simply applies a hunter's ethic of "might makes right." They could not be more wrong. Consider that Mando does not negotiate with the unnamed Mythrol, because he's bringing him in under the legal authority granted by his bounty hunter license.[5] He does not negotiate with Greef Karga or the Mandalorian Armorer, because he respects their positions above him in the hierarchies of the Guild and the coven, respectively. Above all, he keeps the faith with his coven and creed, because "this is the Way."

Taken together, early Mando's moral decisions are based on hierarchy, status, rules, fairness, maximizing benefit, and values. They reflect an ethics of rights, in which logic and reasoning bring deontology, utilitarianism, and virtue ethics into combined action.

"Well, Then I Don't Know If I Want Your Help"

The shift in Mando's decision-making approach occurred gradually, beginning with the impact of a rampaging blurrg. Breaking his typical silence, Mando engaged in lengthy conversation with Kuiil, who clearly confused him. Kuiil extended assistance and care, asked for nothing (or nothing Mando values) in return, and brushed aside Mando's offer of a rights-based reward. He taught Mando one profound lesson about helping people and another about people having different needs and preferences, shutting down any protest with his signature "I have spoken." In opening Mando's mind to notions of care and new forms of cooperation, Kuiil primed him for metamorphosis.

Our map of loyalties, allies, and adversaries connects to the broader ethical scheme of how we relate to others, and Mando's had begun to change. That day provided several further moral shake-ups. Mando was betrayed by the Guild, shot by IG-11, and partnered with the assassin droid in mowing down gazillions of Niktos protecting the asset.

And then, he met the asset.

Looking down into the hovercrib, Mando knew his *rights* with regard to his target, yet also faced a sudden swell of *obligation* marked by conflicting duties to his Client, target, partner, Guild, and the Way. Even Mando could not articulate his sudden objection to bringing this particular bounty in "cold"; it's kinda something you can only express by shooting your partner, y'know?

One reason might've been that the bounty was a child, yet we know that Mando *wasn't* simply protecting the Child as an official Mandalorian foundling (only much later did the Armorer declare it as such). Whatever the cause, upon seeing that little green critter, something clearly stirred in Mando (his facial expression said it all). Both the ethical clash and its resolution must've deeply surprised him.

But this remarkable day was just getting started. Apparently forgetting where he'd parked his blurrg, Mando walked toward the *Razor Crest*, in the meantime surviving an attempt by fellow Guild members to steal his bounty. In the course of an hour, he had been both hunter and prey, and finally – a victim, wronged by Jawas, unethical scavengers who stripped his ship.

At this point, he recalls that he is not alone. Dusting himself off, he seeks Kuiil's help and receives another profound lesson: some situations can be resolved without disintegration. "You can trade," Kuiil explains. Mando objects: "With Jawas? You must be out of your mind!" We can recognize Mando's objection as the plaintive reaction of someone who, having suffered a moral offense, seeks a rights-based remedy from a source of justice.

Kuiil teaches Mando that such situations can be resolved through recognizing that fractured relationships can be restored by setting weapons aside and fostering communication and connection. Restored relationships allow for care and provide outcomes leaving everyone more content than before (and sometimes, flying high on mudhorn egg-yuck fumes).

Mando has taken his first step into a larger ethical world.

"How Uncharacteristic of One of Your Reputation"

The bounty hunter returns to Nevarro a changed Mando; he just doesn't know it yet. In an emotional haze, he even neglects to freeze his bounty. Or was he concerned for its safety? Mando delivers the bounty to the Client, seemingly all business as usual. However, maybe Greef Karga's comment, "I do not know if [the Client] wants to eat it, or hang it on his wall," is churning beneath his helmet. More importantly, we can reasonably believe he's beset by new questions: *What are my responsibilities to myself, and what are my responsibilities to others?*

Mando, beskar prize in hand, watches the Child being floated away. He asks the Client, "What are your plans for it?" At this possible turning point, the Client urges Mando to respect the rules of contract and his Guild's code, take his beskar, and walk away – no questions asked. And, this works … at first. Forty-odd years of moral development, after all, aren't undone instantly.

Mando returns to his ship. Rather than considering what he's *entitled* to – new armor, the next target – he contemplates his *responsibilities*: *What do I owe the Client? The Bounty Hunters' Guild? The Child, who did not know I was its enemy? The Way? Myself?* Remarkably, he resolves these questions in favor of rescuing the Child, breaking ties with the Guild.

Soon providing target practice for the entire Guild, Mando almost pays the ultimate price for his ethical awakening. When his coven rescues him, he realizes his nascent ethical shift is not directly opposed to his upbringing. Whatever else it might include, the Way's doctrine on foundlings represents an untapped well of generalized care for others. In coming out of hiding to support him, the coven reiterates that *to care is ethical*: you shield the Child with your body, and we risk our lives for you, all out of care. They also reinforce the lesson he's slowest to learn: *You cannot go it alone, dummy.*

"You Are a Clan of Two"

Escaping Nevarro with the Child, Mando finally gets it: *You cannot do this on your own; it takes a village.* For a loner like Mando, living "in a village" with others implies new relational and ethical considerations.

Mando begins gathering a figurative village. Kuiil, Peli the mechanic, Cara Dune – with whom he saves an actual village – and others form bonds with him; increasingly, they take each other into greater consideration. He relies on their self-assumed responsibility toward him and the Child, even as he acts out of responsibility to them. Consider the sharp contrast between this new village and the people Mando *used* to associate with. In Chapter 6, "The Prisoner," we see that Ran (Mando's former partner-in-crime), Xi'an (his former lover of sorts?), and the rest of the team gathered to bust Xi'an's brother Qin out of prison are fundamentally disloyal to anyone but themselves.[6] Mando's tangible discomfort with them stems not only from the threat they pose him and the Child, but also from his regretting earlier choices in ethics and relationships. Xi'an and Qin offer a window into Mando's earlier ethics, alluding to a previous heist in which Mando succeeded at the cost of Qin being captured.

"You Have Suffered Damage to Your Central Processing Unit"

Pop quiz: A woman is dying from a disease. A pharmacy has a life-saving drug, but she and her husband cannot afford to buy it. The husband considers breaking into the pharmacy and stealing the drug. What do you think he should do?

Gilligan discovered that male respondents considering this situation tend to focus on the husband's decision, rules about theft, and balances between the rights to life and to property. Females, on the other hand, tend to focus on the relationships involved as well as on the pharmacist's responsibilities. Why is the pharmacist not responding to this woman's needs? These fundamentally different framings of *what this situation is about*, morally speaking, is a dead giveaway that two completely different ethical frames are at work.

What would Din Djarin choose? After all, Djarin acts in ethically iffy ways while protecting the Child, analogous to the husband's choices in Gilligan's scenario. Let's be honest: Djarin leaves a *lot* of bodies lying about, and things often tend to blow up around him. However, he rarely "robs the pharmacy," preferring to pay cash or trade services for help. In one intriguing exception in Chapter 3, "The Sin," Mando hijacks a vehicle at gunpoint to escape the Bounty Hunters' Guild with the Child. The droid-driver refusing to drive him is Gilligan's pharmacist, withholding life-saving means (transportation) at its disposal. Mando not only robs the pharmacy in this case, he endangers the pharmacist and ultimately costs it its life. I know, IG-11 – you were never alive. But still.[7]

"We Gonna Do This in Front of the Kid?"

The hypothetical scenario about the pharmacy illuminates something crucial for understanding Djarin's gradual adoption of ethics of care: often, our choice to *frame* an ethical dilemma through one perspective or another winds up determining our moral *decision*. One aspect of this framing is the very casting of the characters in a hypothetical ethical situation.

In Chapter 9, "The Marshal," Djarin instinctively applies the ethics of rights upon encountering Cobb Vanth clad in Mandalorian armor: my right to reclaim Mandalorian armor supersedes Vanth's rights to property ... and life. Caught up in rights-based thinking, Djarin ignores Vanth's efforts to direct his attention to other responsibilities, like to "the little one" and the bartender. He forgets Kuiil's lesson: *you can trade*. If we think of the Mandalorian creed as his sick wife, the armor as the medication, and Vanth as the "evil" pharmacist, Djarin's duty as the husband is clear to him.

Once violence takes a back seat to communication, Vanth explains that the armor protects the town. If Mando would support this cause and kill the Krayt dragon, Vanth would voluntarily relinquish the armor. From a rights-based perspective, *nothing has changed*. Offering Djarin to risk the same fate as a frog hopping toward Grogu does not change the ethical balance.

However, the new information causes Djarin to recast the entire dilemma through a care-based perspective. *He* is now the pharmacist, with responsibilities toward a husband (Vanth) and wife (the townspeople Vanth seeks to save). The Djarin Pharmacy's drug (fighting skills) can save her life. Can he ethically withhold it? Balancing his responsibility to the Way with responsibilities to Vanth and the townspeople, Djarin decides that the *ethical* course is to work with them to kill the dragon, even if the *easier* way would be to decline Vanth's offer and kill him for the armor.

Reoriented toward care, Djarin even helps Vanth relinquish his own rights-based justifications for fighting the Tuskens in favor of nonviolent communication and joint action. Vanth, in turn, encourages the townspeople to adopt this new mindset regarding the group with whom they share a desert.[8]

"So, What Happens If You Take That Thing Off?"

Once we acknowledge Djarin's shift from a rights-based to a care-based ethical framework – allowing for the fact that old instincts die hard – it's fascinating to explore other decisions he makes along the way. He defends Alliance Lieutenant Devan on a prison ship against his own teammates; he protects Frog Lady's eggs against a voracious green killer seeking to guzzle them down; and he offers or asks Onara, Ahsoka Tano, and finally Luke Skywalker to adopt Grogu.

But having come this far, we have to face why Djarin's ethical metamorphosis is key to answering the series' most enigmatic question: *Can he take it off? Will he?*

The Way seems *very* clear regarding helmet-removal. As the Armorer explains in Chapter 3, "The Sin," helmet rule-observance is ultimate, irrefutable, proof of Mandalorian virtue. Early Mando is so helmet-virtuous, he almost never unhelmets even when alone. Only in Onara's barn does he *finally* grab a bite and let himself look on the Child with his own eyes.

Any helmet-dilemmas, framed in his rights-based language, were simply resolved:

Can I remove my helmet to down a spotchka? The rules say I should not. I will not (note to self: ask Armorer for some sort of beskar drink-straw). Can I remove my helmet to facilitate riding a blurrg and completing my mission? The rules of the Way say I should not, superseding the Guild's creed of "Get 'em!" I'll keep it on (and work harder at blurrging).

Yet as Mando's ethical perspective gradually shifts, he frames helmet-removal dilemmas differently, requiring more complex reasoning: *Might I remove my helmet to connect with Onara? I'm obligated to the Way; I have the* right *to unhelmet, but this would end my* relationship *with the Way and its community. I'm also responsible toward this kind woman and do not want to hurt her. And, what about myself? Could I, as Cara so delicately suggested, just slip off the helmet and settle down here with that beautiful young widow and raise my kid sitting here sipping spotchka – no straw needed?* Only as Onara's fingers gently begin to lift his helmet does he decide: "I do not belong here ... but he does." He resolves his ethical quandary by keeping the helmet on, while still expressing deep relational trust by leaving the Child with Onara.

Later: *Should I remove my helmet for a mission-critical facial scan, in full view of everyone in the Imperial officers' mess, including that jerk Mayfeld? How does all this weigh against my responsibilities to Grogu, alone on an Imperial ship somewhere, waiting for me? What do I owe myself?* Meriting significant deliberation, the resolution of this ethical quandary was heavily weighted in favor of removing the helmet because of Grogu's predicament, held captive by Moff Gideon.

In Djarin's final helmet-removal deliberation, there were no facilitating factors: no technicalities, no conveniently available stormtrooper helmets, and no life-threatening danger.

Do I remove my helmet, in front of just about everybody I know and this cloaked stranger? Do my responsibilities to the Way, myself, and Grogu, allow me – require me, even – to show Grogu the love in my eyes before we part, and ensure that he'll recognize me in the future? His ethical metamorphosis complete, Din Djarin found this final dilemma to be the easiest of all to resolve.

Notes

1 The series only gradually revealed the Child's and the Mandalorian's names; I've attempted to refer to them, throughout, using the names by which they were referred to at the point in time I am referencing. If you were able to follow that sentence, we'll get along just fine.

2 The field of philosophy has also, historically, been a boys' club. Considering psychology and philosophy in tandem, contributions to the study of moral development primarily reflect male participation and paradigms.

3 Carol Gilligan, *In a Different Voice: Psychological Theory and Women's Development* (Cambridge: Harvard University Press, 1982).

4 This was Gilligan's own understanding all along, somewhat obscured by her being identified with her original, gender-differentiating, research. For further, gender-transcending applications of this framework, see Virginia Held, *The Ethics of Care: Personal, Political, and Global* (Oxford: Oxford University Press, 2005).

5 Indeed, under this reasoning, it would be unethical to allow the Mythrol to bargain his way to freedom. Also, unwise. It's 9 ABY, and the song about the last bounty hunter who negotiated with his quarry is still being sung – unrevised – by minstrels the galaxy over.

6 Their degree of mutual ethical care is epitomized by Qin commanding Mayfeld to get him off the ship ASAP, abandoning the others. "What about your sister?" asks Mayfeld. "What about her?" Qin responds.

7 For further discussion of whether droids count as beings with rights or are otherwise subjects of ethical care and concern, see Joshua Jowitt's chapter in this volume (Chapter 16).

8 For all the ethics of care on display, nobody tried talking to the Krayt dragon in search of a more ethical resolution, protecting all the desert-dwellers without reducing one of them to steak and goo. When Krayt dragons gather to hear this story, it is told very differently.

24

Paradox of Faith: The Way of Din Djarin and Kierkegaard

Patrick Tiernan

Can someone be committed to their faith but struggle with what it asks of them? Are duty and desire mutually exclusive? These are questions we find in the story of *The Mandalorian* framed by personal and religious goals cloaked in competing desires and obligations. Din Djarin lies at the center of this dynamic, torn between obligations to abide by the Way of the Mandalore while resigning himself to reuniting the Child, Grogu, with the Jedi. His unwavering faith in pursuing this mission leads him down an existential path questioning his own upbringing and his role as a protector.

Faith or Doubt?

In the opening episode, "The Child," we meet the gun-slinging, soft-spoken, masked mercenary known simply as Mando. His demeanor is calm and calculated with a laser-focus intent on finding his hit and collecting its full bounty. He's concerned only with maintaining anonymity as he pursues his targets with stealth and unforgiving intensity. But, by the episode's conclusion, instead of delivering his latest target and retrieving his bounty from Greef Karga, Mando is gazing down upon the Child like a doting new father. We learn that Mando himself was taken in and cared for by the Mandalorians. Like others before him, he was a "foundling" brought into Mandalorian culture and trained to be a capable warrior, and it's clear that the Mandalorians hold foundlings in high regard. But everything he's grown familiar with

Star Wars and Philosophy Strikes Back: This is the Way, First Edition.
Edited by Jason T. Eberl and Kevin S. Decker.

through his training is thrown into doubt when he encounters the one bounty for which he'll never collect credits.

The moral dilemma Mando faces as he struggles to return the Child to the Jedi Order is illuminated by Søren Kierkegaard (1813–1855), one of the central figures of *existentialism*, a philosophy centered on the belief that individuals define themselves through their actions. The fundamental truths of our lives are not abstract but are lived experiences that challenge our very sense of identity, asking who we are and what we stand for. Our free will generates anguish, as we struggle to find meaning in our lives and take responsibility for our choices.

Kierkegaard's Christian existentialism was critical of the social dynamics and religious models that were supposed to represent authentic religiosity but were actually hypocritical and naive. Religious leaders spoke of virtue but rarely modeled it. Kierkegaard, by contrast, upheld the central tenets of the faith but was humble about what he could claim as objectively true or real. In one of his most well-known books, *Fear and Trembling*, Kierkegaard examines the biblical story of Abraham and Isaac.[1] Highlighting the steadfast faith of the Biblical patriarch Abraham, Kierkegaard views him as an individual who is capable of believing in himself and acting independently. The devotion and commitment of Abraham's faith allows him to have the "power to concentrate the whole substance of his life and the meaning of actuality into one single desire."[2] Abraham is an archetype of someone who resists becoming something other than who they are called to be.

In the moment when God commands Abraham to sacrifice his son Isaac as an offering, he realizes that a single individual is more important than a universal ethical system of right and wrong – what a paradox![3] Kierkegaard calls this the "teleological suspension of the ethical." What does this mean? Well, as an example, let us say that we agree in principle that stealing is not a positive behavior and could lead to a series of poor choices in one's life. If, though, one needed to steal food for one's family, would stealing be permissible? Could it be morally acceptable to ignore this rule – namely, that it'd be morally wrong to steal – at that moment ("suspension of the ethical") because at this given time the purpose of meeting one's family's needs ("teleological") is more important? Throughout the series, Mando becomes a father figure to the Child, echoing the biblical story of Abraham. He's challenged numerous times to give up the Child, and he realizes this is no ordinary being. In handing over the Child, he fulfills his duty but against his better judgment. To keep the Child would risk their safety as well as his allegiance to Bounty Hunter protocol. When faced with the choice to keep the Child, he decides to see the task through of returning him to the Jedi, a decision validated by the value Mandalorians place upon foundlings.

Mercenary or Father?

The word "religion" comes from the Latin *religare*, meaning "to bind" oneself. Throughout his journey, Mando does not just talk about the Way, he lives and embodies it. As a galactic mercenary, Mando's primarily concerned with collecting credits on solicited bounties, no questions asked. Almost mechanically, he takes a formulaic approach: take the puck, bring in the bounty "warm or cold," and collect the credits – no personal entanglements, no social connections, and no hard feelings. To do otherwise would risk abandoning the Mandalorian creed along with his very identity.[4] Traditional Mandalorian culture adheres to the *Resol'nare*, or Six Actions. They consist of wearing armor, speaking the language, defending oneself and one's family, raising one's children as Mandalorians, contributing to the clan's welfare, and, when called upon by the *Mand'alor*, rallying to their cause. Tradition requires that those who desire to be called Mandalorian are to abide by these guidelines and live them out daily. If a Mandalorian does not abide by the *Resol'nare*, they are considered *dar'manda* – someone who's ignorant of their heritage and bereft of their Mandalorian soul. An individual in this state is considered soulless, having no place in *Manda*, the Mandalorian afterlife.[5] Consequently, Mando resists giving in to worldly desires that would only lead him away from these commandments.

Kierkegaard's philosophy speaks of three developmental stages of existence. The first is the *aesthetic stage* in which people are defined by pursuits of the heart and body, and pleasure is discovered in the drama of pretending to be someone else.[6] But eventually, one realizes this is not enough to be fulfilled, leading the individual to despair asking, "Is this all life has to offer?" We're driven to boredom after exhausting desire after desire, unable to attain any sense of fulfillment in our life. In the episode "Sanctuary," Mando lands on the planet Sorgan to hide from the Guild and finds himself helping local villagers defend themselves against Klatoonian Raiders with the help of another mercenary, Cara Dune. During the ordeal, a widow named Omera expresses her gratitude for his help saying, "We want you to stay. The community's grateful. You can pack all this away in case there's any trouble. You and your boy can have a good life. He could be a child for a while. Wouldn't that be nice?" This exchange raises an intriguing possibility regarding the sense of care he's developed toward the Child and about his emerging persona as a father. Settling down and raising a family appears to be a natural desire here, but given his adherence to the Mandalorian creed, he cannot place himself first. In "Redemption," Mando's signet is revealed to be the mudhorn skull representing the great deed accomplished by him and the Child, a clan of two. It also represents a personal challenge to Mando's commitment. Should he abandon the creed for a new life that centers on what many of us seek – committed relationships and personal stability? But what exactly is the good life? What others ask of you? What you desire for yourself? For Mando, there are no such questions, only obedience.

The place of family and the meaning of names are important to note here. Names are also significant in Kierkegaard's writings as he uses several pseudonyms to underscore existential themes of solitude, meaning, and subjectivity that permeate his writings.[7] They also underscore an important existential maxim, namely that to find yourself you must be willing to lose yourself. The tension between finding your purpose in life and staring into the abyss of meaninglessness frames the human condition, and it's played out clearly in the narrative of Din Djarin. For most of the first season, we know very little about Mando until "Redemption," when Moff Gideon calls out the mercenary's birth name. Since he was present at the Siege of Mandalore, Gideon indirectly humanizes Mando by presenting us with his true identity. More is revealed when he becomes injured in the battle with Gideon's troops and IG-11 instructs him to remove his helmet so it can attend to him. As part of the Mandalorian code, he's never allowed to take off his helmet to any living being, but IG-11 notes that it's not a living being. Likewise, it is not until season two's "The Jedi" that we learn the Child's name is Grogu and that he'd been trained at the Jedi Temple on Coruscant and rescued from Order 66. These revelations of names personalize the two main characters. They have moved far beyond the original bounty transaction.

Selfish or Sacrifice?

The persona of Din Djarin evolves in complexity: from enigma, to soldier, to father. He believes in the Mandalorian creed and its rules, but he experiences a personal attachment to Grogu. Indeed, this mutual emotional bond begins to take its toll. Similarly, the existential tradition raises the theme of *authenticity*, the genuine or true way of human existence; specifically, this entails an element of one's own unique self. It's another paradox involving the subjective individual and the objective moral order. Din Djarin commits himself to seeking out other Mandalorians who may help him with his mission. In doing so, he begins to realize that the label "Mandalorian" is not a monolithic ideal, but rather applies to a diverse spectrum of zealots, apostates, and mercenaries universally opposed to oppression of any brand.[8] By discovering his *own way*, Din Djarin also follows *the Way*. This is a specific and unique mark of each Mandalorian going back to the signet each receives. When we witness him collecting enough beskar to fashion an entirely new "iron skin," we might imagine his meetings with Cobb Vanth and Bo-Katan Kryze, both geared in traditional Mandalorian armor, would not be contentious. But these encounters raise the question of what it means to be a true follower of the Way and the responsibilities that come with wearing the Mandalorian armor.

In Kierkegaard's second stage, the *ethical stage*, the individual moves from living for oneself to acting in accordance with moral laws.[9] In this plane of existence, we come to know pleasures that are empathetic, prolonged, and constant rather than the fleeting and limited pleasures of the aesthetic stage. The ethical life actually leads to deeper, more authentic pleasure because we do not suffer from the limits of base indulgences. Appearances seldom determine what's real. When we are first introduced to Cobb Vanth in "The Marshal," we immediately recognize his armor as being from the bounty hunter Boba Fett. When Vanth casually removes his helmet and explains how he acquired the suit, Djarin is unimpressed because this action is not part of the *authentic* Mandalorian creed. The agreement he makes with Vanth to return the armor in exchange for killing the Krayt dragon reaffirms his vow to safeguard all remnants of Mandalorian culture and artifacts. Mando is able to sacrifice because it's in line with his creed and is the right thing to do for the betterment of the Mandalorian Order as a whole. Likewise, in "The Heiress," when Djarin meets Death Watch lieutenant Bo-Katan Kryze and her fellow mercenaries, his horizon of understanding of Mandalore's diversity expands. Bo-Katan has struggled in the past with her desire to obtain the Darksaber when it wasn't rightfully hers to take. Both of these episodes highlight what appear to be selfishly motivated individuals who, in fact, reveal their willingness to sacrifice for the greater good – Vanth wants to save his town and Kryze hopes to redeem herself in the eyes of her soldiers. Appearances can be deceiving. Both Kryze and Vanth mean well but their desires aren't aligned with a higher calling. Their selflessness is clouded by seeking revenge or ensuring their image, respectively. It's in living in accordance with the ethical stage that we can distinguish between the posturing of what's real and the actual representation of someone who lives an authentic life.

Purpose or Futility?

The arc of Din Djarin's character culminates in an intriguing question for the viewer: was his purpose fulfilled in returning Grogu? Or was it a mission in futility? His faith and commitment to the moral precepts of the Way certainly guided his decisions, but he is more than a soldier of fortune. Kierkegaard's existentialism provides a framework to appreciate Din Djarin's moral complexity, a saved individual who in turn saves another. While both the Jedi and Mandalorian Orders echo religious values and ideals, it is not preordained that his mission to return Grogu would conclude successfully. His commitment to uphold the tenets of the Mandalorian Order is absolute, but he's confronted by a mission not of his choosing. He believes he's doing the right thing throughout encounters with Imperial forces and other mercenaries bent on collecting the bounty on Grogu, but he cannot deny the personal attachment he feels for Grogu. The paradox that frames Din Djarin's life culminates in his sacrifice of what he wants for the betterment of the being entrusted to his care – the very act that defines his purpose in life. By never removing his helmet, he maintains his authentic identity and upholds a core tenet of being a Mandalorian. But for Grogu, he is willing to make this sacrifice – twice. In "The Believer," Djarin teams up with Migs Mayfield to infiltrate an Imperial remnant refinery on Morak to acquire more information on Moff Gideon's light cruiser. To log into the network terminal, Djarin must have his face scanned to be recognized by the system. Then in the season finale "The Rescue," he removes his helmet again as the bittersweet reality of saying farewell to Grogu intersects with the realization of his mission to reunite him with the Jedi Order. The literal and figurative way in which Djarin faces this struggle embodies how he defines the true meaning of his existence.

The final stage of life according to Kierkegaard is the *religious*, in which one makes a leap of faith.[10] Here one paradoxically regains one's purpose and desire by giving them up. This tension between faith and reason in Kierkegaard parallels the life of Din Djarin in many ways.[11] Faith ultimately goes beyond the surface and is the task of a lifetime, requiring trust in divine promises, obedience to divine commands, and the teleological suspension of the ethical. Returning to the example of Abraham, from the standpoint of reason, his faith is naive. What would possess anyone to have such a blind adherence to a divine command to commit such a heinous act? Therein lies the paradox in experiences that cause fear, trembling, anxiety, and despair – the journey is never meaningless if one has faith. The leap of faith that Kierkegaard ultimately directs individuals toward goes beyond the aesthetic and ethical and transforms into the religious stage of existence where belief in God transcends everything we know as human beings. This is the Christian paradox that directs the existential narrative of Søren Kierkegaard: to find yourself, you must first lose yourself. Ultimately, these choices form the same moral trajectory for Din Djarin: to become a true Mandalorian, he must abandon the very creed that defines him.

Notes

1 New Revised Standard Version, Gen. 22: 1–14.

2 Søren Kierkegaard, *Fear and Trembling/Repetition*, trans. Howard V. Hong and Edna H. Hong (Princeton, NJ: Princeton University Press, 1983), 42–43.

3 Ibid., 55–57.

4 Karen Traviss, "The Mandalorians: People and Culture," *Star Wars Insider* 86 (2006), at https://mandowords.tumblr.com/post/171049754076/the-mandalorians-people-and-culture-star-wars.

5 In Chapter 5, "Return of the Mandalorian," of *The Book of Boba Fett*, Djarin confesses to the Armorer that he has removed his helmet and she immediately declares that he is "no longer a Mandalorian." The Mandalorian Paz Vizsla, whom Djarin dueled to determine the true heir of the Darksaber, calls him an apostate – one who has renounced a religious belief.

6 Søren Kierkegaard, *Either/Or: Part One*, trans. Howard V. Hong and Edna H. Hong (Princeton, NJ: Princeton University Press, 1987). The example of the aesthetic stage is Don Giovanni (or "Don Juan"), the great seducer of women.

7 By way of example, he wrote *Fear and Trembling* under the pseudonym Johannes de Silencio, allegedly borrowed from the Grimm Brothers' fairy tale *The Faithful Servant*, as a way of attempting to explain the unexplainable: sacrificing your own child. Ironically, Silencio himself struggles to "break the silence" on this matter of faith.

8 Jack Jenkins, "'The Mandalorian' Is an Indictment of Religious Violence, and a Celebration of Pluralism," *America*, December 4, 2020, at https://www.americamagazine.org/arts-culture/2020/12/04/disney-star-wars-mandalorian-religious-pluralism-239404.

9 Søren Kierkegaard, *Either/Or: Part Two*, trans. Howard V. Hong and Edna H. Hong (Princeton, NJ: Princeton University Press, 1987). The example of the ethical stage is marriage, where the aesthetic views it as boring and routine while the ethical views it as an eternal agreement.

10 Søren Kierkegaard, *Stages on Life's Way*, trans. Howard V. Hong and Edna H. Hong (Princeton, NJ: Princeton University Press, 1988). Kierkegaard contrasts two perspectives in writing on the religious stage: "Religiousness A" (how one uses reason to discern absolute truth) and "Religiousness B" (what authentic Christianity looks like).

11 Merold Westphal, *Kierkegaard's Concept of Faith* (Grand Rapids, MI: Eerdmans, 2014), 101–117.

25

Reading the Mind of Din Djarin: The Music of *The Mandalorian*

Lance Belluomini

> Emotions of any kind are produced by melody and rhythm; therefore music has the power to form character.
>
> —Aristotle, *Politics*

In the memorable opening scene of *The Mandalorian* a lone figure tracks a fugitive on an icy planet. As he steps into a cantina bar, the masked and armored Mandalorian bounty hunter soon draws his blaster during a brawl with alien thugs who have taken an interest in his beskar armor. When one thug attempts to flee, the hunter trips him with a grappling line then fires his blaster at the door controls, causing the door panels to shut, slicing the alien in half. The Mandalorian's bounty fugitive has seen all this, and the hunter unforgettably tells him, "I can either bring you in warm, or I can bring you in cold." We then cut to the title card logo of the show: *The Mandalorian*. This is our introduction to the heroic main character: Din Djarin (aka "Mando").

Many artistic elements contribute to the beauty of this opening sequence. Of course there are the visual effects of the stunning environments as well as the costume design – the standouts being Din's helmet, armor, weapons, and flowing cape. But composer Ludwig Göransson's exotic music makes the greatest contribution to the aesthetics of this opening scene. His choice of primitive instruments to produce almost tribal music perfectly captures the lone aspect of Din's character.[1]

When Din walks through the cantina door, Göransson delivers Din's first motif to us played by a bass recorder (part of a musical cue titled "Hey Mando"), a flute instrument. Göransson uses the instrument

Star Wars and Philosophy Strikes Back: This is the Way, First Edition.
Edited by Jason T. Eberl and Kevin S. Decker.

to generate organic sounds of wind whistling through trees and hollows of the earth, contrasting associated intimate and human feelings with the modern visuals on screen. The beautiful rhythm of this motif, reminiscent of Ennio Morricone's spaghetti Western scores, evokes a quintessential Western whistle or the tension-filled musical motif of a cowboy standoff. We think of a lone man's journey – a man initially, like Clint Eastwood's iconic character, "with no name." The ancient sounding two-note interval of the piece has a distinct melancholy howl, and from this melody Göransson weaves a variety of harmonies carrying different emotions and moods throughout the show.

After Din secures his bounty capture, we are introduced to his second motif (part of "*The Mandalorian* Theme"), starting with the dramatic heartbeat-like pulse drop "bum-bummm!" This opening tune uses the interval of a fourth between notes, a dissonant repeating interval creating tension and getting us ready to leap into Din's adventures.[2] We hear the next part of the show's theme on top of the pulse sound through instruments played by Göransson: a bass recorder, electric guitar (an animal-like growl), drums (a rhythmic march), dramatic piano (a counter-melody with the bass), and electric keyboard (adding a soft magical feeling). This combination evokes feelings of heroism and strength. But Din's two motifs in this track also serve to express Din's thoughts, feelings, and struggles on his missions. This is necessary because, as Göransson says, "For this show you are just following one man and his perspective the whole time. And you do not get his facial expressions because he's wearing a helmet. So I knew there was a lot of ground to cover with different music, which essentially had to convey that."[3]

But do we really pay attention to the music when watching *The Mandalorian*? Most of us aren't consciously aware of its value and impact on us; our attention is usually focused on the action or the dialogue. This chapter looks at how Göransson's motifs emotionally move us, but also how the music "reads the mind" of Din. In conveying meaning musically, Göransson's compositions enhance our aesthetic appreciation of *The Mandalorian* and further our emotional investment in Din's story.

Grogu's Music Through Din's Eyes

Throughout history, people have been captured by the extraordinary effects of music. The ancient Greeks included music in education because they believed it perfects our soul or nature. Aristotle (384–322 BCE) discusses the purpose and value of music in the eighth book of his *Politics*, where he says that music imitates emotion and thus affects our emotions. This is important because learning to govern our emotions is necessary for perfecting our nature and rationality. Aristotle writes, "Rhythm and melody supply imitations of anger and gentleness, and also of courage and temperance, and of the other qualities of character, which hardly fall short of the actual affections, as we know from our own experience, for in listening to such strains our souls undergo a change."[4]

Notice how Göransson's music imitates emotions that we feel and recognize. It captures the emotions that Din is experiencing, allowing us to enjoy good emotional dispositions (something that, according to Aristotle, music does for us).[5] But how? Consider when Din first encounters Grogu at the end of the first chapter. Here, the music reads Din's mind – it imitates and communicates what he's feeling and thinking. We hear the first of several motifs included in "Grogu's Theme." When Din tells IG-11 of their target, "We'll bring it in alive," a sad melody ("The Asset") kicks in. The music is like a broken children's tune, played by dramatic piano and the plucking strings of an electric guitar. It then swells and reaches a crescendo with a variation of Din's first motif layered on top.

Clearly, the music informs us that Din has mixed feelings about this mission. It provides Din's unseen facial bewilderment over what he's gotten himself into. It also conveys his conflicted thoughts on whether he should turn the child over to the Imperials to obtain his beskar reward. Yet we also get a sense from this music that Din feels emotionally connected to Grogu. This is because, according to Aristotle, the music imitates Din's feeling of compassion, familiarizing us with this balanced emotional movement. The rhythm and melody of the broken children's tune reveals Din's feelings of empathy and sadness in the face of Grogu's helplessness and innocence. Din then acts on his caring instincts by dispensing with IG-11, also reflected in the music. We hear Mando's first motif mixed with Grogu's opening melody, expressing their immediate bond – the music corresponding with the chapter's final image of Din standing over the floating crib as the two reach out to one another – evocative of Michelangelo's "The Creation of Adam."

Grogu's motif repeats throughout *The Mandalorian* season one, most noticeably in "The Child" where Grogu uses the Force to save Din from the charging mudhorn. When Grogu Force-lifts the beast into the air, the music expresses Din's puzzled state as to what's going on. To further highlight their emotional connection, this piece ends with a blend of Din's first motif. Another version of this motif is heard in "Redemption" when Grogu uses the Force to deflect the flames of an incinerator trooper to save Din's heroic team. This time the motif plays in a slower tempo using a symphonic orchestra, imitating feelings of heroism and triumph.

Another popular musical motif associated with Grogu involves the use of soft bell-like tones that sound both old and new. In the final moments of "The Child," when Din checks on Grogu asleep in his cradle, the camera shifts to Din's mask staring at Grogu and we hear soft bell-like sounds. This childlike motif represents how Mando perceives Grogu – an innocent child full of mysterious and magical abilities.

Göransson uses a Fender Rhodes piano keyboard to create the soft alternating back-and-forth bell-like sounds, conveying nostalgic and magical feelings that provide a fairy-tale quality to the piece. Göransson has revealed that he took inspiration from John Williams's *Star Wars* music, which often features bell-sounding instruments (the celeste and glockenspiel, among others), to convey powerful feelings associated with the Force. In *The Empire Strikes Back*, the "Yoda and the Force" cue begins when Yoda says to Luke, "For my ally is the Force and a powerful ally it is." The bell-like sounds on top of the familiar "Force Theme" create nostalgic, mysterious, and magical feelings.

In *The Mandalorian*, Göransson recreates these feelings. Grogu's soft bell-like motif is a powerful piece showing up in different musical shapes. But it does not only play in scenes featuring Grogu. In "Redemption," when IG-11 attempts to remove Din's helmet to heal his head wound, Din says, "It is forbidden. No living thing has seen me without my helmet since I swore the Creed." We then get IG-11's captivating response, "I am not a living thing." When IG-11 removes Din's helmet, we briefly hear Grogu's soft bell-like motif, signaling the end to the mystery about Din's true visage. We see he's just a man who's been injured, a man who looks sad, scared, and vulnerable. Aristotle would rightly point out that it's the mysterious bell-like music that imitates the emotion of compassion which moves us and elevates the power of this scene.

Music, Emotion, and Din's Virtuous Way

Aristotle mentions that another purpose of music is to provide us with pleasure from the relaxation it provides. And from this delight comes another advantage: music influences our moral character. Aristotle claims that this happens when we are emotionally stirred by certain kinds of music.[6] In fact, as previously mentioned, the pleasure we find in music can lead us to the enjoyment of better emotional dispositions: "Since then music is a pleasure and virtue consists in rejoicing and loving and hating aright, there is clearly nothing which we are so much concerned to acquire and to cultivate as the power of forming right judgments and of taking delight in good dispositions and noble actions."[7] Aristotle is telling us that the pleasure of music can lead us to enjoy what he calls well-ordered emotions (such as joy) that are properly measured or balanced. Since good music familiarizes us with balanced movements of emotions, it fosters virtue. Put another way, because good music moves us emotionally and gets us used to true pleasures, it leads us toward being virtuous.

This is precisely what Göransson's music in *The Mandalorian* does. Consider the scene in "The Mandalorian" when the Ugnaught Kuiil helps Din learn how to ride a blurrg at his outpost. During Din's second attempt at mounting the blurrg, we hear Din's first motif by strings (in the cue titled "You Are a Mandalorian"), which imitates the feeling of triumph. But the music fades away when the blurrg throws him, signaling to us that Din is not yet ready for the challenge. But Kuiil reminds him of his people's history, saying to Din, "You are a Mandalorian. Your ancestors rode the great Mythosaur." Inspired, Din faces his fears. As he successfully tames and mounts the blurrg, we hear Din's first motif again but this time with a sweep of symphonic orchestration. Next, as Din and Kuiil set out on their mission riding the blurrgs, *The Mandalorian* theme plays in full glory – a symphonic march with trumpets carrying most of the melody and harmony along with electric and bass guitars which help drive the orchestra. The instrumentation imitates joyful and triumphant feelings.[8]

Because Göransson's music in this scene imitates well-ordered emotions that we enjoy, Aristotle would say his music disposes us toward being virtuous. This coincides with one of the more general appeals of the show: that we should aim to lead a virtuous way of life like Din does. *The Mandalorian* says, among other things, that living virtuously is what defines us. Sure, Din's adherence to his tribe's Way is critical to him, but the show continually highlights Din's moral character. This is seen through his natural impulse to care for Grogu, an impulse he extends to other communities. Certainly, it's the virtue of care, and other virtues he possesses, that truly define Din. Throughout the series he shows courage, bravery, perseverance, honor, trustworthiness, and gratitude.

Din's Theme as a Symbol of Strength and Confidence

In addition to the pleasure we feel from enjoying well-ordered emotional movements of music, Aristotle mentions another kind of pleasure we can feel from music: intellectual enjoyment.[9] This occurs when we find delight in contemplating the appropriateness of the emotions or feelings imitated by the music. Aristotle says that our delight in sensing aesthetic order (between music's imitation of the feeling and the feeling itself) is driven by our natural desire to know.[10]

Recall that at the start of season two, Göransson's music imitates Din's newfound feelings of confidence and optimism while also expressing his emotional attachments. In effect, the music tells us a story – from Din's lone man's journey to embracing a new quest with an unlikely companion with whom he develops a strong paternal connection: Grogu. But the music does not just transmit important narrative information. It also gives us intellectual enjoyment.

In the opening of "The Marshal," Din is walking down a darkly lit street in an industrial city with Grogu hovering at his side. Strange beasts are watching them. But in the musical cue "Mando is Back," instead of the motif playing on a bass recorder as in season one (where it expressed Din's lone man's journey), it is now played by amplified electric guitars and synthesizers – expressing Din's strength, confidence, and his paternal bond with Grogu. The music tells us they are now a team, a "clan of two."

The electric guitars lend this motif a rock 'n' roll and heavy metal feel: this is the strength Din now possesses. Additionally, the layered techno and electronic synth sounds provide us with Din's perceptions of the dangerous and gritty underworld he now faces along his quest. But the synth palette also bolsters Din's confidence and optimism, on display moments later during the fight club scene where he wards off alien assassins interested in his beskar armor. Here the synth sounds play in a faster tempo and are accompanied with big percussion hits that accentuate Din's confidence, signaling that he's reached "invincible warrior" status.

We also experience pleasure in realizing that we are being moved by the music in a way which is in tune with Din's confident and optimistic feelings. We recognize and appreciate the appropriate emotional order created in the musical composition. In other words, we intellectually enjoy seeing the relation that exists between Din's confident feeling and how the musical piece imitates this confident feeling.

In fact, Göransson provided us with intellectual enjoyment when he played the guitar version of Din's first motif at the end of season one, foreshadowing Din's new identity, strength, and confidence in season two. This occurred during the emotional flashback to Din's childhood during the Clone Wars attack when he was saved by Mandalorian forces. In the scene where a Mandalorian lifts young Din from a bunker, Göransson's instrumentation (full of low frequencies from the distortion and reverb on the electric guitars) reveals to us that Din and the Mandalorians are all about confidence, strength, and survival.

Interestingly, because Göransson repeatedly uses the recognizable main character themes in each chapter (played with different harmonies and instrumentation), he musically and thematically makes the episodes of the show feel like one continuous movie. In doing so, Göransson accomplishes something aesthetically unique and musically complex. While he gives each chapter of *The Mandalorian* its own distinct musical identity, he also gives the show its own distinctive sound.[11] Unquestionably, we are emotionally moved by the complex musical structure and style of these beautiful distinct harmonies and counterpoints from the show's main themes – which augment our aesthetic admiration for the show as a whole.

Din and Grogu's Emotional Farewell

The music in *The Mandalorian* also arouses our emotions through the sheer beauty of the exotic melodies, rhythms, and harmonies. Peter Kivy and other philosophers who write about music refer to these types of emotional responses as "emotions of appreciation." They're present when we feel awed or amazed by well-crafted musical compositions.[12]

Who can forget the heartbreaking farewell scene between Din and Grogu in the season two finale "The Rescue?"[13] There's an emotionally powerful moment when Din takes off his helmet to say goodbye to Grogu, who's off to learn the ways of the Force with Luke Skywalker. Din says to Grogu, "That's who you belong with. He's one of your kind. I'll see you again. I promise." After Grogu reaches his hand out to touch Din's helmet, and Din starts to remove it, the musical cue "Come with Me" transitions into a dreamy and gentle synthesized version of Grogu's broken children's tune, imitating Din's sadness. But Göransson also includes a few bell-like sounds when Din says, "All right, pal. It's time to go. Do not be afraid." This cue also emotionally connects Din and Grogu's final scene together with their first encounter. Then, the same broken children's tune was played by electric guitars to evoke Din's sadness over Grogu's helpless predicament. In effect, this sad tune connects the two characters together.

But things become more complex when the droid R2-D2 appears. Grogu's main motif evolves into a string-heavy orchestral suite touching on many of the recognizable pieces of music in the show. By tying the themes together, Göransson not only highlights the closure of Din and Grogu's storyline, he also pays homage to the harmonic language of John Williams's *Star Wars* music from which most of Göransson's music departs. Like Williams, he skillfully builds emotional tension by changing the tempo of the music. What's more, when Luke carries Grogu away and Din locks eyes with his former charge, we hear a new triumphant and heroic version of Din's first motif. The beauty of the orchestration (led by dramatic violins), the intricate instrumentation, the blended themes, and Din's motif express the joy and sadness that Din and Grogu are feeling, heightening the emotions of the visuals. Göransson's ingenuity and the beauty of his craftsmanship in this musical composition trigger this positive emotional response in us. And being emotionally moved is the primary effect of *The Mandalorian's* music.

A New Sound for *Star Wars*

The music of *The Mandalorian* is a combination of organic and electronic instruments played on top of one another, the distorted synthesizers together with the more traditional sounds of a symphonic orchestra. The music fits with the grittiness of Din's environments; it ties the narrative together; it imitates certain emotions that allow us to enjoy good emotional dispositions. It even steers us toward being virtuous, which supports the show's moral argument. But our discussion has also shown us that the music succeeds in conveying the intimacy of Din's story, his self-development, and his state of mind beneath the helmet – his facial expressions, feelings, and thoughts. It's refreshing and fun for us to hear music that captures the adventure of *Star Wars* but uses completely different and unorthodox methods. Göransson gets the feel of *Star Wars* and is not afraid to give us new sounds that guide us on our journey in a galaxy far, far away. As Din and his tribe would say, "This is the Way."[14]

Notes

1 It comes as no surprise that Göransson has won two Emmy awards for his work on two different chapters of The Mandalorian in the category of Outstanding Music Composition for a Series.
2 Notice that through the mixture of organic, electronic, and percussion-heavy sounds of this opening scene, Göransson expands the musical world of Star Wars (a departure from John Williams's classical and romantic themes), bringing the franchise into the future with new musical styles, compositions, and instrumentation that nicely align with the nature of the show as a "space Western."
3 Bill Desowitz, "The Mandalorian: How Ludwig Göransson's Retro-Futuristic Score Created a New 'Star Wars' Mystique," IndieWire, August 13,2020athttps://www.indiewire.com/2020/08/the-mandalorian-ludwig-goranssons-score-1234579780.
4 Aristotle, Politics, trans. C.D.C. Reeve (Indianapolis: Hackett, 2017), chapter 5, 1340a23; b18–19.
5 Note that the emotional dispositions we experience aren't always good. At times, Göransson's music imitates unpleasant emotions that Din feels, such as fear and anger.
6 Aristotle, Politics, 1339b40–1340a15.
7 Ibid., 1340a16–a19.
8 In this scene, Din's moments of strife followed by perseverance are reminiscent of the training montages from the Rocky films where the music showcases moments of breakthrough for Rocky, highlighting his commitment to win.
9 Aristotle, Politics, 1339a30–1339a34.
10 Aristotle, Metaphysics, trans. Richard Hope (Ann Arbor: University of Michigan Press, 1952), chapter 1, 980a21; chapter 2, 982a19.
11 It's worth noting that John Williams also accomplished this feat. His musical themes ("The Imperial March," "The Emperor's Theme," "The Force Theme," and "Yoda's Theme") all contribute to the overall continuity of the nine-film Skywalker saga as well.
12 For more on "emotions of appreciation," see Peter Kivy, *Music Alone: Philosophical Reflections on the Purely Musical Experience* (Ithaca, NY: Cornell University Press, 1990).
13 The director of "The Rescue," Peyton Reed, revealed that this emotional moment of Din and Grogu's goodbye was meant to parallel the heartbreaking farewell of Elliott and E.T. in Steven Spielberg's 1982 movie *E.T. the Extra-Terrestrial.*
14 I wish to thank Jason Eberl, Kevin Decker, and Bill Irwin for their helpful comments with earlier versions of this chapter.

Part VI

EPISODES VII–IX

26

Awakening Race, Culture, and Ethnicity in a Galaxy Far, Far Away

Edwardo Pérez

The original trio of Luke, Leia, and Han might've been played by White actors, but *Star Wars* has always been diverse, highlighting actors of color in various, often significant roles: not just heard (like African American actor James Earl Jones as Darth Vader, African American actor Ahmed Best as Jar Jar Binks, or Kenyan/Mexican actress Lupita Nyong'o as Maz Kanata), but *seen.*

In *The Empire Strikes Back*, African American actor Billy Dee Williams turned the trio into a quartet as Lando Calrissian (a role Donald Glover later effortlessly stepped into in *Solo*). Samuel L. Jackson's prequel trilogy character, Mace Windu, was Yoda's equal, and wielded the coolest purple lightsaber the galaxy's ever seen. Indeed, Williams and Jackson did not just represent Black actors and the Black community as Lando and Jedi Master Windu: they gave fans heroic, consequential characters to root for, characters who instantly became as iconic and as legendary as the original cast.[1]

In *The Last Jedi*, we see Kelly Marie Tran and Veronica Ngo (both of Vietnamese heritage), following Chinese actor Ken Leung in *The Force Awakens* and Chinese actors Donnie Yen and Wen Jiang in *Rogue One*. The latter also featured Mexican actor Diego Luna, Riz Ahmed (of British Pakistani heritage), and African American actor Forrest Whitaker as Saw Gerrera. The sequel trilogy featured British Nigerian actor John Boyega and Oscar Isaac (of Guatemalan heritage), while *Solo* also featured Thandie (now Thandiwe) Newton of British Zimbabwean heritage – and we have not even covered the voice actors and characters from the animated series and Disney+ shows![2]

Star Wars and Philosophy Strikes Back: This is the Way, First Edition.
Edited by Jason T. Eberl and Kevin S. Decker.

Despite all of this diversity, casting Boyega as stormtrooper FN-2187 (christened "Finn") in *The Force Awakens* raised some interesting questions regarding cultural representation in *Star Wars* – because while we'd seen TIE fighter pilots (and later Death Troopers) with black armor, we'd never seen a helmetless stormtrooper with black skin. This fact wasn't lost on Boyega, who's criticized the treatment of his character, framing his criticism (and his experience filming the sequels) through a racial lens.

For Jamaican British sociologist Stuart Hall (1932–2014), viewing Black subjects like Finn through a racial lens requires "the recognition that 'black' is essentially a politically and culturally constructed category,"[3] one rooted in "the common legacy of struggle and resistance that, as [W.E.B.] Du Bois put it, is the 'social heritage of slavery,' alongside the distinctive forms of life shaped by the subjection to a 'common disaster,' and the depth and intensity with which black expressive cultures have been formed by what [Du Bois] called 'one long memory.'"[4] If Hall and Du Bois are right, how can this lens help us see how Finn is constructed in the sequels? How does he represent the heritage/disaster/memory that Hall and Du Bois recount?

"You Do Not Know a Thing about Me"

In the prequels, clone troopers were established as clones of Jango Fett, played by Maori-descended actor Temuera Morrison in *Attack of the Clones* (who's currently Boba Fett in *The Mandalorian* and *The Book of Boba Fett*).[5] Yet, in the sequels, stormtroopers aren't grown in a cloning facility – they are taken as children and indoctrinated into the First Order. So, we not only get Boyega's Finn, we also get former stormtrooper Jannah (played by Naomi Ackie, a British actress whose family is from Grenada) and others who defected from Company 77 and settled on Kef Bir. Regardless of whether they are cloned or taken from homes, the life of a stormtrooper is forced servitude. They aren't just military troops trained to follow orders – and shoot with really bad aim – they are slaves and are treated as such. Stormtroopers are free labor and can be replaced or reconditioned; they do not have autonomy or agency. This is the legacy Finn is thrust into and it's significant – not just because Finn is the first Black stormtrooper we see, but because of what being an enslaved Black man (who was taken as a child) means outside the *Star Wars* narrative.

For example, Hall observes that racism "creates a seductive black-and-white symbolic universe," framed through the oppositions of "them and us, primitive and civilized, light and dark."[6] Seeing Finn as a Black stormtrooper recasts this symbolic opposition. On one hand, this sight creates some cognitive dissonance, especially if we consider how stormtroopers in every trilogy reference the Nazi *Sturmabteilung* known as the SA, Brown Shirts, or Storm Troopers (*Sturmtruppen*). It's difficult to picture Black men as Nazi soldiers. On the other hand, knowing that Finn was taken as a child and enslaved, his character references the Atlantic Slave Trade of the seventeenth through nineteenth centuries.

For African American writer Saidiya Hartman, "the most universal definition of the slave is a stranger."[7] This does not just describe the reality of a slave as a nonhuman living among humans in an existence that's always outside and othered. It's also the reality of how slaves are made; as Hartman observes, theirs is an origin rooted in loss, especially of their mother: "To lose your mother was to be denied your kin, country, and identity. To lose your mother was to forget your past." Hartman adds that "the history of the transatlantic slave trade" could be summed up by the recognition that slaves were not just strangers, they were orphans.[8] She notes that for fugitives of slavery, "old identities sometimes had to be jettisoned in order to invent new ones." This meant that "your life just might depend on this capacity for self-fashioning," and that "naming oneself anew was sometimes the price exacted by the practice of freedom."[9]

Finn's certainly lost whatever family he once had and he's definitely a fugitive, but it's Poe who names him. Finn accepts the name and the individual agency that goes with it – and while Finn initially lies to Rey and BB-8 that he's part of the Resistance, this is an identity he ends up legitimately embracing. As Finn, he begins a journey that transforms him from First Order Stormtrooper FN-2187 to Resistance General Finn. And since everyone in the First Order still recognizes him (albeit as a traitor!), his survival does not depend on his capacity to refashion himself. Instead, it depends on accepting his new identity and on defining that identity through his commitment to the Resistance – to the point that he becomes known to Rose not as Finn, but as "The Finn" in *The Last Jedi*.

He's "The Finn" not just because he helped the Resistance blow up Starkiller base, but because he embodies one of the most significant narrative aspects of the sequel trilogy – it's not *just* that stormtroopers are no longer cloned, it's that they are able to think for themselves.

Finn is not part of a (mostly) mindless collective, blindly following orders.[10] Rather, he's able to contemplate the morality of an order and choose not to follow it.

Sadly, this theme never really gets developed in the sequel trilogy. We do see Jannah, in *The Rise of Skywalker*, confess to disobeying an order in a way that's similar to Finn's disobedience in *The Force Awakens*. Yet the only explanation we get is that she had "a feeling," which Finn, upon reflection, attributes to "the Force." Finn, it seems – like Maz and "Broom Boy" Temiri Blagg from *The Last Jedi* – is Force-sensitive. But like everything else with Finn, this never gets fully developed.

What's paramount, though, is that Finn's conscience speaks not just to his capacity to refashion himself, it also serves as a rebuke to how Black existence has historically been framed, especially in America. As Joe R. Feagin observes, systemic racism in the United States is rooted in persistent beliefs of Black inferiority and White superiority, what Feagin calls the *white racial frame* – "the dominant racial frame that has long legitimated, rationalized, and shaped racial oppression and inequality in [America]."[11] Thus, in showing freedom of thought (or freedom of any kind), Finn claims equal status, a status that Kylo Ren acknowledges, that Rose idolizes, and that Poe (and Rey) embrace – but one that Boyega, in spite of all this, seems frustrated with.

"You Know Fuck All"

In an interview on NPR's "Fresh Air," Boyega expressed concern that the character of Finn was "bypassed," not just in the films but also in the marketing – notably, when his image was minimized in the Chinese poster for *The Force Awakens*. As Boyega notes, "I was just like, well, I'm in the movie [...] and I guess a lot of people forgot that, at the time, I was the only Black guy on the cast."[12] Or, as he put it in a *GQ* interview, "I'm the only cast member who had their own unique experience of that franchise based on their race [...] nobody else had the uproar and death threats sent to their Instagram DMs and social media, saying, 'Black this and black that and you should not be a Stormtrooper.' Nobody else had that experience."[13] As Boyega explained in comments aimed at Disney, "Like, you guys knew what to do with Daisy Ridley, you knew what to do with Adam Driver. You knew what to do with these other people, but when it came to Kelly Marie Tran, when it came to John Boyega, you know fuck all. So what do you want me to say?"[14]

Certainly, there are plenty of criticisms that could be leveled about the sequel trilogy (if not the entire *Star Wars* saga), and Boyega's take on how Finn is treated is valid – not just because Finn is initially depicted in *The Force Awakens* as a co-lead with Rey (and reduced to comic relief), but because Boyega is a solid actor whose talents, at times, are wasted. Nevertheless, while Boyega's frustration is aimed at Disney, it might also have to do with the issue of *colorism*.

"I Was Raised to Do One Thing"

Novelist and social activist Alice Walker coined and defined colorism as the "prejudicial or preferential treatment of same-race people based solely on their color," according to Kimberly Jade Norwood and Violeta Solonova Foreman.[15] For Norwood and Foreman, colorism, at root, is concerned with the lightness and darkness of skin tone, with preference given to whiteness. Historically, Nina G. Jablonski explains, "Great meaning was attached to human blackness, because black had consistently negative connotations in Indo-European languages, and darkness – such as the darkness of night – had a long standing association with evil."[16] So … in *Star Wars* … light side equals good and dark side equals … yeah, maybe Jablonski has a point, but does this really account for how Boyega's Finn has been treated? If so, is it intentional, historical, or just an unfortunate coincidence?

Colorism in the United States took root during the period of slavery, when the "coalescence of needs, beliefs, justifications, and practices had the effect of placing white skin at a premium and dehumanizing black skin."[17] Norwood and Foreman add, "These beliefs and preferences hold true today. The closer one's skin color is to white, the closer one is to being treated with elevated status."[18] This gives us an interesting take on Boyega's Finn and Ackie's Jannah, does not it? For how are we supposed to see them? Are we supposed to be surprised that they were Black stormtroopers? Is their color supposed to matter? Is it meant as a reference to slavery and slave rebellion? And given this history of servitude, is it appropriate (or maybe even racially insensitive?) that Finn and Jannah were Black stormtroopers?

While the parallels to slavery are clear, the sequel trilogy never explores how (or why) children are taken and trained to become stormtroopers in the First Order. It's not until the season one finale of *The Bad Batch* ("Kamino Lost") that we learn the Empire destroyed

Kamino and its cloning facilities, which at least explains why the First Order troopers aren't clones. Clones or not, what's key to the story is that Finn and Jannah claim their agency and an identity beyond an alphanumeric designation. Indeed, Finn and Jannah portray the humanization of the stormtrooper. They're no longer expendable clones, but unique individuals whose color should not matter.

Yet, if we laud Finn and Jannah for having the courage to claim an identity, we have to also criticize them (and every Resistance member in the sequels) for their indifferent treatment of every other stormtrooper in the sequel trilogy. Why is not one of the goals of the Resistance to assist other troopers in being freed or finding their autonomy? Why must every other stormtrooper besides Finn and Jannah be indiscriminately killed, or, for comic relief, shown to be weak-minded through Rey's use of Force abilities? And given the stunt-casting of Daniel Craig, Tom Hardy, Ed Sheeran, and Princes William and Harry (all White celebrities), how seriously are we to take the nature of stormtroopers and the issue of slavery?

"For the First Time I Have Something to Fight For"

Other than its being morally unjustifiable, slavery is problematic in *Star Wars* because of its inconsistent portrayal within the narrative. In general, it's all but ignored, even by the Jedi. So when it surfaces (whether in droids, humans, or clones) there is not any clear message. Droids are bought and sold, Clones are indiscriminately killed, and humans like Anakin are freed, but not his mother. L3-37 leads a revolt and Finn and Jannah escape, but slave rebellion is not the type of rebellion *Star Wars* is about.[19] This is what makes Finn (and later Jannah) perhaps the most interesting and compelling characters of the sequel trilogy – and the most wasted in terms of narrative potential, as Boyega observes.

Ironically, Finn's story is more of an "awakening" than Rey's, especially when she finds she's not Luke's daughter. Rey seems to be clearly positioned as Luke's daughter in *The Force Awakens*, but she's retconned to being "no one" in *The Last Jedi*, until she's retconned yet again to being Palpatine's granddaughter in *The Rise of Skywalker*. This is not interesting, it does not subvert expectations: it's lazy writing. Finn, as a stormtrooper who escapes the First Order and joins the Resistance is arguably a better (and more timely) story – or at least it was in *The Force Awakens*, because in *The Last Jedi*, Finn becomes inconsequential, as Boyega contends. Rose may refer to him as "The

Finn," yet he does not really seem to have a place in the Resistance (other than being a living encyclopedia of First Order knowledge) until he meets Jannah in *The Rise of Skywalker*. Still, his role in all three sequel films often drifts into comic relief – which, at times, borders on what's called "the minstrel stereotype."

"I'm the Guy that Used to Mop It"

Jennifer Bloomquist writes that there is "a protracted history of Whites creating Black caricatures," which includes "underdeveloped Black characters" in American entertainment.[20] As Bloomquist explains, entertainers known as "Ethiopian delineators" were "all-White, all-male casts in blackface," adding that the "comedy hinged on gross misrepresentations of what the actors determined to be (southern) Black culture, including singing, dancing, and delivering comedic speeches."[21] As Bloomquist notes, these shows were not only based on stereotypes, they were also used "as a tool to further malign Blacks and to promote justifications for slavery."[22] Among the archetypes developed in such shows are "Zip Coon, Jim Crow, Uncle Tom, and Sambo," but the most potent weapon minstrel shows utilized to "demoralize, dehumanize, and subjugate Blacks" is so-called "Black language."[23]

To be fair, Finn is not dancing, singing, or delivering comedic speeches (though he does have some comedic dialogue) and he does not speak in a "negro dialect" or appear to be a caricature or stereotype. However, Finn *could* be seen as resembling an "Uncle Tom," especially as defined by Folklorist Patricia A. Turner. She views "Tom" as "having a supposed identification with his masters/employers and ... contempt for his own (black) kind ... (having) racial self-hate ... willing to 'sell out' blacks in order to placate whites and improve his personal well-being."[24] Is it a stretch that Finn is selling out First Order stormtroopers? That the stormtroopers who call him a "traitor" might as well be calling him an "Uncle Tom"? As for Finn's speech, it's worth noting that Boyega adopted an American accent rather than use his native British accent. Why cannot Finn speak with the same "received pronunciation" as Rey or Jannah?[25] Much ado was made about Rey speaking in a British accent (with initial fan theories suggesting she was related to Obi-Wan), yet her accent does not make sense on Jakku and Finn's does not make sense in the First Order either.

As Bloomquist notes, the so-called "negro dialect" was exaggerated in minstrelsy "in an attempt to underscore widely held White beliefs about Black intelligence, integrity, and morality."[26] Included in this is the depiction of Black men as "always sexually preoccupied," especially with White women. Finn is certainly enamored with Rey – to the point that it drives his narrative decisions in all three sequel films. Does this make Finn some sort of Mandingo stereotype who cannot control his urges for Rey? And consider how Rose, after calling Finn a hero, quickly turns to assuming he's a coward trying to escape. Or how Finn, especially in *The Last Jedi*, gets negated by Rose throughout the narrative. Being "The Finn" is not enough to give him the benefit of the doubt and speaking in an American accent perhaps makes it easier not to take him seriously. If so, is Finn the victim of linguistic racism?

Most heroic characters in *Star Wars* (Luke, Han, Lando, Mace, Poe, Anakin) speak in American accents. So, there's nothing inherently wrong or racist in having Finn speak in an American accent. Still, if Jannah could keep her British accent (which makes narrative sense) why could not Finn? Other than not wanting Rey and Finn to talk like two Brits in *The Force Awakens* (for American audiences' sake?), there's no good narrative reason. It might not be racist or an intentional effort to deny Finn any privilege that White characters enjoy. Yet, when taken into the fuller account of Finn's narrative, it at least seems like another missed opportunity to develop his character.

"I'm in Charge Now, Phasma, *I'm* in Charge!"

Ultimately, Boyega's concerns about Finn seem justified. Yet, Boyega overlooks the presence of culture and the representation of other races and ethnicities throughout the *Star Wars* films and even throughout the various television series. It's unfortunate that Boyega had such a negative experience, as Finn is a heroic, admirable character. It's also unfortunate that the sequel trilogy (especially *The Last Jedi*) squandered the opportunity to develop what could've been a more significant character and narrative. Yet, with shows like *The Mandalorian*, *Ahsoka*, *Andor*, and *The Book of Boba Fett* – which all feature prominent actors and characters of color – it seems like Disney might have heard Boyega's criticism and reacted. All they need now is a series that focuses on Finn and Jannah traveling through the galaxy helping First Order troopers reunite with the families they have lost. Maybe this could be the basis for a genuinely new order throughout the galaxy, one that remembers the horrors of slavery and makes sure that it never happens again – to humans, nonhumans, and droids.

Notes

1 Also Hispanic actor Jimmy Smits (of Puerto Rican and Surinamese descent) made his Bail Organa character (the "dad" of Princess Leia!) notable in the prequel trilogy and *Rogue One*.

2 For example, in *The Mandalorian*, aside from Morrison's Fett, the title character of Mando is played by Chilean American actor Pedro Pascal, and features African American actor Carl Weathers, Chinese American actress Ming-Na Wen, and Rosario Dawson, of Puerto Rican and Afro-Cuban descent.

3 Stuart Hall, *The Fateful Triangle: Race, Ethnicity, Nation* (Cambridge: Harvard University Press, 2017), 76.

4 Ibid., 77.

5 It's also worth noting that fellow Maori Keisha Castle-Hughes was featured in *Revenge of the Sith* as Queen Apailana.

6 Hall, *The Fateful Triangle*, 71.

7 Saidiya Hartman, *Lose Your Mother: A Journey Along the Atlantic Slave Route* (New York: Farrar, Straus and Giroux, 2007), 5.

8 Hartman uses the African word *obruni* ("stranger"), and as Hartman notes: "The domain of the stranger is always an elusive *elsewhere*." Hartman, *Lose Your Mother*, 4, 85.

9 Ibid., 234.

10 To be fair, this generalization about clone troopers does not apply in every instance, as witnessed throughout the *Clone Wars*, *Rebels*, and *The Bad Batch* animated series. For discussion of clone troopers' individual personalities and moral identities, see Patricia Brace's and Tim Challans's chapters in this volume (chapters 8 and 5, respectively).

11 Joe R. Feagin, *The White Racial Frame: Centuries of Racial Framing and Counter-Framing*, 2e (New York: Routledge, 2013), x.

12 Sam Sanders, "Actor John Boyega on 'Star Wars', 'Small Axe', and Telling 'Stories of the Untold.'" http://NPR.org, May 19, 2021, at https://www.npr.org/2021/05/19/998219668/actor-john-boyega-on-star-wars-small-axe-and-telling-stories-of-the-untold.

13 Jimi Famurewa, "John Boyega: 'I'm the Only Cast Member Whose Experience of Star Wars Was Based on Their Race,'" http://GQ.com, September 2, 2020, at https://www.gq-magazine.co.uk/culture/article/john-boyega-interview-2020.

14 Ibid.

15 Kimberly Jade Norwood and Violeta Solonova Foreman, "The Ubiquitousness of Colorism: Then and Now," in Kimberly Jade Norwood, ed., *Color Matters: Skin Tone Bias and the Myth of a Post-Racial America* (New York: Routledge, 2014), 9.

16 Nina G. Jablonski, *Living Color: The Biological and Social Meaning of Skin Color* (Berkeley: University of California Press, 2012), 136.

17 Norwood and Foreman, "The Ubitquitousness of Colorism," 15.
18 Ibid., 15.
19 For further discussion of L3-37's droid revolt, see Joshua Jowitt's chapter in this volume (Chapter 16).
20 Jennifer Bloomquist, "The Minstrel Legacy: African American English and the Historical Construction of 'Black' Identities in Entertainment," *Journal of African American Studies* 19.4 (2015), 411.
21 Ibid., 411.
22 Ibid., 411.
23 Ibid., 413.
24 Patricia A. Turner, *Ceramic Uncles and Celluloid Mammies: Black Images and Their Influence on Culture* (Charlottesville: University of Virginia Press, 2002), 69.
25 Or Emilia Clarke's Qi'ra, Paul Bettany's Dryden Vos, Phoebe Waller-Bridge's L3-37, Felicity Jones's Jyn Erso, most of the Death Star personnel, most of the First Order personnel, and C-3PO.
26 Bloomquist, "The Minstrel Legacy," 413.

27

The Last Jedi's Despair: Did Episode VIII Ruin Luke Skywalker?

David Kyle Johnson

That's how we are gonna win. Not fighting what we hate. Saving what we love.

—Rose Tico, *The Last Jedi*

Some fans have suggested that the titles of the Skywalker Saga films are in the wrong order. *Episode IV: A New Hope* should've been "Return of the Jedi" – since the Jedi begin to make their return after being all but wiped out. *Episode VI: Return of the Jedi* should've been "The Last Jedi" – since, once Yoda dies, Luke is the last living Jedi. And *Episode VIII: The Last Jedi* should've been "A New Hope" – since Luke's sacrifice in his battle with Kylo gives Rey and The Resistance a new hope in their struggle against the First Order. As Poe puts it, "He's doing this for a reason. He's stalling so we can escape. … We are the spark that'll light the fire that will burn the First Order down. Skywalker's doing this so we can survive."

But *The Last Jedi*'s title is far from its most controversial aspect. Consider how Luke Skywalker is portrayed. He's a recluse who's seemingly given up hope, tossing aside Anakin's lightsaber and calling for the Jedi to end. This seems to betray Luke's character. As Mark Hamill himself put it to *The Last Jedi* (*TLJ*)'s director Rian Johnson, "I fundamentally disagree with virtually everything you have decided for my character."[1] Many fans echoed Hamill, thinking this character change came out of left field. *Medium* writer Joseph Choi said that *TLJ*'s Luke

Star Wars and Philosophy Strikes Back: This is the Way, First Edition.
Edited by Jason T. Eberl and Kevin S. Decker.

was "a terrified and cowardly old man committed to dying alone wallowing in regret ... a big middle finger to anyone who grew up believing in Luke Skywalker."[2] Indeed, many fans said *TLJ* ruined Luke Skywalker.[3]

Did it really? Or was *TLJ*'s depiction of Luke not only predictable, but spot on? Maybe, far from ruining anything, it helped make *The Last Jedi* (as Mark Hamill eventually admitted) "the most sophisticated Star Wars movie since *Empire*."[4]

We Should Have Seen It Coming

Before the release of *TLJ*, David Goodner, at the website *Waging Nonviolence*, said "It would ... betray his character arc, if Luke Skywalker became anything other than a staunch pacifist in *The Last Jedi*."[5] Why? Think about what happens at the end of *Return of the Jedi* (*ROTJ*). Emperor Palpatine tells Luke that acting violently is the way to the dark side: "Take your weapon. Strike me down with all of your hatred, and your journey towards the dark side will be complete." He's delighted as Luke fights Vader, especially when Luke goes on the offense. It's only once Luke rejects violence, and literally *throws away his lightsaber*, that he becomes a Jedi and gains his victory. This was the culmination of Luke's character arc, nearly the last thing we saw him do in the original trilogy. Before, he used violence, but now he's like older Obi-Wan, who for the most part used nonviolent methods (e.g. mind tricks and distractions) to achieve his goals. Everyone wondered how Luke would react to being offered his lightsaber by Rey at the end of *The Force Awakens* (*TFA*). But we should've expected him to throw it away – just like he did before – and to eventually, nonviolently, sacrifice himself, just like Obi-Wan did in *A New Hope* (*ANH*).

In *TLJ* however, Luke is not only a pacifist; he's rejected the way of the Jedi, even calling for the Jedi Order to end. Could we have seen *this* coming? I did, in January 2016, after watching *TFA*.[6] How? In *TFA*, Han clarifies that Luke "...was training a new generation of Jedi. One boy, an apprentice turned against him, destroyed it all. Luke felt responsible ... He walked away from everything. The people who knew him the best think he went looking for the first Jedi temple."

To defeat that apprentice – Ben Solo/Kylo Ren – Luke wasn't going to train more Jedi, since they might turn just as easily as did Ben. But why did not Luke, as he put it in *TLJ*, "walk out with a laser sword and face down the whole First Order?" Because that would probably just make things worse.

Something that struck me about *TFA* was how, over the time since *ROTJ*, the Force and the Jedi had become myths, something that not even Rey thought was real. In the prequels, the Jedi were so established, and their abilities so obvious, that Force-use was more like a science. But since the fall of the Empire – really since its inception – the Force and Force powers were relegated to the status of myth. Consider how those around Vader reacted to him in *ANH*: "Do not try to frighten us with your sorcerer's ways, Lord Vader. Your sad devotion to that ancient religion..." And that's what it is: a religion. That's why Vader finds their "lack of *faith* disturbing." The Jedi Order is a religious order – as is the Sith. And this is especially true at the beginning of the sequels, where those who believe in the Force, like Lor San Tekka, do so without any evidence – by faith.

But this means that all the chaos and bloodshed we saw in the prequels, and even the original trilogy, was a result of two religious factions bidding and fighting for political power. The Clone Wars, Order 66, the creation of the Empire, the destruction of Alderaan, a Super Star Destroyer, and two Death Stars – all of this due to one religious faction running the show while the other one wanted to.

This is reminiscent of how religions fought for political power in seventeenth-century England. Then, the Church of England was in power, but the Puritans wanted to take over the government in the name of what they saw as God's will. To do so, Oliver Cromwell called for the head of Charles I (and got it) and a bloody civil war ensued. When Cromwell died a decade later, the resulting power vacuum led to even more violence. Things eventually resolved, but not before another rebellion and a couple more exchanges of power. Religious factions fighting for political power produce a lot of war and bloodshed.

Witnessing such events inspired Thomas Hobbes (1588–1679) and John Locke (1632–1704) to write prolifically on the role of government and religion's relationship to it. Hobbes (loyal to the Crown and the Church of England) argues in *Leviathan* that, to prevent religious wars, the sovereign (the King or government) should choose a religion (it does not matter which one) and impose it on everyone with an iron fist.[7] This might not be ideal – what if the "wrong" religion is imposed? But it's preferable to the bloody alternative.

In his *Two Treatises of Government*, Locke argues for a better solution: a separation of religious and political power.[8] Religion should be a private affair; politics and government should be a secular (nonreligious) matter. If religion is mixed with government, a fight for power between religious groups is inevitable. And since religious matters cannot be settled by reason and argument, they can only be settled by violence. So we'd all be better off if religion had nothing to do with government. No religious belief should be outlawed, Locke argues, unless it's violent or endangers the life, liberty, or property of others – but it should remain something that individuals choose. It's not something that should be imposed through political power. Locke's work inspired the United States' founding fathers (as Thomas Jefferson puts it) to erect a "wall of separation" between religion and government.[9]

After watching *TFA* and learning about Luke's self-imposed exile, I wondered whether Luke had concluded something similar. The Jedi and Sith fighting for power cost the galaxy billions of lives. Maybe, like Locke, Luke concluded that we'd be better off if devotion to the Force was merely a matter of private conscience – if neither the Jedi nor the Sith had anything to do with government. So he resolved to make his Jedi devotion a merely private affair. Or maybe, like Hobbes, Luke concluded that it does not matter which religious faction is in charge, as long as none are fighting for power. It's not ideal, but the Sith imposing their version of order on the galaxy might be preferable to the chaos of trying to overthrow them in the name of the Jedi.

It seems I wasn't that far off. Consider Luke's words from the film's novelization (that echo what he says in the film):

> If you strip away the myth and look at their deeds, from the birth of the Sith to the fall of the Republic the legacy of the Jedi is failure. Hypocrisy. Hubris ... At the height of their powers they allowed Darth Sidious to rise, create the Empire, and wipe them out ... it was a Jedi Master who was responsible for the training and creation of Darth Vader ... [After Vader and Palpatine died] [f]or years there was balance. I took no Padawans, and no darkness rose. But then I saw Ben, my nephew ... In my hubris I thought I could train him...[10]

We all know how that worked out and perhaps can understand why Luke thought it time for the Jedi Order to die.

Guilt by Association (with the Jedi)

In fact, Luke may have taken it a step further. In 2017, I wrote about the question of guilt by association – the moral culpability that goes along with group membership.[11] This is different that the ad hominem logical fallacy "guilt by association," where a person's argument is dismissed because of a similarity they share with another (bad) person.

The question I am concerned with is, if a group you belong to acts in ways that are morally wrong, must you leave that group if you do not want to be somewhat guilty of the atrocities yourself – even if you yourself did not perform them? After all, isn't such a fear of "guilt by association" why many lifelong Republicans left the Republican party before and after Trump's presidency? Isn't this why people left the Catholic Church in the wake of the child sexual abuse scandal?

This question seems especially acute for religious affiliation. If a Muslim concludes that Islam is sexist, are they obligated to reject the faith or be guilty of sexism themself? What level of culpability do you have as a Hindu, who promotes the idea that cows are sacred, for those who beat Muslims to death because they eat beef?[12] Such questions do not have easy answers, and it's probably a matter of degree. Someone who believes that God exists but does not belong to any specific religion does not share as much culpability as, say, someone who belongs to the Westboro Baptist Church (the "God Hates Fags" people who protest military funerals and Jedi-worshipping comic-cons). But an atheist, who openly renounces belief in God, does not bear any guilt by association for moral crimes done in God's name.[13]

According to the novelization of *TLJ*, Luke sought out the Jedi texts, not to study them but to destroy them; he just had not been able to bring himself to do it. He was contemplating his last failure to do so when Rey arrived at Ahch-To. So it seems not only that Luke wants to avoid guilt by association by renouncing the Jedi, but also that – like many who leave their religious faith in the wake of realizing how much damage it has done – he's actively trying to tear it down. Sure, religion does some good – it inspires charity and love in some and comforts others. But it's also responsible for three Crusades, the Inquisition, the Salem witch trials, 9/11, countless jihads, the KKK, the Thirty Years War, Manifest Destiny (i.e. the slaughter of Native Americans), the French Religious Wars, the Armenian genocide, the aforementioned English civil wars, abortion clinic bombings, and it contributed to the Holocaust – and these are just events in the Middle East and the West. We could begin an Eastern list with the Thuggee murders and Buddhist atrocities against Rohingya Muslims in Myanmar. Religion: many would argue that we'd be better off without it. Similarly, Luke could argue, would not the galaxy be better off if the Force, the Sith, and the Jedi remained a matter of myth and legend? And this, perhaps, is why Hamill concluded that *TLJ* is so sophisticated: it's the first film to entertain the notion that the Jedi are anything but perfect saints.

Luke Skywalker: Pacifist

So far, we have seen where Luke's head is at the beginning of *TLJ* – why he does not immediately jump at the opportunity to fly off and help Rey the moment she arrives. But he's eventually spurred into action. Does this mean he changed his mind and abandoned his previous views? About the Jedi, yes – it seems so. As he gladly tells Kylo, during their battle on Crait, "I will not be the last Jedi." Maybe he concludes the Jedi do more good than harm after all. But about his pacifism, it seems not; his response to the threat of Kylo and the First Order was truly that of a pacifist.

To understand why, it will be important to understand a bit more about pacifism and the varieties in which it can come. Absolute pacifism is the idea that all violence and war is morally unjustified and thus should be avoided at all costs. Now, some pacifists are not absolutists; some are opposed to war but think that personal violence can, sometimes, be justified – like in self-defense. But among the absolutists, there are different camps. There are *deontological* pacifists who think that violence and war are never justified, in principle, regardless of the consequences. For them, nonviolence is a moral duty. And then there are *consequentialist* pacifists who think violence should always be avoided because it always makes matters worse. If violence caused more benefit than harm, it would be justified – but it just never does. And this latter view, it seems, describes *TLJ*'s Luke Skywalker.

To understand Luke's position, it's important to understand that (contrary to popular opinion) pacifism is not a call to inaction; when something wrong occurs that could be stopped by violence, the pacifist is not obligated to stand around and do nothing. Especially when it's an act of violence, the pacifist is obligated to stop it. To do so, though, they must take nonviolent action. For a deontological pacifist, this is because violence is always inherently wrong. For a consequentialist pacifist like Luke, it's because violent action always makes matters worse.[14]

This tracks with a very common pacifist argument against war. Think about the Korean and Vietnam Wars. They were fought mainly because of Truman and Eisenhower's "domino theory" – the idea that, once one capitalist society fell to communism, they all would. But not only did preventing North Korea from "communizing" South Korea not prevent North Vietnam from trying the same thing with South Vietnam, the later failure to prevent Vietnam from becoming a communist country had very little long-term negative effect. Not only did it not lead to a domino effect of capitalist nations turning communist, but Vietnam is now a peaceful nation in good standing with the United Nations. They have an embassy in Washington, DC, and the United States has one in Hanoi.

In making this argument, the pacifist is not saying that communism is a better system than capitalism, or that South Koreans would've been better off under communism. Instead, the suggestion is that Korea (and the world) as a whole would've been better off, all things considered, had military action never been taken in Korea at all. And if this is true, that would've left Korea communist. Whatever benefits South Korea has seen under capitalism, the consequentialist pacifist thinks these aren't enough to justify the horrors of the Korean War; Korea would now likely be no worse off than Vietnam or China.

While the pacifist might be right about Korea or Vietnam, complete absolute pacifism is difficult to defend in all circumstances. Take World War II. "A nonviolent movement," President Obama once pointed out, "could not have halted Hitler's armies."[15] Nevertheless, Luke seems to be a consequentialist pacifist in *TLJ*, right to the bitter end. Think of how he defeats Kylo Ren. He does something that cannot possibly be violent: he appears as a "Force projection" that cannot touch Kylo – only distract him. This is the quintessential example of a proactive, nonviolent action that stops a violent one. Indeed, if Luke's view changed at all over the course of the film, it was in rejecting the misconception that pacifism called him to inaction, and instead realizing that it called him to action of the nonviolent type.

A Novel Pacifism

Defenses of pacifism are overt in the novelization of *TLJ*. Consider what Poe thinks to himself after Finn demands that they go out and help Luke in his fight against Kylo:

> Was this the same Finn who'd insisted he wasn't here to join another army? And not so long ago, he [Poe] would have reacted the same way – looking for anything he could fly and blasting off across the plains. But he'd learned there were other ways to fight – and that those who chose them were not less brave.[16]

The novel opens with Luke having a dream about what his life would've been like had he never gotten involved (in *ANH*). He lives on Tatooine, married to a woman named Camie, managing his uncle Owen and aunt Beru's moisture farm (who both got to live a full life).

The galaxy is "at peace" under Imperial rule, and he lives a perfectly contented life.[17]

Later, Luke tells Rey that sailing ships have arrived on the island of Ahch-To for their monthly raid on the caretaker's village. When she demands they spring to action, Luke says,

> Do you know what a true Jedi would do right now? Nothing. If you meet the raiding party with Force, they'll be back next month – with greater numbers and greater violence. Will you be here next month? [...] That burn inside you, that anger thinking what the raiders are going to do? The books in the Jedi library say ignore that. Only act when you can maintain balance. Even if people get hurt.[18]

As is also revealed in the deleted scene shot for the film, it turns out the "raid" is actually a monthly feast – which is perhaps what the monthly raids turned into over time, in the absence of a violent response. Luke's philosophy, it seems, was best captured by Rose, after she saved Finn from sacrificing himself: "That's how we are gonna win. Not fighting what we hate. Saving what we love."

The Last Jedi: A New Hope

Ultimately, Mark Hamill, after conversations with director Rian Johnson, agreed with Johnson's take on Luke: "I was surprised at how he saw Luke. And it took me a while to get around to his way of thinking, but once I was there it was a thrilling experience. I hope it will be for the audience too."[19] Interestingly, the idea that Luke would question – in his old age – the violent role that he and the Rebellion played in the Empire's demise is not contrary to the vision of the original creator of *Star Wars*, George Lucas. According to Peter Sciretta at Slash Film, the story that Lucas pitched to Disney for Episode VII was one where "30 years after the fall of the Empire, Luke had gone to a dark place and secluded himself in a Jedi temple on a new planet ... meditating, reassessing his whole life."[20]

And this is perhaps the best reason for retitling Episode VIII "A New Hope." Luke gives the Resistance a new hope not only by sacrificing himself, but also by showing Rey a different way to be a Jedi. Granted, it takes her a while; she goes on the violent offensive quite a few times early on in Episode IX, but every time it's clear that she's acting, wrongly, in anger – like Luke did. In her battle with Palpatine, however, her combat moves are mainly defensive – only deflecting and dodging blaster bolts to let the Emperor's guards kill each other, and repelling the Emperor's Force lightning back at him while Palpatine wants her to kill him in anger. That Rey, by the end, is a new kind of Jedi is symbolized by the color of her lightsaber: "yellow optimism."[21]

Of course, at the end of Episode IX, the Resistance wins the day with an impressive show of violence. This, perhaps, highlights the objection to pacifism that those who are pacifists only have the freedom to be such because of the efforts of those who act violently. At the same time, however, we have to wonder whether the victory earned by the Resistance will be as short-lived as the Rebellion's victory in *ANH* or even *ROTJ*. How often does violence actually make things better? We're told that it does – that it's often necessary – but Palpatine also told Anakin that resurrecting the dead was a dark side ability; Episode IX taught us it comes from the light. Perhaps those in power – like the Canto Bight elite – who profit from violence are manipulating us just like Palpatine manipulated Anakin. Perhaps that's also what those who say "*TLJ* ruined Luke Skywalker by making him nonviolent" are doing. Instead, I suggest that Luke's growth as a character into a pacifist, one who recognizes the real consequences of violence, solidifies his status as the definitive guardian of peace and justice. Perhaps Luke Skywalker is not the last Jedi, but the ultimate Jedi.

Notes

1 Christopher Hooton, "The Last Jedi: Mark Hamill 'Fundamentally Disagrees with Virtually Everything' Written for His Character," *Independent*, April 20, 2017, at www.independent.co.uk/arts-entertainment/films/news/last-jedi-plot-luke-skywalker-script-mark-hamill-jedi-a7692386.html"www.independent.co.uk/arts-entertainment/films/news/last-jedi-plot-luke-skywalker-script-mark-hamill-jedi-a7692386.html.

2 Joseph Choi, "The Last Jedi: On the Character Assassination of Luke Skywalker," *Medium*, December 17, 2017, at https://medium.com/@josvchoi/the-last-jedi-on-the-character-assassination-of-luke-skywalker-38fe0190d01a.

3 David Kyle Johnson, "The Greatest Teacher, Failure is." Why Hate the Last Jedi? *Psychology Today*, March 27, 2018, at https://www.psychologytoday.com/us/blog/plato-pop/201803/the-greatest-teacher-failure-is-why-hate-the-last-jedi.

4 Eric Kohn and Jenna Marotta, "Mark Hamill Says Luke Skywalker Was 'Demoralized' in New Doc About 'The Last Jedi' Production," *Indie Wire,* March 13, 2018, at https://www.indiewire.com/2018/03/mark-hamill-the-last-jedi-demoralized-the-last-jedi-sxsw-2018-1201938578.

5 David Goodner, "Will 'The Last Jedi' Betray Luke Skywalker's Turn Toward Nonviolence?" *Waging Nonviolence*, December 8, 2017, at https://wagingnonviolence.org/2017/12/will-last-jedi-make-luke-skywalker-reject-turn-toward-nonviolence/#:~:text=But%20his%20refusal%20to%20kill,in%20%E2%80%9CThe%20Last%20Jedi.%E2%80%9D.

6 David Kyle Johnson, "Star Wars: Answering the Big Questions," *Psychology Today*, January 27, 2016, at https://www.psychologytoday.com/us/blog/plato-pop/201601/star-wars-answering-the-big-questions.

7 Thomas Hobbes, *Leviathan: Revised Student Edition*, ed. Richard Tuck (Cambridge: Cambridge University Press, 1996).

8 John Locke, *Two Treatises of Government*, ed. Peter Laslett (Cambridge: Cambridge University Press, 1988).

9 "Jefferson's Letter to the Danbury Baptists, The Final Letter, as Sent," Library of Congress, at http://loc.gov/loc/lcib/9806/danpre.html.

10 Jason Fry, *The Last Jedi* (New York: Del Rey, 2018), 146–147.

11 David Kyle Johnson, "Moral Culpability and Choosing to Believe in God," in B. Anderson, ed., *Atheism and the Christian Faith* (Wilmington, DE: Vernon Press, 2017), 11–32.

12 "Hindu Mob Kills Muslim Man after Rumours He Was Eating Beef," *The Guardian*, September 30, 2015, at https://www.theguardian.com/world/2015/sep/30/hindu-mob-kills-muslim-man-eating-beef.

13 Whether the atheist bears moral responsibility for evil done by atheist nation states is an issue I address in my 2017 chapter on moral culpability – see note above.

14 Because there are two kinds of utilitarianism, act and rule, there would be two kinds of such pacifism. One would say that acts of violence always lead to worse consequences; the other would say that acts of violence, on the whole, or "in general," make matters worse (and thus that all acts of violence are unjustified, even if certain ones would lead to more good than harm). It's not clear to me which version Luke is in *TLJ*.

15 Barack Obama, "Barack Obama Receives Nobel Peace Prize: Speech in Full," *Telegraph*, December 10, 2009, at www.telegraph.co.uk/news/worldnews/barackobama/6780104/Barack-Obama-receives-Nobel-Peace-Prize-speech-in-full.html.

16 Fry, *The Last Jedi*, 298.

17 It should be noted, however, that in the dream, to establish this "peace," the Empire destroyed not only Alderaan, but Mon Cala and Chandrilla. (Is that worse than what the Rebellion and Resistance did to topple the Empire and First Order? I'll leave that up to you.)

18 Fry, *The Last Jedi*, 148.

19 Dirk Libbey, "What Mark Hamill Really Meant When He Criticized Luke Skywalker's Direction," *Cinema Blend,* June 16, 2017, at https://www.cinemablend.com/news/1671010/what-mark-hamill-really-meant-when-he-criticized-luke-skywalkers-direction.

20 Peter Sciretta, "Our Only Look at George Lucas' Vision for the 'Star Wars' Sequel Trilogy," *Slashfilm*, December 19, 2017, at https://www.slashfilm.com/george-lucas-sequel-trilogy.

21 Kirsten Acuna, "The 'Star Wars: The Rise of Skywalker' Visual Effects Team Describe Rey's New Lightsaber and the Small Detail You May Have Missed in It," *Insider,* January 7, 2020, at https://www.insider.com/star-wars-the-rise-of-skywalker-rey-new-lightsaber-explained-2020-1.

28

Deleuze, the Force of Becoming, and *The Last Jedi*

Corry Shores

Who's the *real* Luke Skywalker? Rian Johnson, director of *The Last Jedi* (*TLJ*), raised that question for *Star Wars* audiences, resulting in a heated debate among fans. Prior to the sequel trilogy, filmgoers saw Luke grow from a whiney farm boy in *A New Hope* (*ANH*) to a formidable Jedi Knight in *Return of the Jedi* (*ROTJ*). He played a major role in overthrowing the Empire, defeating one of the most powerful Force-wielders that the galaxy ever saw – his father, Anakin – turning this committed Sith back to the light side. He was also charged with a cosmically important mission by his dying master, Yoda. As the last of the Jedi, Luke must now pass on what he has learned of the Force, presumably to restart the Jedi Order. In the imaginations of many, Luke simply *must* have continued his rise, becoming one of the most powerful living beings in the universe.[1] Yet, the Luke of *TLJ*, more than 30 years older, appears at first as a broken, cynical coward, hidden away after his Jedi training temple was destroyed, all while the First Order begins taking over the galaxy in his absence. To the shock of many fans, Luke had given up on the Force altogether, proclaiming: "I will never train another generation of Jedi. I came to this island to die. It's time for the Jedi to end." Mark Hamill, who for many has become synonymous with the Luke character he plays, reports confronting Johnson about these very lines, telling him that "Luke was the most optimistic, hopeful character. [...] A Jedi does not give up!"[2] Hamill even came to think of his character as no longer "Luke" but rather as some other, "Jake" Skywalker.[3]

Is it possible that Hamill, along with the many fans who share his views, may not have seen the greatness of Johnson's Luke? We'll try

Star Wars and Philosophy Strikes Back: This is the Way, First Edition.
Edited by Jason T. Eberl and Kevin S. Decker.

(despite Yoda's contrary teaching) to answer this question by considering Gilles Deleuze's (1925–1995) notion of the *forces of becoming* to see that, perhaps, Luke bore a power even greater than the Force itself, namely, the ability to drastically self-deform and *become-other*.

A Tale of Two Lukes

To characterize the different sides in this debate, let us consider the arguments made by some of its strongest voices: Niatoos Dadbeh of the YouTube channel *Star Wars Theory*, on the one hand, and Zak Koonce and Craven Moorhaus of the *Auralnauts Podcast*, on the other. Like Hamill, Dadbeh strongly believes that the Luke of the original trilogy is an entirely different person altogether from the one in *TLJ*. He says that certain (now non-canon) novels and comics written after *ROTJ* had Luke "create a Jedi temple, and he became this *unbelievably super-powerful* being." For this reason, Luke served as a "beacon of hope" and empowerment for many fans who found inspiration in his great ability to overcome adversity.[4] Johnson then at least mischaracterizes the Luke character that fans came to know following the original trilogy. But even worse, Dadbeh accuses Johnson of failing to uphold his "moral responsibility" to continue this known arc, as it does such incredible damage to fans' emotional relationship with their beloved character.[5] Dadbeh also thinks that Luke's final act of Force projection in *TLJ*, when he confronts Kylo Ren as no more than a mirage cast light-years across the galaxy, was simply a pathetic effort, as it ultimately killed Luke when instead he could've flown to the planet to defeat Kylo in person.[6]

Koonce and Moorhaus, however, found Johnson's portrayal of a broken Luke to be his best possible development, given his particular background in the original trilogy. Also key is the storyline laid out in *The Force Awakens*, where Han reported that Luke "just walked away from everything" after Kylo crushed his hopes to revive the Jedi Order. They argue that Luke's character progression in *TLJ* is entirely consistent with the original trilogy version of Luke, who started his Jedi training much too late in his life. In fact, he never even properly finished it, because doing so required that he confront Vader. Yet Luke was only able to defeat him by acting, *not like a Jedi*, but with an intense, burning fury drawing from the dark side. They also note that Luke was never really portrayed as a great master of the Force in the original trilogy, but much more like an undisciplined amateur. So, there's no basis in the films to expect Luke to become an ultra-powerful being who could single-handedly restart the whole Jedi Order. Frankly, at the time of Yoda's death, Luke wasn't an especially promising Jedi, just the last one available.[7]

Koonce and Moorhaus also point out that Luke's flight into hiding was hardly unprecedented for a Jedi master. The only two Jedi he ever knew, Obi-Wan and Yoda, both did exactly the same thing, all while the Empire rose in power. Yoda himself even says in *Revenge of the Sith*, after being bested by Palpatine, "Into exile, I must go. Failed, I have." Beyond this, as Luke learned more about Jedi history, including their corruption and inability to prevent the Empire's rise despite drastically outnumbering their Sith opposition, he became disillusioned with the Jedi Order itself and had legitimate questions about whether it was worth rekindling. Koonce and Moorhaus thus conclude that Johnson's Luke perfectly follows his given trajectory. They also believe, contrary to Dadbeh, that Luke's Force projection in his final battle with Kylo is one of the most potent Jedi feats ever shown in the films. Not only is it so great a task as to prove lethal to Luke, it also holds true to the Jedi virtue that the less one actually engages in physical combat – while yet still prevailing – the better.[8]

Koonce and Moorhaus's observations form a strong case for portraying Luke at this stage in his life as beaten down and disillusioned. At the same time, it's also perfectly conceivable that Luke's life could've gone in the opposite direction – one that Dadbeh envisioned and as depicted in the post-*ROTJ* "Legends" novels, with him becoming incredibly powerful and hopeful. Neither of these paths is exclusively authentic to Luke; *both* are equally possible outcomes of his development. If there's one thing that characterizes the Luke of the original trilogy, it's that he demonstrates these highly divergent tendencies. In *ANH*, he's a hopeless and weak farm boy whining about Tosche Station but *also* the hero of the Trench Run who uses the Force to destroy the Death Star. In *The Empire Strikes Back*, he's the headstrong underdog who stands up to Vader while *also* being the discouraged quitter who gives up on raising the X-Wing. And in *ROTJ*, we see him using his greatly advanced Jedi skills and composure to rescue Han but also later hiding from Vader during their climactic battle, only emerging when he loses control of his aggressive emotions. So, if there's anything we might say to characterize Luke Skywalker, it's that he has a remarkable capacity for self-variance. His arc does not follow a straight line like Han's development from selfish smuggler to altruistic general to sacrificial father;

instead, it erratically shifts between his potentials at various moments. How are we to understand such an inconsistent Luke?

The Tensions that Bind Us

To answer this question, we should take a closer look at the Force. Yoda teaches Luke that "Life creates it, makes it grow. Its energy surrounds us and binds us," and that it lies "between you, me, the tree, the rock, everywhere." Similarly, Luke tells Rey that the Force is "the energy between all things, a tension, a balance, that binds the universe together." Deleuze's idea of "force" is not too dissimilar from this, although it has a slightly different way of operating, because it effects a different kind of change.

Deleuze draws his notion of the *forces of becoming* partly from German philosopher Friedrich Nietzsche (1844–1900), who says that the world is "a monster of energy, without beginning, without end" that "only transforms itself" as "a play of forces and waves of forces … a sea of forces flowing and rushing together, eternally changing … with an ebb and a flood of its forms." This "eternally self-creating," "eternally self-destroying" world, Nietzsche concludes emphatically, "*is the will to power – and nothing besides!* And you yourselves are also this will to power – and nothing besides!"[9]

Might this mean that *we ourselves* are composed entirely of forces of transformation? Deleuze's interpretation is that all bodies, all physical things, are "nothing but forces" defined solely by their activities of affecting – and being affected by – other things with which they interact.[10] There's never a singular force but always competing combinations of forces, with *power* as their capacity to alter each other. When forces are bound together in a certain kind of power competition, they form a larger entity, which can combine with others to produce an even larger body, and so on, up to and beyond the scale of our own bodies and the things of our everyday world with which we interact.

This means that your own body is not mere "crude matter," as Yoda puts it, but rather a "whirlwind of forces," all acting in competition with one another, yet doing so in a way that they also hold together.[11] *Energetic beings are we*, as Yoda might say. You remain alive as a unified creature because every part of you is a confrontation of competing forces, all in a continual process of mutation. Whether you notice them or not, you always carry around these powers of transformation within you, waiting to be unleashed.

Learning the Force would be – in Deleuze's philosophy – something like coming to sense our powers of *becoming-other* and making productive use of the inner instabilities of our forces in order to creatively "deform" ourselves and our relations to others. One example is overcoming alcoholism, something Deleuze knows from experience, which requires drastically altering our inner psychological and physiological workings while at the same time forming new relations.[12] This means breaking from the pub we frequent, for instance, and forming new habits in different places with different people. Another illustration is learning how to swim. Our bodies are already a swirl of disruptive forces when we jump into the sea for the first time. We're then met with the tumultuous forces and movements of the choppy waves in the water. To survive, we must recompose ourselves by changing the "mechanics" of the interactions among our body's parts so that our forces and each wave's forces become more accommodated to one another; in that way, we and the wave form a larger, composite body of dynamically altering forces as we swim within it.[13]

Which Side Are You On?

It'd be tempting to think that we become "one with the wave," so to speak. For Deleuze, it's not so simple, because there's so much more tension, difference, and deformation involved. He distinguishes two different kinds of "combat" in which forces may engage, with each type having a different sort of power. Forces that are in *combat-against the Other* are unable to coordinate their mutual influences to form larger units, but are rather destructive to each other's capacities. This is a "base" sort of will to power that's really just a "will to dominate." It generally leads to our own and others' destruction, by leaving us unable to deform and adapt to changing circumstances – like the Sith, we deal in *absolutes*. Deleuze illustrates this with the Russian fable of the frog and the scorpion, as told by Orson Welles in the film *Mr. Arkadin* (1955).[14] The scorpion wants to CROSS a river and asks the frog to carry him. The frog first refuses, saying that the scorpion will surely sting and kill him. Still, the scorpion convinces the frog by noting that if he does so, he too will drown. Halfway across the river, the scorpion does in fact sting the frog, killing them both. What's the scorpion's explanation? *He cannot change his character*.[15]

At the end of *ROTJ* when the Emperor is shocking Luke to near death with Force lightning, he's like the scorpion, ultimately just bringing about his own demise. Instead, it's Anakin who prevails because he's able to reconstitute himself to the light side, rejoining the Jedi. This is a "nobler" kind of will to power, the *will to become--other*. For Deleuze, it involves *combat-between oneself*, whereby "a force enriches itself by seizing hold of other forces and joining itself to them in a new ensemble: a becoming."[16] There's still a *competitive* exchange of forces, but they act to create new compositions and relations with others in a mutually empowering way. This use of power would be Deleuze's equivalent of the light side of the Force: "the good is outpouring, ascending life, the kind which knows how to transform itself, to metamorphose itself according to the forces it encounters, and which forms a constantly larger force with them, always increasing the power to live, always opening new 'possibilities'."[17]

How might we look again at Rian Johnson's Luke, using Deleuze's idea of force? On account of his Skywalker lineage, Luke is endowed with exceptional Force potential. He was living on Ach-to, on an island housing the first Jedi temple, so he was constantly surrounded by a potent influence of the Force, all while being highly attuned to it naturally. Under these conditions, it would seem almost impossible for him to cut off his connection to the Force; at least, life would probably demand a constant, incredible exertion of effort on his part. Also, he would have to reconstitute himself drastically, so as not to feel that intense presence of the Force always surrounding him. In light of this, we might say that his forces of transformation were so powerful they even proved stronger than the Force itself, as he successfully overcame its potent and relentless influence upon him. Also, for him to perform the incredible feat of Force projection at the end of the film, requiring him to suddenly reawaken his contact with the Force in a most profound way, shows yet again how great his powers of transformation are. Perhaps Dadbeh, Hamill, and the many others who were disappointed with Johnson's Luke could also adopt this different perspective and regard him as an "unbelievably super-powerful being," if they took into consideration his incredible powers with – and also *against* – the Force itself. Couldn't this self-transformative Luke be an even brighter "beacon of hope" for those facing adversity?

Abilities Some Considered to Be Non-organic

It would seem that we are dealing with two very different things: the Force of *Star Wars* and Deleuze's *forces of becoming*. For Deleuze, forces are "non-organic," meaning that they act primarily to break down and deform given compositions; the Force, however, is what binds things together.

But maybe – from a certain point of view – these two notions are in fact compatible and overlap in large part. For one thing, the forces of becoming aid things in cohering together, even though this is a tense and combative sort of interaction. And though these forces are non-organic for Deleuze, he considers them to have a "non-organic *vitality*" because they allow things to mutate into more adaptable beings.[18] If living creatures did not have this capacity to deform and radically *become-other*, they might simply die out. Consider, for instance, the Great Oxidation Event. Between 2.3 and 2.5 million years ago, there was an overabundance of oxygen in the early stages of life on Earth, which was killing off the many anaerobic organisms responsible for this overproduction. This destructive trend was only reversed when new oxygen-consuming creatures emerged and restored balance.[19] In this case, the non-organic vitality would be found in the genetic mutations and deformations of life-forms that served to advance life on the whole rather than make so many species go extinct. If there's any killing here, it's more like Kylo Ren's admonition to Rey: "Let the past die. Kill it if you have to. That's the only way to become what you were meant to be." Becoming something other by using our forces of transformation is a sort of dying because we must say goodbye to our previous selves. Yet, it can still be a "vital" dying, if we emerge in a newer, wiser, more capable form, in fruitful combinations with others. So, perhaps Deleuze's forces of becoming aren't so different from the Force understood as "the energy between all things, a tension, a balance, that binds the universe together," so long as we emphasize that it's this *dynamic tension itself* that serves as the binding factor.[20]

Notes

1 Niatoos Dadbeh, "Real Talk – *The Last Jedi* – Unedited," *Star Wars Theory*, July 5, 2019, at https://youtu.be/8cnJEDy8z_Y.

2 Mark Hamill, "Mark Hamill on *The Last Jedi*, His Favourite Character and the Dark Side!" *KISS FM UK*, December 14, 2017, at https://youtu.be/-umb4cyFFSE.

3 Ron Dicker, "Mark Hamill Rips His Role in 'Last Jedi': He's Not My Luke Skywalker," *Huffpost*, December 22, 2017, at https://www.huffpost.com/entry/mark-hamill-last-jedi-luke-skywalker_n_5a3cf644e4b025f99e16864d.

4 Dadbeh, "Real Talk."

5 Ibid.

6 Niatoos Dadbeh, "Not My Luke Skywalker: A Love Letter to the Sequels," *Star Wars Theory*, July 11, 2020, at https://youtu.be/sJC63tFpxB4.

7 Zac Koonce and Craven Moorhaus, "Auralnauts Podcast – Ep16: *The Last Jedi*," *Auralnauts*, 2018, at, https://soundcloud.com/auralnauts-1/auralnauts-podcast-ep16-the-last-jedi.

8 Ibid.

9 Friedrich Nietzsche, *The Will to Power*, ed. Walter Kaufmann, trans. Walter Kaufmann and R.J. Hollingdale (New York: Vintage Books, 1968), 549–550.

10 Gilles Deleuze, *Cinema 2: The Time-Image*, trans. Hugh Tomlinson and Robert Galeta (London: Continuum, 2005), 135.

11 Gilles Deleuze, *Essays Critical and Clinical*, trans. Daniel Smith and Michael Greco (Minneapolis: University of Minnesota Press, 1997), 134.

12 Gilles Deleuze and Claire Parnet, "B as in Beverage," in *Gilles Deleuze from A to Z*, dir. Pierre-André Boutang, trans. Charles Stivale (Los Angeles: Semiotext(e), 2012); Gilles Deleuze and Félix Guattari, *A Thousand Plateaus*, trans. Brian Massumi (London: Continuum, 2004), 484.

13 Gilles Deleuze, "Spinoza: The Velocities of Thought / 13," *The Deleuze Seminars*, March 17, 1981, at https://deleuze.cla.purdue.edu/seminars/spinoza-velocities-thought/lecture-13.

14 Deleuze, *Cinema* 2, 135–137; Deleuze, *Essays Critical and Clinical*, 131–132.

15 Orson Welles, dir. *Mr. Arkadin* (Filmorsa, 1955).

16 Deleuze, *Essays Critical and Clinical*, 132.

17 Deleuze, *Cinema* 2, 137.

18 Deleuze, *Essays Critical and Clinical*, 131, emphasis mine.

19 Richard Blaustein, "The Great Oxidation Event: Evolving Understandings of How Oxygenic Life on Earth Began," *BioScience* 66 (2016), 189.

20 I am deeply grateful to Kevin Decker, Jason Eberl, William Irwin, and Giles Flitney for their substantial improvements to the content and style of this chapter.

29

Passionate Love, Platonic Love, and Force Love in *Star Wars*

James Lawler

In *Attack of the Clones* (*AOTC*), Senator Padmé Amidala asks Anakin Skywalker, "Are you allowed to love? I thought that was forbidden for a Jedi." Anakin replies, "Attachment is forbidden. Possession is forbidden. Compassion, which I would define as unconditional love, is central to a Jedi's life. So you might say we are encouraged to love." Anakin is playing with two meanings of love, the passionate love that he feels for Padmé and the dispassionate, detached, "Platonic love" of the Jedi warrior. Anakin is therefore deeply conflicted.

This conflict expresses the Jedi teaching of "the Force" – the life-generated power with which the Jedi are able consciously to connect. The Force is an energy field that surrounds and penetrates all living beings; it binds everything together. Modern physics extends this Jedi teaching to the entire universe. According to Sir Isaac Newton (1643–1727), it is the force of *gravity* that binds the universe together. In his Law of Gravity, each body attracts every other body in direct proportion to the mass of the bodies, and in inverse proportion to the square of the distance between them. This means that every individual being exerts power over every other being and exists in relation to the force of gravity of the universe as a whole.

If we were able to tap into that power and use it for ourselves, imagine what we could do! The Jedi have a natural ability to tune into the Force to a greater degree than ordinary humans, and through their special training learn to exercise and control this power. The heart of this training is to close your eyes and feel the Force within you. Since

Star Wars and Philosophy Strikes Back: This is the Way, First Edition.
Edited by Jason T. Eberl and Kevin S. Decker.

everything is connected to everything else, this feeling will guide you in relation to everything else, whether a dangerous object hurtling toward you or finding important targets at a distance from you.

Philosophy Begins with Passion

Gravity is, by definition, a force of attraction, not a force for repelling objects, disrupting them, or pushing them away, although this is a possibility. A small mass contains an enormous destructive force, as Einstein's formula $E = mc^2$ expresses. Imagine a brick falls from 10 ft above you – how much damage could it do to you if it were to land on your head? The brick picks up speed as it falls. Suppose it was falling at the speed of light and then square that number. That's the total amount of force in a single brick. This is why the small amount of mass of the atomic bomb can devastate a city. The force of gravity is the sum of the inner powers of all bodies in the Universe. Fortunately, it normally acts by the quiet force of attraction that one body exerts on another, rather than by the force of one body crashing against another.

In Lucas's universe, the Jedi have a special capacity to connect with the Force. But all of us feel the Force in very ordinary ways when we fall in love. There is nothing more powerful in human psychology than the power of attraction in the love of one person for another. In love the Force is internalized and becomes conscious in the feeling of attraction of one person for another. The Force is not only an external physical power but also the inner reality of human feelings and intuitions. In another scene from *AOTC*, Anakin tells Padmé, in words worthy of Shakespeare's *Romeo and Juliet*: "I'm haunted by the kiss you should never have given me. My heart is beating, hoping that kiss will not become a scar. You are in my very soul, tormenting me. What can I do? I will do anything you ask."

Padmé was right when she said she thought the Jedi were forbidden to fall in love. The power of passionate love between persons – sexual love or love of the body – is experience of the Force. But the Jedi teach that this kind of love belongs to the dark side and needs to be shunned. This side of the Force is held to be negative, destructive, taking all rational control away from those who are caught up in its power. It's this side of the Force that Anakin feels for Padmé. Its prohibition leads him to abandon the Jedi and join the Sith, who use the Force for control and domination.

But the Jedi also teach their trainees to have a detached, compassionate love for others that is sometimes called "Platonic love." It's the kind of love that lets others go, even lets them die. In *Revenge of the Sith*, Yoda counsels Anakin, "Death is a natural part of life. Rejoice for those around you who transform into the Force. Mourn them, do not. Miss them, do not. Attachment leads to jealousy. The shadow of greed, that is ... Train yourself to let go of everything you fear to lose." Anakin can't follow this advice and decides to use the powers of the dark side to save his beloved. The result is his transformation into Darth Vader.

The two sides of the Force can be found in an allegory by Plato (ca. 428–348 BCE) in the dialogue *Phaedrus*, in which the human soul is compared to the driver of a chariot with two horses pulling in opposite directions. One horse pulls the chariot in an upward direction, toward greater beauty, goodness, and understanding. The other pulls the chariot downward toward evil and madness. The charioteer must choose between following the upward-moving horse, symbol of the rational soul's pure dispassionate love, or the downward-moving one, symbol of the body's sensuous and egotistical love.[1]

In Plato's *Symposium*, however, this teaching of two opposing forces in human life is presented with greater complexity. The *Symposium* tells the story of a gathering of friends around cups of wine. They decide to challenge one another for the best account of the nature of love. Socrates explains the teaching he received from a wise woman, Diotima, who teaches Socrates that to become a philosopher it's first necessary to fall passionately in love with someone: "For he who would proceed aright in this matter should begin in youth to visit beautiful forms; and first, if he be guided by his instructor aright, to love one such form only. Out of that he should create fair thoughts."[2]

Diotima's introductory course in philosophy begins with loving someone, for only then will a person's thoughts become beautiful. This starting point has its dangers, however, since we shouldn't get stuck on this first step in understanding love. Love for only one person tends to blind the lover to what's beautiful in other persons and in other things. More advanced philosophy must go beyond this initial love; otherwise it will become a violent, overwhelming force. We need to climb the ladder of love to higher and higher levels, to see the beauty of institutions, laws, and the sciences. The advanced student of philosophy will then not be

> like a servant in love with the beauty of one youth or man or institution, himself a slave mean and narrow-minded, but drawing towards and contemplating the vast sea of beauty, he will create many fair and

> noble thoughts and notions in boundless love of wisdom; until on that shore he grows and waxes strong, and at last the vision is revealed to him of a single science, which is the science of beauty everywhere.[3]

According to this teaching, Anakin's love of Padmé should've been welcomed by his Jedi teachers as a necessary beginning, but one that needs eventually to be channeled to wider and higher degrees of comprehension of the universal nature of the Force first experienced in passionate love. Instead, the Jedi condemn students who naturally feel the attractions and power of such love. As a result of this negative attitude, the students of the Force become divided into two groups: the proponents of the light side, who condemn passionate love, and those who fall under the spell of the dark side, and cultivate the darker emotions, including anger and hatred as well as passionate love. Instead of combining together and composing, as Palpatine tells Anakin in *Revenge of the Sith*, "a larger view of the Force," the two groups fight against one another in acts of mutual self-destruction.

Fulfilling the Prophecy

Anakin's transformation into Darth Vader seems to contradict a prophecy about him: that he's the Chosen One who would bring balance back to the Force. If the sequel trilogy of *Star Wars* lays out this framework, the original trilogy shows how Anakin's love of Padmé, along with his turn to the dark side, begins to fulfill the prophecy. *Return of the Jedi* concludes with Darth Vader's turn against his master, Emperor Palpatine, out of compassionate love for his son Luke – one of the twins, along with Leia, born from his union with his beloved Padmé.

The pursuit of a middle ground between the two sides of the Force culminates in the Force love of *The Rise of Skywalker* that unites Rey, granddaughter of Palpatine, and Kylo Ren, son of Leia Organa and Han Solo and grandson of Anakin Skywalker. The two sides of love that are first divided and set in opposition to one another become intertwined. Ren explains to Rey: "My mother was the daughter of Vader. Your father was the son of the Emperor. What Palpatine doesn't know is we're a dyad in the Force, Rey, two that are one." The love comprising the dyad of Rey and Ren realizes the balance of the Force begun by the love of Anakin and Padmé.

Plato again provides the framework for this conception of love as a destiny arranged by the Force, giving us the playwright Aristophanes's story of the origin and nature of love. We've mentioned Socrates's account of Diotima's teaching on the same subject. Aristophanes, the author of comedies, gives an account that remains at the level of the passionate love between two people, but evolves and deepens over many lifetimes. According to Aristophanes, human beings were once much more powerful than we are today. We had four legs and four arms and faces on both sides of our heads. We moved very quickly by turning cartwheels at high speed. The gods were afraid of us, for we threatened their power. And so Zeus decided literally to cut us down to size, splitting us in half.

Ever since, we "halflings" have been searching over many lifetimes for our original other half. We might find someone who's similar to our other half and we might have a friendly, congenial love with them. If we pursue a good life, avoiding excesses and being responsible citizens, we'll eventually find our true other half: "And when one of them meets with his other half, the actual half of himself ... the pair are lost in an amazement of love and friendship and intimacy." Aristophanes concludes, "I believe that if our loves were perfectly accomplished, and each one returning to his primeval nature had his original true love, then our race would be happy."[4]

A Love Story in Three Acts

Star Wars doesn't leave the original love, Anakin's passionate love for Padmé, behind. Its nine episodes follow Aristophanes's progression in which the truly perfect love is found at the end of the story. In effect, *Star Wars* is a love story in three acts. Anakin and Padmé's passionate love is at the heart of the prequel trilogy. The Platonic love of the twins Luke and Leia is at the core of the original trilogy. The Force love of Rey and Ren concludes the drama of love that finally achieves the balance of the Force in the sequel trilogy. This is when Rey and Ren overcome the dualism and seeming contradiction of the dark side and the light side. Rey, child of the dark side who turns to the light, joins forces with the Jedi, Kylo Ren, child of the light side who turns to the dark, seeks to conquer the universe as the leader of the First Order. And then Rey and Ren, the third such dyad of love in *Star Wars*, join forces.

Rey and Ren's conflicting and converging paths provide one of the two main themes of *The Rise of Skywalker*. The other is the clash of armies: the Republican forces with Leia at their head and Rey as their main fighter, and the First Order forces led by Kylo Ren, with Palpatine lurking in the background. The two themes intertwine as alternate pulses of the final film, the former one loud and strident in bright daylight, the latter one quiet and introspective, taking place mostly in dark shadows. Rey and Ren are, after all, leaders of armies as well as a dyad of mutual attraction in a struggle over the direction of the future of the galaxy.

It's this other side of the story, the clash of armies, that's addressed in Plato's notion of the widening of forms and objects of love. While passionate love plays a necessary role in the unfolding of human history, the love of freedom at the level of the state is equally important. In the *Symposium*'s final part, the friendly combat over love's nature is interrupted by the appearance of Alcibiades, one of the most brilliant, powerful, and wealthy Athenians. He's also known for his good looks. Alcibiades insists on telling a story of his own confused love for Socrates, in which higher and lower motives collided. Alcibiades, spellbound by Socrates's ideas, came to be mesmerized by him, to the point of realizing that his own pursuit of fame, fortune, and power conflicted with the pursuit of goodness, beauty, and knowledge. He confesses,

> I am conscious that if I did not shut my ears against him, and fly as from the voice of the siren, my fate would be like that of others. He would transfix me, and I should grow old sitting at his feet. For he makes me confess that I ought not to live as I do, neglecting the wants of my own soul, and busying myself with the concerns of the Athenians; therefore I hold my ears and tear myself away from him.[5]

Failing to follow Socrates's teaching and climb the ladder of love, Alcibiades remained fixed on the first rung, and tried unsuccessfully to get Socrates to join him there.

In the war between Athens and Sparta, Alcibiades betrayed his fellow Athenians by going over to the Spartans. Athens was the leader of the city-states of Greece run by its free male citizens. Sparta was the leader of the forces of aristocracy and slavery. When the war ended with their defeat, Athens's leaders, seeking to deflect responsibility from their own shoulders, focused on Alcibiades's treason. As Alcibiades was thought to be Socrates's student, they charged Socrates with responsibility for leading Alcibiades astray. The portrayal of Alcibiades's rejection of Socrates's teachings in the *Symposium* is one side of Plato's defense of Socrates. In the *Apology*, Plato presents Socrates's defense at his trial, where he was accused of corrupting the youth and not believing in the gods of the city. The most prominent of these youth who'd supposedly been corrupted was the known traitor, Alcibiades.

In the *Apology*, Socrates explains the problem with Athens: too many Athenians, especially the rich and powerful, failed to understand the upper reaches of the ladder of love and focused instead on individualistic goals, as Alcibiades had done. Socrates is therefore the true patriot: "I think that no better piece of fortune has ever befallen you in Athens than my service to God. For I spend my whole life in going about and persuading you all to give your first and chiefest care to the perfection of your souls, and not till you have done that to think of your bodies, or your wealth; and telling you that virtue does not come from wealth, but that wealth, and every other good thing which men have, whether in public, or in private, comes from virtue."[6]

The rich Athenians, Alcibiades and others, put their own interests above the city's. Virtue, Socrates teaches, must come first: devotion to the good of all. This is the secret of lasting wealth. A society in which individuals put their self-interest first will be divided and weak. A society in which individuals join together for the good of all will be rich and powerful. Love between separate individuals, however beautiful it is in itself, mustn't be isolated from the more general kind of love that has its own kind of passion and force, the greater Force that shines forth when individuals join together for a higher cause.

In the final confrontation over the galaxy's fate, Finn, an escaped First Order stormtrooper, whose love for Rey creates a commitment to the Resistance, bonds with Jannah, a leader of refugees who are also former stormtroopers. Finn explains to Jannah how the power of the Force has brought them together in a unity based on the commitment of individuals to the higher good that Socrates called virtue:

JANNAH: All of us here were stormtroopers. We mutinied at the Battle of Ansett Island. They told us to fire on civilians. We wouldn't do it. We laid our weapons down.

FINN: All of you?

JANNAH: The whole company. I don't even know how it happened. It wasn't a decision, really, it was like...

FINN: An instinct. Feeling.

JANNAH: A feeling.

FINN: The Force. The Force brought me here. It brought me to Rey. And Poe.

JANNAH: You say that like you're sure it's real.

FINN: It's real. I wasn't sure then ... but I am now.

Overcoming Death through the Force of Love

In the end, Rey summons the Jedi of the past to destroy Palpatine, exchanging her life for his death. Ren finds Rey's body, as Romeo found Juliet in Shakespeare's tragedy. Thinking Juliet had died, Romeo kills himself to join her, as Juliet does when she awakens from her drug-induced sleep to find her lover dead. Rey is really dead, but Ren revives her by exchanging his life for hers. Ren doesn't die a natural death however. Simultaneously with his mother, Leia, his body evaporates under its shroud. Linked together in life, they become one with the Force without losing their identities. Luke and Leia appear to Rey when she buries their lightsabers. After being just Rey with no family name, she takes the Skywalker name as her own. It turns out that Yoda was wrong about death after all. The dead don't transform into the Force. The Force transforms into them.

Notes

1 Plato, "Phaedrus," in *The Collected Dialogues of Plato*, ed. Edith Hamilton and Huntingdon Cairns (Princeton: Bollingen/Princeton University Press, 1961), 475–525.
2 Plato, Symposium, in Hamilton and Cairns, eds., The Collected Dialogues of Plato, 210b.
3 Ibid., 210d.
4 Ibid., 193b.
5 Ibid., 216a.
6 Plato, Apology, in Hamilton and Cairns, eds., The Collected Dialogues of Plato, 58b.

30

The Rise of Rey Skywalker: The Importance of Community and Friends in *Star Wars*

James M. Okapal

I'm Rey. … Rey Skywalker.

Thus ends the nine-movie Skywalker Saga. It's the story, in part, of three different children from desert planets and the communities they join. Anakin Skywalker leaves his enslaved mother to join the Jedi Order. He then joins the Sith and helps destroy the Order after years of questionable choices. Luke Skywalker leaves his home after stormtroopers murder his aunt and uncle, embarking on a quest to save the galaxy from tyranny by joining the Rebellion. He then attempts to revive the Jedi Order, but fails. Rey, the granddaughter of Emperor Sheev Palpatine, leaves the battle-scarred wasteland of Jakku as a matter of self-preservation. By the time she arrives at the sacred island on Ahch-To, she realizes her actual quest is to discover her place in all this – the saga, the galaxy, and her own life. And in the end, she seems to defy Lor San Tekka's wisdom that "you cannot deny the truth that is your family" when she makes the choice to claim the Skywalkers as her family and the Jedi as her community.[1]

"They're My Friends. I've Got to Help Them"

To understand Rey's search for relationships and community we can make use of Aristotle's (384–322 BCE) theory of friendship, which has three forms: friendships of utility, of pleasure, and of virtue.[2] Each is

Star Wars and Philosophy Strikes Back: This is the Way, First Edition.
Edited by Jason T. Eberl and Kevin S. Decker.

defined, in part, by the motivation for the friendship. When the relationship is founded on its usefulness or advantage – like any friendship the pirate king Hondo Ohnaka would have – it's a friendship for utility. If it's grounded in having jointly pleasurable activities – like those shared by members of Jabba the Hutt's court – you have friendships for pleasure. If the ground of the friendship is the mutual pursuit of goodness and flourishing – based on the desire for friends to be the best that they can be, as seen in the triads of Anakin, Obi-Wan, and Padmé, Luke, Leia, and Han, or Rey, Finn, and Poe – then you have a virtuous friendship.

Friendships for the sake of virtue differ from the other two forms of friendship. These imperfect friendships are fundamentally *self-regarding* and often *short-lived*. In contrast, each member in a virtuous friendship has both self-regarding and other-regarding motivations; they want both their friend and themselves to flourish. This other-regarding element of a virtuous friendship is "a concern on the part of each friend for the welfare of the other, for the other's sake, and that involves some degree of intimacy."[3]

The "for the other's sake" part is integral to the entire idea of virtuous friendship: a virtuous friend is willing to ignore their own interests in favor of another's. Paradigmatic examples of this are the sacrificial actions of Jedi Knights Obi-Wan Kenobi and Kanan Jarrus, who sacrificed their lives so others could thrive. Nevertheless, it can be hard to sort through our immediate motivations to ensure that our actions are actually done for the sake of a friend and not merely for our own welfare. This seems to be the point when Luke prepares to leave for Cloud City. Luke's stated reason for leaving is, "They're my friends. I've got to help them." But more important is Yoda's reply: "If you leave now, help them you could, but you will destroy all for which they have fought and suffered." Luke's motivation at this moment seems to be merely the welfare of Han, Chewie, Leia, and C-3PO, as Luke perceives it. But it is not for *their* sake, nor for *their* interests, that he's trying to help them. Luke has not yet learned what Ezra Bridger finally accepts about Kanan's sacrifice in the *Rebels* episode "A World Between Worlds." Ezra wants to save Kanan, but Ahsoka points out that "Kanan gave his life so that you could live. If he's taken out of this moment, you all die. … I'm sorry Ezra, but you must see, Kanan found the moment when he was needed most and he did what he had to do for everyone." Despite appearances, saving Kanan would not truly be acting for Kanan's sake. Friends for virtue must sacrifice their self-regarding interests: Obi-Wan must sacrifice himself to allow Luke to fulfill his destiny; Kanan must sacrifice himself to save others who'll help bring down the Empire; Ezra must sacrifice a future with his mentor; and Luke, if he'd listened to Yoda, would've had to sacrifice his friends to continue his Jedi training and not face Vader prematurely.

"We Are What They Grow Beyond"

The motivations of usefulness, pleasure, and virtue do not exhaust the important elements that define our relationships. In addition, Aristotle recognizes the importance of the *larger communities* in which friendships take place as well as the role of *choice* in friendships. These choices are more important than just entering into a relationship; they are also choices of a value system. In *The Force Awakens* (*TFA*), Finn gives a speech about choices as he tries to convince Rey to leave with him for the Outer Rim:

> I'm not Resistance. I'm not a hero. I'm a stormtrooper. Like all of them, I was taken from a family I will never know. But my first battle, I made a choice. I wasn't going to kill for them. So I ran. Right into you. And you looked at me like no one ever has. I was ashamed of what I was. But I'm done with the First Order. I'm never going back. Rey, come with me.

Finn, while not part of the Resistance (yet), knows that the First Order's values – which begin with the destruction of communities, relationships, and people such as the Tuanul on Jakku – do not represent a community to which he can *choose* to belong. He realizes that Rey is someone who has an ability to connect with others, even droids. Rey exemplifies the value of community building, even though she's an isolated junk trader, while the vast membership of the First Order exemplifies the opposite.

In other words, each friendship includes two communities. Both communities are defined by values. Intimate friendships include values of virtue, pleasure, or usefulness. Background communities provide a larger tapestry of values that influence the intimate relationships which form within them. In the *Star Wars* universe, characters make choices about both these intimate and wider communities, and in doing so choose a set of values. If the choice of an intimate relationship is also a choice of a wider community and the community's values, the weight of such a choice becomes apparent. Rey's choice to claim the Skywalker name is significant as she's making a choice between two communities with irreconcilable values: the Jedi and the Sith.

What sort of values does she have to choose between? The Jedi have a rich and complex set of values with other-regarding motivations at their core. In *The Jedi Path*, Grand Master Fae Coven states that the Jedi Code is "a pledge of protection to the citizens and inhabitants of the Republic."[4] The Jedi Code concerns a Jedi's relationships with wider communities, not merely within the Order itself. A Jedi is oriented to think about the interests of others and interpret all aspects of the Jedi Code in terms of other-regarding ideals, particularly those that break down the barriers of self and other. The precept "There is no passion, there is serenity" becomes operationalized as "a reminder not to elevate the self above the mission," which is, according to Chief Librarian Restelly Quist's comment, a vow "to defend its ideals of exploration, knowledge and justice."[5] As Obi-Wan tells Luke, the role of the Jedi in the Republic was service to others as guardians of peace and justice. The Jedi's purpose is to help create conditions of flourishing for themselves and others. The precept "There is no chaos, there is harmony" requires that Jedi see that all life is united and each life has its own purpose, its own version of flourishing. A Jedi's relationship with the Force is a reminder that all Jedi are "part of an energy larger than ourselves, and we play roles in a cosmic fabric that outstrip our incarnate understanding."[6]

There are, of course, other virtues the Jedi find valuable. Courage is tested by the Jedi Trials.[7] Morrit Ch'gally, Jedi recruiter, notes that Jedi attire, the outward symbol of the Order, is meant to evoke humility in its simple fabric, colors, and style; the usefulness of Jedi to others is indicated by their utility belt.[8] Throughout *The Jedi Path* are examples that highlight additional Jedi values such as peace, knowledge, serenity, harmony, self-discipline, compassion, tenacity, and loyalty. Each of these values would be easily recognized by Aristotle as important virtues.

The Sith, unsurprisingly, disavow or disfigure these values. Sorzus Syn, a Dark Jedi, constructed the Sith Code as follows: "Peace is a lie. There is only passion. Through passion I gain strength. Through strength I gain power. Through power I gain victory. Through victory my chains are broken. The Force shall set me free."[9] Perhaps the most significant element of this Code is the use of the singular pronoun, "I." Unlike the Jedi Code, which uses plural pronouns like "we" and "our," and which references communities such as all living things, the Sith Code is entirely self-regarding. There's no wider community of concern, only self-aggrandizement acquired through exclusion. Strength and power aren't used to help others, but to gain victory *over* others. A Sith elevates himself to the position of Sith Lord, indicating that all others are inferior.

With this victory, the Sith Lord achieves the ultimate goal of freedom for himself at the expense of others, a freedom of pure license, unbound by mores, laws, or even petty concepts such as good and evil.

Consider Darth Bane's comments about the relationships that should be cultivated by a Sith Lord. The wealth amassed by the Sith must be used "to hire spies, scholars, assassins, trainers, guards and thieves. All will prove useful."[10] In other words, the Lord only seeks friendships for use. This is true even for the master's relationship with the apprentice: "This is the Rule of Two: One Sith must contain all the power of the dark side. One Master must decide how that power shall be used. Sharing power is an act of weakness and a violation of the Sith Code."[11] The apprentice, like all other beings, is merely useful, ensuring that the line of Sith continues and grows in power. As Darth Sidious indicates in his marginalia to the *Book of Sith*, "Darth Maul, Darth Tyrannus, Darth Vader. Each useful in his own way. Each easy to replace when his purpose has reached its end."[12] The Sith apprentice understands all of this and likewise sees the master as merely useful. The apprentice has one goal, to become powerful enough to kill the master and carry on the Sith legacy.[13] This is a perversion of Yoda's wisdom that "[Masters] are what [apprentices] grow beyond." A Jedi master gets out of the way so their apprentice can grow. A Sith apprentice sees their master as an impediment or chain to be removed to achieve freedom. Understanding this contrast between the Jedi and Sith helps us understand events of the sequel trilogy, particularly its conclusion.

Sidious's goal is to achieve unlimited power and immortality so that the Rule of Two can be transformed into the Rule of One. He comes to the precipice of achieving his goal on Exegol. He's been using Sith alchemy to make clones of himself to find a new vessel for his soul. He goads Rey to submit to her hate and anger. If she strikes down his physical form, he'll thereby come to possess her and achieve immortality. To a Sith, even a blood relative is nothing more than a useful vessel, to be manipulated or even destroyed in the quest for immortality and unlimited power.

"The Belonging You Seek Is Not Behind You. It Is Ahead"

The sequel trilogy is, in large part, several stories about a new generation of characters – Rey, Ben Solo, Finn, and Poe Dameron – trying to find their place in the world by searching for a community in which they can take an important role. But that choice cannot be made early in one's life, cannot be made for you, and must factor in making mistakes. For example, Finn, once seeing the true nature of the First Order, makes his choice to leave but too closely attaches himself to one person, Rey, and makes poor choices before being saved by Rose Tico in the climax of *The Last Jedi* (*TLJ*). But Rey's story emphasizes that "people cannot be friends if they do not choose the friend knowingly and responsibly." Rey, not knowing who she is at the beginning of *TFA*, cannot knowingly choose the relationships that'll define her. She must first embark on the hero's journey of *self-discovery*.

Rey is constantly confronted with choices of friendship and community. In *TFA*, Finn offers her the choice of a relationship running from the First Order in the Outer Rim. This scene is bookended by two other offers to form relationships. Han offers Rey a job with him and Chewie as a second mate, an opportunity to trade her life as a junk salvager for that of a smuggler; she declines the offer due to her continued hope of reuniting with her parents. After Finn decides to leave, Rey is offered another choice: to follow the path of the Force. She's drawn to the Skywalker lightsaber which gives her a Force vision of past and future. The vision ends with Obi-Wan saying, "Rey, these are your first steps." Maz Kanata explains the experience, "The belonging you seek is not behind you, it is ahead. Take the lightsaber." But Rey, unprepared to make that commitment to a wider world, replies, "I do not want any part of this." Each offer is a choice involving different values and a different life.

Following the way of the Force requires additional choices. Luke and Leia represent one option: follow the light side and become a Jedi. Ben, Snoke, and Rey's grandfather represent the other option: follow the dark side and become a Sith. Throughout *TLJ*, everyone keeps telling Rey to forget what came before and find a different path. Luke rebuffs her, telling her that he cannot be her teacher, that the Jedi path is a failure that needs to end. She experiences multiple Force connections with Kylo Ren that turn out to be ploys by Snoke to lure her to the dark side. During another, Kylo tries to convince Rey that she needs to choose, as he did, to forget her connections with others and to kill those who represent the past if necessary – which aligns with the self-regarding nature of Sith values. Rey rejects Kylo's offer twice, rejoining what's left of the Resistance but, notably, neither of the communities related to the Force.

Rey cannot choose a community yet because she still does not know from where she comes. She cannot choose between the dark and the light sides *knowingly* because she does not know her own past. When Luke asks where she's from in *TLJ*, she says "nowhere." In the cave on Ahch-To, she wants to see her parents and gain insight into her family connections, but is only shown reflections of herself. Kylo says he knows the truth: her parents were filthy junk traders, nobodies. He says, "You have no place in this story. You come from nothing. You're nothing." But this is not entirely true, and these gaps in her self-knowledge mean Rey cannot choose knowingly between the light and the dark.

And so we first see Rey in *The Rise of Skywalker* chanting "Be with me" repeatedly in the hope of connecting with the Jedi of the past. At this point, she concludes that "They're not with me." She believes it is not possible "to hear the voice of the Jedi that came before," indicating that she is not really part of their community despite all her training with Leia and her scouring of the Jedi texts for insight. They're not with her because she still does not know her past. The first clue about her past is the vision she receives during a frustrated training session: she sees an image of herself on the Sith throne. The second clue comes when, in her confrontation with Kylo on Passana, she inadvertently uses Sith lightning to destroy a transport. Eventually, Kylo tells her she's Palpatine's granddaughter. Finally, when she touches a Sith holocron, she confronts her dark self, who says "Do not be afraid of who you are." It's only after gaining the information about herself and her past, and accepting this as the truth, that Rey can *knowingly* choose between the light and the dark.

When confronting her grandfather on Exegol, she calls again, "Be with me." This time she hears Jedi voices. Amidst the welcoming voices of Yoda, Obi-Wan, Anakin, Luke, Kanan, Ahsoka Tano, Adi Gallia, Aayla Secura, and Luminara Unduli, one stands out. Qui-Gon informs her that "every Jedi who has ever lived, lives in you. ... We stand behind you." Now that Rey knows her past, she can knowingly choose her path, that is, knowingly and responsibly join the Jedi community and adopt its values. In the grand Jedi tradition, she chooses not to hate, not to kill Sidious directly, but using Luke's and Leia's sabers together, absorbs Sidious's Sith lightning. Sidious's life ends through her other-regarding sacrifice: a sacrifice for the good of her friends, the Resistance, and the galaxy.

In other words, Rey made her choice knowing why both the light and the dark paths were open to her. By birth, she could follow the Sith. However, she chose the light and, in doing so, she heeded the wisdom of Luke and Leia. Leia trained Rey knowing Rey was a Palpatine because she "saw [Rey's] spirit, her heart" and knew, as Luke did, that "some things are stronger than blood." Rey's genetics were not her destiny, but instead formed the background of a meaningful choice.

"And I, I'm All the Jedi!"

Rey, of course, does not stay dead. After being revived, Rey returns, not to her old homeworld of Jakku or Naboo, where her grandfather began, but to Tatooine, the home of Anakin and Luke Skywalker. She buries the Skywalker lightsabers at the Lars homestead, symbolically putting both Luke and Leia to rest. In this, she claims the Jedi as her wider community. She claims peace, justice, compassion, harmony, and other-regarding values as her guides in life. She values others for who they are and pledges to make the galaxy a place where virtue can thrive and individuals can flourish. It's at this moment, when asked who she is, that she fully embraces the Jedi and the Skywalkers as her friends, her community, her family. As Lor San Tekka said, Rey "cannot deny the truth that is her family." She was born a Palpatine. But, because she knowingly chose a different family, a different set of values and ideals, to be the one through whom all the Jedi live, the one who finally defeated the Sith, the one that may finally bring balance to the Force, she is the embodiment of the greatest familial line of the Jedi. She is Rey Skywalker.[15]

Notes

1 These aren't the only three individuals in search of community. We see this theme of community repeated time and again in many of the stories told in the *Star Wars* universe. In *Rebels*, a ragtag group form a community that fights the Empire and comes to realize they are part of an even larger Rebel Alliance. In *Rogue One*, Jyn Erso reconnects with both her biological father, Galen, and adoptive father, Saw Gerrera, only to find a home, however briefly, in the Rebellion. Similar themes are found in *The Bad Batch* with Omega and Clone Force 99, *The Mandalorian*'s "Clan of Two," and the growing family in *The Book of Boba Fett* of Boba, Fennec, Krrsantan, Cobb Vanth, and the Mods biker gang trying to protect Mos Espa.

2 Aristotle, *Nicomachean Ethics*, especially books VIII and IX (Cambridge: Harvard University Press, 2003).

3 Bennett Helm, "Friendship," in *Stanford Encyclopedia of Philosophy* at https://plato.stanford.edu/entries/friendship.

4 Daniel Wallace, *The Jedi Path: A Manual for Students of the Force* (Bellevue, WA: Becker & Mayer, 2017), 6.
5 Ibid., 9.
6 Ibid., 7.
7 Ibid., 99.
8 Ibid., 52–53.
9 Ibid., 47.
10 Daniel Wallace, *The Book of Sith: Secrets from the Dark Side* (Bellevue, WA: Becker & Mayer, 2013), 74.
11 Ibid., 66.
12 Ibid., 72.
13 Ibid., 75.
14 Michael H. Mitias, *Friendship: A Central Moral Value* (New York: Rodopi, 2012), 67.
15 I want to thank Jason Eberl, Kevin Decker, and William Irwin for their comments. Your support helped create the best version of this chapter, demonstrating that you are each, truly, friends of philosophical virtue.

Index

Star Wars and Philosophy Strikes Back: This is the Way, First Edition.
Edited by Jason T. Eberl and Kevin S. Decker.